News from Nowhere

News from Nowhere

THEORY AND POLITICS OF ROMANTICISM

Edited by
Tony Pinkney, Keith Hanley
and Fred Botting

1995
Romanticism,
Theory, Gender

RYBURN PUBLISHING
KEELE UNIVERSITY PRESS

First published in 1995
by Ryburn Publishing
an imprint of
Keele University Press
Keele, Staffordshire

© Contributors

Transferred to digital print 2013

Composed by
Keele University Press
Printed and bound by CPI Group (UK) Ltd
Croydon, CR0 4YY

ISBN 1 85331 089 1

Contents

News from Nowhere: Theory and Politics of Romanticism

Editors: Tony Pinkney, Keith Hanley, Fred Botting
The Wordsworth Centre, Department of English
Lancaster University, Lancaster LA1 4YT, UK

News from Nowhere is the journal of The Wordsworth Centre, Lancaster University. It is published annually by Ryburn Publishing, an imprint of Keele University Press. Contributions and correspondence should be addressed to the editors at the address above. Orders and distribution inquiries should be addressed to the Publishers at Keele University, Staffordshire ST5 5BG, UK.

Call for papers: 'Romantic Masculinities'

The Wordsworth Centre at Lancaster University, which has been sponsoring political and theoretical revaluations of Romanticism since its international conference on 'Romanticism and Revolution' in 1989, invites contributions on the topic of 'Romantic Masculinities' for a conference it is hosting in 1995. The conference will form the basis of next year's volume of *News from Nowhere*, as with the current issue, which was based on two events – 'Wordsworth and the Shapes of Theory' and 'Theory Gender Romanticism' – organised by The Wordsworth Centre.

Preface

The journal *News from Nowhere* was founded in Oxford in 1986. The project was two-fold: to criticise and reform the outmoded conceptions of English Studies which then prevailed at Oxford, and to publicise and develop the new critical practices which were utterly transforming the discipline. By issue 8 *News from Nowhere* had adopted the subtitle 'Journal of Cultural Materialism' to announce a broad but never doctrinaire allegiance to the literary-critical and cultural interventions represented by the work of Raymond Williams. In autumn 1991, however, the dispersal of the original group of editors left the journal in a state of cryogenic limbo.

We are now defrosting *News from Nowhere* with the subtitle 'Theory and Politics of Romanticism' as the annual journal of the Wordsworth Centre at Lancaster. It will both represent and serve to define the Centre's programme in the years to come. By developing the implications already contained in the title itself, *News from Nowhere: Theory and Politics of Romanticism* continues to celebrate the utopian vision of William Morris as a decisive moment in the labyrinthine passage of Romanticism from the nineteenth to the twentieth century.

In its earlier form, the journal was well known not only for providing a forum for new kinds of work in literary and cultural studies, but also for seeking to turn them to practical account in a series of lively, polemical interventions in the present. The new subtitle demands a continuation of that tradition. 'Romanticism' is not simply the name of a restricted historical and literary field – 1780 to 1830, say. It *is* that, of course, and the journal will certainly aim to cultivate new kinds of critical, theoretical and political approaches to the writings and culture of that period. But Romanticism is also the name of a dense cluster of signs, meanings, values and impulses which survive beyond the initial moment of their formulation, albeit in often strange ways, and retain a force in actual practice and utopian aspiration in our own society as in the 1790s. Jean-François Lyotard, for example, describes the postmodern as lying, not at the end of modernity, but in its nascent moment. Associated with the terrific irruptions of the sublime which, like the postmodern within modernity, 'puts forward the unpresentable in presentation itself', the relationship between postmodernity and modernity remains inextricably bound up with the political, cultural and philosophical shocks addressed in Romantic writing.[1]

In all sorts of ways Romanticism inhabits and informs the realism, modernism and postmodernism which, ironically, at the level of explicit conscious polemic often militantly oppose it. Indeed,

> a veritable romantic *unconscious* is discernable today in most of the central motifs of our 'modernity'. Not the least result of romanticism's indefinable character is the way it has allowed this so-called modernity to use romanticism as a foil, without ever recognizing – or in order not to recognize – that it has done little more than rehash romanticism's discoveries.[2]

Exploring the survivals and resurgences of Romanticism involves more than a simple recognition of (post)modernity's present in a Romantic past characterized as a simple revolt against reason and the state: the 'literary Absolute' that Romanticism evokes 'aggravates and radicalizes the thinking of totality and the Subject. It *infinitizes* this thinking, and therein, precisely, rests its ambiguity.' (*Literary Absolute*, p. 15) In terms of social as well as cultural practice, Romanticism remains a current and driving force in our own historical moment, emerging in debates on education, national culture, democratic rights, global ecology and sexual politics. With the crisis of a Marxist politics which thought it had seen off Romanticism from the historical field, the vigour and topicality of that submerged Romantic tradition has become abundantly evident in both utopian and dystopian ways.

There can, of course, be no easy way of reinventing Morris's Romantic anti-capitalist tradition in the uncertain present of postmodernity. Images of fourteenth-century craftsmen and unalienated labour do not fit comfortably into the mass-mediatised hyperspace of the society of the spectacle. Or, rather, they fit all *too* comfortably, as just one more depthless image of a dehistoricised Western commodity culture. As Fredric Jameson has argued of contemporary utopianism, 'a vision of something that has content, that is a full representation, may tend to arouse suspicion, because all representations are rigged in the first place. So the blank notion of the possibility of utopia … might be a little safer for the moment'.[3] Yet Morris's own apparently nostalgic plenitude might, through reading differently, be more productively hollowed out than at first glance. In many ways, his *News from Nowhere* darkly undercuts the achieved positivity of its own utopian vision. Morris's Gothic reads itself against the grain, and cheerful Ruskinian craftwork is haunted by latent uncertainty and paranoia, by a form of Gothic with a more disturbing hue. In questioning the truth of Ellen's utopian proofs, the narrator calls up a disturbing flicker of doubt: 'a glimmering of fear of what might follow; of anxiety as to the remedy which this new age might offer for the missing of something one might set one's heart on.' This reading of the text – problematising assumptions about its sunny official self-image – would disclose it as a writing of conversations, a matter of dialogues and questionings, as the interrogation of possibilities rather than a total and monolithic directing of desire: *News from Nowhere* thus appears as much a heterotopia, an 'other space' in a Foucauldian sense, as the happy Hobbitland it is often taken to be.[4]

Morris's powerful yoking of romantic utopian projection and interrogative critical suspicion may serve as a model of our own professional practice as Romantic scholars in the late twentieth century. The visionary gleams of high Romanticism, its cleansing of the doors of perception and intimations of the light that never was on land or sea remain striking moments of cultural aspiration – visions and values that no contemporary radical politics could for a moment do without – and, at the same time, dark reminders of an insistent wish for a Romantic oneness that remains shadowed, terrorised, by spectral images of its other. Politically, the Morrisian social blueprint would have to be profoundly reworked among the complexities of our contemporary image and information culture; Raymond Williams used to observe that socialism would deliver a more complex, not a more simple, society. So, too, must Romantic texts be interrogated and reworked in the light of the most sophisticated modes of reading initiated by recent literary theory – Marxist, feminist, and poststructuralist above all. That such a reworking is already underway in as well as on those texts needs little restating, though it is important to acknowledge how such processes of traversal, critique and reimagining continue to address, compellingly and complexly, the perturbed *fin de siècle* we inhabit. Wordsworth, so punishingly subject to an array of critical examinations in the last two decades, remains crucial in this project of Romantic revaluation, as the amount of attention he receives in this volume indicates, precisely because he so conspicuously consolidates two dominant Romanticisms: that which immerses itself in 'obstinate questionings' and that which shuns 'Utopia – subterranean fields' for the constructions of contemporary reality.

Given that feminism, critically as well as politically, has, over the last twenty years, most notably driven academic debates concerning cultural, institutional and individual change, it seems appropriate that the first issue of the relaunched *News from Nowhere* should devote itself to 'Romanticism, Theory, Gender'. Far from homogeneous, these terms and the following essays which diversely address them, provide points of intersection for discussions of text, culture, history, sexuality and criticism itself. If there is no easy way to dialogise Romanticism, there remains much work to be done analysing and historicising it according to contingencies of the present as well as the past; and some of that work is begun in this issue. If Romantic constructions of sexuality and subjectivity hold a certain sway over contemporary formulations, they may also disclose the terminal and hidden limits around which the present circulates. Similarly, though Romantic nature may be currently invoked by eco-friendliness, careful reading of Romantic represen-tations, or a patient tread along the tracks of its spatial orientations and movements, may engender different relations between natural, cultural and subjective worlds.

A contemporary radical politics doubtless does not wait upon the efforts of small bands of professional Romantic scholars. Yet if the 'recovery' of Romantic utopianism helped fund the New Left Project of the 1950s and 1960s, then it may be that continued theoretical meditation on Romanticism across the entire range of its tradition(s) can play at least a bit part in holding open that empty and menaced utopian space in which, even yet, in the epoch of late capitalism and 'the end of history', different formations may begin to flower. We inhabit a dilemma: while, to adopt Walter Benjamin's dictum, every generation is endowed with a *weak* Messianic power, other urgent voices are arguing that there are newer constraints and injunctions on even the most modest assumptions of power which call for a belligerent attitude towards all claims of totality.

Motivating all our explorations, however, is the project of both the journal and the Centre: to retheorise, as far as possible, ideas about communal politics and social engagement that have traditionally found expression in Romantic anti-capitalism: 'we are all, still and always, aware of the *Crisis*, convinced that "interventions" are necessary and that the least of texts is immediately 'effective' ['*opératoire*']; we all think, as if it went without saying, that politics passes through the literary (or the theoretical). Romanticism is our *naiveté*.'[5]

Notes

1   Jean-François Lyotard, *The Postmodern Condition*, tr. Geoff Bennington and Brian Massumi (Manchester: Manchester University Press, 1984), pp. 79–81.

2   Philippe Lacoue-Labarthe and Jean-Luc Nancy, *The Literary Absolute*, tr. Philip Barnard and Cheryl Lester (New York: SUNY Pr., 1988), p. 15.

3   Fredric Jameson, 'Postmodernism and utopia: an interview', *News From Nowhere* 9 (1991), p. 8.

4   Michel Foucault, 'Of Other Spaces', *Diacritics* 16.1 (1986), pp. 22–27.

5   *Literary Absolute*, pp. 16–17.

Wordsworth and the
Shapes of Theory

Paul Hamilton
University of Southampton

Two of the conclusions prompted by the recent history of critical theory sit rather uncomfortably beside each other. One is the reminder that Romanticism has claimed a formative influence on the shapes it has taken. The other is that Romantic criticism has come upon some of the more recent turns in critical theory quite late.

Cultural materialism and feminism are obvious examples of critical initiatives still fairly novel in academic studies of Romantic literature. Anne Mellor's new book on Romanticism and gender can with some justice bill itself as the first full-length feminist reading of the subject. And that further reminds one that an earlier book of hers, *English Romantic Irony*, was able, again plausibly, to describe itself as the first work exclusively devoted to that area, which seems even more extraordinary. In the case of feminism, both the predominantly male canon of the Romantic period's most influential genre, poetry, and its trope of figuring a stereotyped female sensibility of 'wise passiveness' or 'negative capability' as the sign of a fully activated poetic faculty, could perhaps resist feminist critique longer than other literatures. Nevertheless, the time-lag before getting a full discussion of the ironic trope which powered so much critical theory from the New Critics to deconstruction remains puzzling.

Equally, recent critics' eagerness to see the Romantic period as a decisive influence on critical theory is there for all to see. It seems immediately justified by Romantic poets' *sentimental* rather than *naive* literary self-consciousness, and their conspicuously programmatic approach to their art in manifesto and polemic. Furthermore, the ongoing debates about the nature of literature to which they gave unusual impetus seem focused at both the most popular and the most recherché ends of critical debate by one dispute: not Byron against Bowles, Jeffrey against the Lakers or Hazlitt against almost everyone, but the disagreement outlined at the opening of *Biographia Literaria*.

> But of the objects I proposed to myself, it was not the least important to effect, as far as possible, a settlement of the long continued controversy concerning the true nature of poetic diction; and at the same

time to define with the utmost impartiality the real *poetic* character of
the poet, by whose writings this controversy was first kindled, and has
since been fuelled and fanned.[1]

Coleridge, looking for *the* example, target or focus for his enormously
overdetermined work on critical theory, chooses Wordsworth. Here he
set in motion a tradition which could not share the complexity of his
personal reasons but which has matched him in almost all other respects.

As I have suggested, this has included the taking of the Romantic
debate as somehow formative of the subsequent shape of critical theory.
For example, Don Bialostosky's important new book, *Wordsworth, dialogics
and the practice of criticism*, assumes a number of Romantic matrices for
his and any other contemporary critical argument.[2] The general point
is, he thinks, self-evident: an 'intersection of Wordsworthian, Roman-
ticist, and theoretical interests ... by now so well known in England and
America that I would expect most readers who pick up this book to
recognize it and many to participate in it' (p. xiv). Bialostosky's book
above all emphasizes the divided voices which are to be heard at the
heart of this formative moment. The Wordsworth so useful for critical
theory which we have inherited has been too much Coleridge's creature.
The dialogue which his poetry richly fosters, and to which Bialostosky
welcomes us readers from the start, has too often been reduced to
monologue through Coleridge's influence, and, in particular, through
Coleridge's famous pronouncement on poems like 'The Sailor's
Mother' that there is 'an abrupt downfall' in the transition from the
speech of poetic narrator to lower-class character which had been better
elided. Since the 'real language of men' attempted by this transition is,
for Coleridge, an illusion (even this most authentic try, says Coleridge,
has been 'freed from provincialisms') the result is 'a species of ventril-
oquism, where two are represented as talking, while in truth one man
only speaks' (II, 54, 109).

I'll return to Bialostosky's defence of Wordsworth's dialogism later.
His general point about the Romantic genealogy of contemporary
critical theory can be supported by a number of texts which help
place his own intervention and to make more visible the characteristics
of the phenomenon. Here are some examples, not all of which he uses.
In the French post-structuralist tradition, Jean-Luc Nancy and Philippe
Lacoue-Labarthe see literature itself as something instituted under the
pressure on high idealist philosophy to disown areas for which it could
not legislate. The limits of its authority became less vulnerably obvious
when the ideal, aesthetic realm took responsibility for its own discourse.
The Kantian failure to get on adequate terms with 'ideas' was thus
excused.[3] A more down-to-earth notion of the institution of literature is
at work in Allon White's and Peter Stallybrass's *The Poetry and Politics of*

Transgression, when they detail Wordsworth's formative part in the construction of modern authorship. Bialostosky quotes their description of this project of showing how 'authorship ... was produced *over against* the popular, as embodied in the festive scene of the fair and the carnival and as embodied in popular drama' (p. 26). Here things are viewed the other way round from Nancy and Lacoue-Labarthe: literature seeks to publicize its affinities with higher vocations, like philosophy, rather than grab the chance of proclaiming its difference and so its other affinities with lower, more popular discourses. Bialostosky finds support for his general point in Jonathan Arac's *Critical Genealogies* when it declares confidently that Wordsworth 'did more than anyone to establish a vocation of literature in relation to which ... our own culture's idea of the literary critic took shape'.[4] More particularly, Stallybrass's and White's vocation of the author, an elitist soliloquizer, is clearly at odds with Arac's and Bialostosky's anti-Coleridgean picture of a writer whose work is 'constituted' (their word) in an exemplary manner by its mutually critical voices. Presumably James Kenneth Stephen's satirical pastiche on Wordsworthian voices merely compounds the Coleridgean error – 'Two voices are there: one is of the deep ... / And one is of an old half-witted sheep / Which bleats articulate monotony ... / And Wordsworth, both are thine'. Far from this mishearing, Wordsworthian voices now orchestrate complex dilemmas which expose criticism other than the dialogic as simplistic or forced. Bialostosky argues that in 'The Solitary Reaper', for example, the reaper's untranslated gaelic song and the speaker's over-anxious imperatives to listen set up an irresolution which may be aporetic but is still historically voiced. 'The Solitary Reaper' provides us 'not with a too easy image of the solitary reaper, but with an almost too difficult image of the deracinated poet caught between a traditional society he cannot recover and a contemporary society he cannot persuade' (p. 151). Dialogics, Bialostosky might say, can do the critical police, both deconstruction and new historicism, in different voices.

However, this is to go too quickly. Critics like Arac and Bialostosky claim that the formative influence of Wordsworth and Romanticism on critical theory was much more monologic and uniform than this, hence the need for their dialogic intervention. Even if one does not accept the existence of a Romantic ideology, it seems undeniable that ideology itself, as a self-justifying belief system, gets a good run in the Romantic period. At any rate, this notion of ideology as a Romantic construction links otherwise divergent critical efforts such as deconstruction and new historicism by providing their common targets. The work of Paul de Man seems infused with materialist content if it can be described as a 'critique of aesthetic ideology'. The critical object of new historicist study stays in one place if the dominant writings of the period, in all their miscellany, coagulate in a Romantic ideology. And for some new historicists, the ideology is far-reaching. For Jon Klancher, even the reviews like *Blackwoods* manifest the 'project of imperializing mental energy', a process of acculturation by which the review's middle-class audiences reassure themselves that everything speaks to them and connives at their interests. Klancher describes the circularity as 'the middle-class reader's growing capacity to turn the form of a discourse into its own content'.[5] This circularity extends the poetic communion of the Romantic imagination with itself to figure the aspirations of ordinary, self-made people. And the analogy of their self-image with poetry either euphemizes their grasping materialism or worryingly dissolves it in an unreal, fictional realm. Hence Klancher has the period's bourgeoisie, people on the make, mirroring 'the ultimately contentless activity of the mind's self-discovery' (p. 60); and, going in the other direction from poetry to class, Marjorie Levinson has John Keats 'go about the business of making himself into that nonsense thing, the middle class'.[6] In both cases, Romantic self-reflexivity both excludes potential competition and deprives itself of any means of external or communal legitimation. It is self-defeating because so single-mindedly self-enhancing. It is indeed a nonsense.

For more explanation of this alarming or extreme verdict we have to go still further back in the history of recent critical theory. It echoes the young Marx's twin attack on German idealism and the German bourgeoisie in his *Critique of Hegel's Philosophy of Right*. He attacks exactly the same mentalism and self-servingness of roughly the same historical period: 'the real seed life of the German people has up to now only flourished in its cranium. In a word: *You cannot transcend [aufheben] philosophy without realizing [verwirklichen] it.*'[7] Criticism only adds to the substance of what is criticized. New historicism attacked criticism held to show precisely this kind of undialogical participation in Romanticism. When Jerome McGann published *The Romantic Ideology* in 1983 the targets were clearly the Yale school and, behind them, M. H. Abrams and the same new critical tradition which Frank Lentricchia in *After the New Criticism* saw as a baleful influence taking its cue from the Romantic idealism of Coleridge. Bialostosky regards himself as coming in to remedy the failure to separate Wordsworth out from this general Romantic ideology. He thinks this crucial mistake results from the failure of critical theory to examine the historical, Romantic character of the origin of its own ideas. Critical theorists, in other words, extrapolated from Romantic theory to critical theory in general without realizing that they should first have checked: they should have done more Romantic criticism in order to understand the full implications of their theoretical positions.

Before considering further where Bialostosky is at and raising some questions about the dialogical solution to ideological problems, I'd like to look briefly at the representative of the Yale school most influential on recent critical theory. Bialostosky gives Paul de Man the longest and most careful treatment of any critic in his book, including Coleridge, especially Coleridge! In 1966, in his lecture on 'Wordsworth and Hölderlin', de Man confidently asserted that 'the problem of romanticism continues to dominate the other problems of historiography and literary criticism. The main points around which contemporary methodological and ethical arguments circle can almost always be traced directly back to the romantic heritage.'[8] The 'problem' in its mature form for de Man is encapsulated by the character of poetry as disfiguration. Disfiguration denotes first of all the maimed, ineffectual, 'blinded with an eye' aspect of a discourse deprived of real referents. Secondly, disfigurement denotes poetry's attempts to efface its inescapably figural character. This disfigurement is bound to fail, for all language is figural for de Man, but it is also, therefore, a disfigurement which will *figuratively* disfigure, producing grotesqueries, violence and distortion of all kinds, thus rigorously drawing attention to the impossibility of literalism or normalcy. Bialostosky calls de Man's critical vocabulary 'Gothic' with some reason. De Man's famous and much more urbane conclusion at the end of chapter one of *Allegories of Reading* conflates literature and criticism as partners in rigor and unreliability. The violence in the process he describes thus gets effaced as he repeats the Romantic strategy. In so doing, though, he repeats the Romantic dilemma: either he is out of touch with what he purports to describe, writing in a bogus metalanguage which actually floats, ungrounded, above nothing; or else *his* disfiguration, described with relative innocuousness here, sublimates the violence he does to texts whose figural nature it shares. For him to dress up his readings in this way is to disguise their violence and forced quality; yet immediately you begin to criticize de Man, as Bialostosky does, the incorrigibility of his method becomes apparent. He is unsinkable. Think how the disclosures about his war-time journalism legitimate his later scepticism by the violence with which they disfigure the preferred image of his life's work.

Faced with a critical buoyancy of this kind, it is easy to be provoked to a critique of ideology and yet to feel, like Marx, that theory itself is incriminated or framed by its intellectual selfishness and that we really ought to change the subject. Anyone for economics? Bialostosky clearly thinks that it is a blanket condemnation of this order which de Man has provoked: all Romantic poetry and critical theory are equally ideological, whether Coleridgean or Wordsworthian. The comprehensiveness of such dissent is too sweeping for Bialostosky. We should discriminate more, listen for the conflictual voices within the Romantic canon, and resurrect the drama of their disputes.

I have no major disagreement with this. I am suspicious that, like the new historicism and its target, Wordsworthian dialogics is too sweeping in its claims both to diagnose a 'problem' and to propose a remedy. Bialostosky tries to equate dialogics with a proper sensitivity to the institutions within which one speaks and therefore with a discreet relativising of any critical judgement. This seems to generate an admirable openness. Bialostosky's chapters hold 'symposia' on various of Wordsworth's poems. He is unusually fastidious in attributing any new critical opinion or interpretation to its original author. This, he says, is not simply 'the scholarly obligation of doing one's homework', and so not presenting as mine what was published some years ago; the patient working through of a series of readings of 'The Solitary Reaper' or the sonnet 'Upon Westminster Bridge' or 'It is a beauteous evening, calm and free', is also, says Bialostosky, 'to provoke [critics] to become self-conscious contributors to the critical community that enables and challenges their cultural practices' (p. 124). This sounds very much like, indeed affirms itself to be, the academy talking to itself, or, more specifically, the American academy in seminar. As a result, even taking Bialostosky on those terms, I think there are two main problems which arise from his approach and attitude, one specific, one more general. First of all, one wants to be sure that he has got the other schools with which he disagrees correct; secondly, is he really positioned at the end of the critical tradition he describes, or have other less manageable but perhaps more potent critical animals come out of the Romantic defile? To answer the first question, I would like to consider his reading of 'The Sailor's Mother', and then, with the second query in mind, to try a wider survey of recent developments across the field of Romantic studies.

In his dialogic reading of 'The Sailor's Wife', Bialostosky's initial target is Coleridge; secondarily he invents a reading which he somewhat playfully attributes to Jerome McGann. In these corrections of former article readings, real and imagined, Bialostosky extends the activity of the poem itself: the speaker in the poem, we hear, 'reports his speech and hers, then, in the satisfaction that arises from her correction of his first impression; he hears himself ironically, as he hears her words with continuing pleasure in her pleasure' (p. 69). No de Manian violence happens here, but rather an extension and repetition in the critical activity of Wordsworth's 'grand elementary principle of pleasure' of which the poem and its reading are both instances. For, contrary to a mystifying Coleridgean tradition, Bialostosky's Wordsworthian tradition would let us teach poetry as a pleasurable verbal and cultural practice that self-consciously cultivates powers inherent in the ordinary verbal and cultural experience of our students (p. 37). However pleasingly democratic this sounds (and there are major democratic moments in Coleridge's *Biographia Literaria* too), the seamless unity of writer and critic recalls once more the spectre of ideology. Having certainly seen off the elitist element of Coleridge's criticism of the poem, Bialostosky now has to dispel any notion that his reading is vulnerable to ideological critique. Correction, after all, has lost its sting in his account: instead it has become an incorrigible pleasure. We weren't disagreeing, you and I, we were engaging in dialogue, sharing its pleasures. Isn't Bialostosky an easy target for the new historicist who argues that this dereliction of judgement, this overcoming of criticism by pleasure, is just what it is the purpose of Romantic ideology to excuse?

Bialostosky tries to turn the tables by turning the new historicist into a sitting duck instead. This critic reduces 'the many voices' dialogic readings reveal to 'the self-indulgent single voice of the ideologue' (p. 73). Bialostosky thinks there is historicism enough in his own reading and that further historicist 'correction' of the speaker would mute the poetic polyphony. Taking, now, the case of 'The Sailor's Wife', the imaginary McGann's 'dialectical certainty' would dismiss the elementary pleasure in the 'singing-bird' which, by implication, replaces the slightly bombastic elevation of tone and feeling with which the narrator casts the sailor's wife as 'like a Roman Matron'. McGann would only be able to sustain his critique by repeating Coleridge's charge of 'abrupt downfall' in the poem's shift of register and by extending it to include disapproval of the speaker's covert elevation of the woman by another ideological device. The 'grand elementary principle of pleasure' moves into place to console the mother and exonerate the narrator when his Burkean rhetoric cannot be sustained. (Bialostosky reminds us that Burke likens Marie Antoinette to 'a Roman Matron' in *Reflections*.) The reality of shared pleasure is denied in this reading because, some might say, pushing Bialostosky's McGann a bit further, the Burkean voice has successfully appropriated it. In its Burkean apposition, the 'elementary principle of pleasure' must enforce a conservative political view of the organic integrity of society, a view which elides real repression and discrimination and with which we cannot sympathise.

As soon as we begin to push the historicist reading further, though, Bialostosky's McGann begins to look more formidable. Bialostosky is saying that we lose more than we gain by accepting an ideological reading. To be unable to acknowledge 'natural' pleasures transcending social class is to give a victory to the ideologies we were out to expose. Yes, we might say, but doesn't the poem implicitly acknowledge this and allow us to take the pleasure back, although in a precarious form? We have to undergo the ideological rite of passage, if you like, but at the other end we can emerge grasping intact the comforts stolen from us. The 'Roman Matron', after all, is Burke's typical appropriation from French Revolutionary rhetoric of a classical, republican idiom. The dazzling impropriety of Burke's application of the 'Roman Matron' epithet to Marie Antoinette works exactly through his monstering of the revolution and revolutionaries so that their unnaturalness makes

historical and even political difference look comparatively trivial. This
licence of appropriation contrasts with most French Revolutionary art
in a republican mode; its echoes were much more literal and severe.
Arguably, the poem awakens us readers rather than the speaker to the
fact that there *is* a frail inheritance of pleasure – a dead man's singing-
bird in a cage carried aimlessly by his mother of 'little wit' – a 'delight'
free of Burkean pride and ownership. But how frail the legacy looks,
surrounded by much stronger appropriative energies, ready, like the
speaker, to seize upon it. The same poetic form, differently voiced by
the speaker's own words and then his remembered words for the mother,
registers different things: the confident appropriation of the speaker and
then the fragile resistance which the woman's emblematic possibilities
pose to the speaker's politically Burkean design. Against Burke's politics,
but in keeping with his rhetorical strategies, she hangs on to her pleasure
on her own terms. The confident, almost Horatian section of the
narrator is weakened by the uncomfortable assimilation of the mother's
speech to this inappropriately hegemonic verse-form. That stylistic
discomfort, verging on bathos and twitter (especially that last couplet),
is all we have to measure her independence; but then we should remember that some of Burke's other images for Marie Antoinette – as Gothic
victim, say – are also fairly abject, his chivalry forced. We don't have to
read Wordsworth's poem as just the effusion of a patronising narrator;
nor must we see the awkwardness of his incorporation of the mother
as signalling a successful conversation, dialogically and improbably
democratic. Rather we are witnesses to a Burkean exercise in appropriation, licensed to cut both ways, though certainly not in equal portions.
In that case, in the Romantic game of critical trumping or *Aufhebung*
maybe the new historicist still has another card to play?

I have tried, somewhat provocatively, to galvanise a new historicist
reading against Bialostosky mostly because of my interest in the second
question I raised earlier. It isn't too hard to revive a critical position and
have it pop up further down the line than Bialostosky's dialogue, but the
most recent developments in Romantic scholarship question his linear
progress of criticism, suggesting instead that a lateral expansion may be
what is needed.

Any review of current Romantic *criticism* has to acknowledge that a
vast amount of scholarship is now occurring concerning the contemporary alternatives to the period's hegemonic discourse, writings ignored
by Romanticism's conversation with itself, however multivocal or equivocal. The question then is this one. Can contemporary critical theory
also shape the consequences of this Romantic ignorance of other kinds
of writing during the period?

Briefly, these consequences were firstly a critical failure of reading
which we inherit today and which we compound by failing to appreciate

the challenge of often highly popular writings felt then by major Romantic authors. Innovative commentators and anthologists of Romantic writing repeatedly question now whether or not we know how to read a mass of writing of the time, especially 'sentimental' or women's writing, scientific writing and political economy. Secondly, past failures to provide rationales for non-canonical literature, critical methodologies which match the philosophical sophistication of Romantic theory, consigned the redefinition of cultural values to ostensibly inhospitable discourses – scientific, positivistic, economic. Romanticism's stark antagonism to their materialism, coupled with its own eventual bankruptcy, cast them unfairly as catastrophes: the inappropriate and exclusive media in which its humanistic cultural values were left to find an unlikely subsistence. New theorists, from Marx onwards, were well able to rescue the real nature of the new materialism from Romantic demonization. Lost, however, along the way were the alternative voices which accompanied the previous Romantic ascendancy. Their rationale lay outside Romanticism's binary opposition of itself to a materialism it styled as unacceptably mechanistic, deterministic and reductive.

Current scepticism about the distinctiveness and value of literature, the canon, criticism and its theory reworks that original Romantic crisis. Both the story of Romanticism in English, and present problems in defining English as an independent subject amongst the claims of other media, throw light upon each other. Our understanding of the Romantic period grows more complex the more sensitive new, multi-media scholarship makes us to Romanticism's instability and to its extra-canonical opposition. Equally, the current relativizing of literary studies by studies in other media no longer looks necessarily like cultural devaluation or the failure of the humanistic project once we have historically situated the Romantic habit of regarding this endeavour as literature's prerogative, and better understood Romantic literature as a result.

It is plausible to argue that Romanticism has focused the most radical departures of critical theory during the last twenty-five years, from Derrida's deconstruction of Rousseau onwards. But now that the study of Romanticism has for a while settled on those writings excluded from its canon and consequently neglected by theory, theory itself is challenged by its old ally. When the Romantic idealists were attacked by the materialists who succeeded them, there appeared to be no alternatives, simply an ending, the 'war on thought' declared in *The German Ideology*. Of course literature of a Romantic kind survived in English, and the most rigorous of materialisms generated new theories. With hindsight we should avoid that deceptive Romantic cul-de-sac today and realise that cultural studies places rather than replaces the value of literature, and that this judgement encourages more disabused and better reading of the original texts.

Is this merely another self-serving argument though, saving the text yet again in order, like Geoffrey Hartman, to provide one more safe-house for a critical theory? Historians of critical theory vary in degrees of cynicism, but one frequently held position is that every ostensibly impartial reinterpretation of the past is always in the business of bolstering the latest critical methodology. Don Bialostosky quotes Bruce Robbins to this effect (p. 38). I have tried here to keep seeing things the other way round, breaking the hermeneutical circle or Romantic merging of history and philosophy, the object and its critique. This more materialist line would imply that changes in our own circumstances, like the revolutions in communicative media, show up the inadequacies of our inherited theories of cultural value. The new theories we evolve as a result make us alive to the non-canonical features of the past, previously unnoticed or marginalised. Part of the pastness, though, of these new objects of theoretical attention is to challenge, in their turn, the adequacy of our modern/postmodern theories of them. In other words, the new theories raise *general* questions about how we might place canonical Romanticism in an intelligible setting, simultaneously revising our notions of *its* intelligibility. Literary historical research specifies the *particular* problems involved. Because these problems are historically different, they demand further theoretical flexibility and originality from us: reading outside the Romantic mainstream in the 1790s or 1820s is very different, say, from studying popular culture today. We can learn from the different form this general opposition of 'high' and 'low' art took in the past and sharpen our current reading-practices accordingly.

And so the dialectic continues. I am less cynical about this outcome than some American new historicists, and less sanguine about its residual idealism than Bialostosky because I think that the critical institutions of the academy have sometimes to decide not to converse with other voices. Let's have dialectic rather than dialogue. Not that critical theorists should mount a Mallarméan *grève*. English is not defending itself very successfully at the moment, hence its vulnerability to government ideologues. Yet to restore the old cultural hierarchy, with English at the top, would be to play into the Government's hands. Maybe what is required is a critical theory which can convince that a more sympathetic and comprehensive understanding of literature and its privilege is achieved, that literary value becomes more visible, as the play of other discourses which creates that value, although they have their own values, is revealed. Or, yet again the other way round, we should show that more of canonical literature's value-creating power (more of Wordsworth), whatever we think of that power or those values, remains *hidden* the more unquestioningly we accept its Romantic self-esteem.

Notes

1   *Biographia Literaria*, ed. J. Engell and W. J. Bate in *The Collected Works of Samuel Taylor Coleridge* (London: Routledge and Kegan Paul, 1983), 2 vols., I, 5.

2   Don Bialostosky, *Wordsworth, dialogics and the practice of criticism* (Cambridge: Cambridge University Press, 1992).

3   Jean-Luc Nancy and Philippe Lacoue-Labarthe, *The Literary Absolute: the Theory of Literature in German Romanticism*, trans. with an introduction by Philip Barnard and Cheryl Lester (Albany, New York: SUNY Press, 1988).

4   Jonathan Arac, *Critical Genealogies: Historical Situations for Postmodern Literary Studies* (New York: Columbia University Press, 1987), p. 3.

5   Jon Klancher, *The Making of English Reading Audiences 1790–1832* (Madison: University of Wisconsin Press, 1987), pp. 58–9.

6   Marjorie Levinson, *Keats's Life of Allegory: the Origins of a Style* (Oxford: Basil Blackwell, 1988), p. 26.

7   Karl Marx, 'Critique of Hegel's Philosophy of Right' in *Early Writings*, trans. R. Livingstone and G. Benton (Harmondsworth: Penguin, 1975), p. 250.

8   Paul de Man, *The Rhetoric of Romanticism* (New York: Columbia University Press, 1984), p. 48.

'Jerusalem was the omphalos of mortality': Gender and Thomas De Quincey's Hysteric Phantasies

Elisabeth Bronfen
University of Zurich

But the deep deep tragedies of infancy, as when the child's hands were unlinked for ever from his mother's neck, or his lips for ever from his sister's kisses, these remain lurking below all, and these lurk to the last. Alchemy there is none of passion or disease that can scorch away these immortal impresses ... every man probably will meet [this truth] experimentally who passes through similar convulsions of dreaming or delirium from any similar or equal disturbance in his nature.[1]

Making verdant things that express death

I want to begin with two quotations, so as to frame my discussion of gender and Thomas De Quincey's hysteric phantasies. The first is from Freud's *Studies in Hysteria* (1893–95). In his case history of Emmy v. N. Freud at one point records that 'the night before she had had horrible dreams. She had had to lay out a number of dead people [*so viele Tote schmücken*] and put them in coffins, but would not put the lids on [*wollte aber nie den Deckel darauf geben*]'.[2] What we have here is the self-representation of a hysteric, dressing, adorning, indeed one could say embellishing the dead, at the same time that in this dream phantasy she also commemorates the presence of the dead amongst the living by virtue of leaving the coffins open. I invoke this image because I will want to present De Quincey's autobiographical writings – especially his *Suspiria de Profundis* – as an example for male hysteric phantasy-work.

In order to do so, however, I need to recall for you that before Freud's work, hysteria was considered to be a so-called 'disorder' that performs the problematic relationship between identity, gender and representation. The English physician Thomas Sydenham, one of the first to write on this illness during the period of the Enlightenment, propounds the notion that hysteria is an illness of imitation, it 'imitates other diseases', indeed imitates culture. As the critic G. S. Rousseau puts it, hysteria is 'produced by tensions and stresses within the culture surrounding the patient ... the symptom leading to the condition of

22

hysteria "imitated" the culture in which it (the symptom) had been produced'.[3] Since the middle of the 19th century, in addition to this definition of hysteria as an illness of imitation, it was also considered to be the suffering from mnemonic traces of a psychic trauma whose origin is unknown or repressed. While the French psychiatrist Pierre Janet apodictically calls hysteria a *maladie par representation*, on the one hand constructed by the cultural images it imitates and on the other hand engendering condensed and displaced repetitions of an originary psychic disorder, Freud brings into play the concept of pathogenic memory.[4] He argues that when there is no satisfactory abreaction of a psychical trauma, the memory of it retains the affect which it originally had and leads to symptom-formation. Given that he found in his hysterical patients 'nothing but impressions which have not lost their affect and whose memory has remained vivid', he concluded that hysterics suffer from reminiscences: they can not get free of the past, and for its sake they neglect what is real and immediate (*Hysteria*, p. 37).

What is common to all these definitions is that the hysteric performs the problematics entailed in mimesis, to be more precise, the disturbance often inscribed in the project of self-representation, of autobiography. The hysteric uses the body to repeat by proxy an earlier trauma, and in the course of this imitative self-representation oscillates between restoring the past and obliterating the present, between a feminine and a masculine self-definition, between revitalizing what is dead and mortifying what is living. One could say, with the help of body-symptoms the hysteric decorates the past and its dead, keeps it from being buried – notably by virtue of fits of excitation and paralysis, hallucinations, absences of consciousness, as well as the histrionic display of phantasy scenes, the dissimulation of various roles contingent upon a *belle indifférence* to each. The hysteric thus lives a double consciousness in the sense that she or he vacillates between conscious and trance-like self-representations. As a result the hysteric performs a fluid exchange with the past, with the difference it inscribes in the world of the living, with a commemoration of mortality.

Freud's interpretation of Emmy v. N.'s dream is that it 'obviously' represents a recollection of the death of her husband. If, however, one looks more closely at the case history he presents, and given also that Emmy v. N. speaks about the dead in the plural, it would be more accurate to see this dream as representing the many encounters with mortality that have informed her identity[5] – when (aged five) her brothers and sisters often threw dead animals at her, when (aged seven) she unexpectedly saw her sister in her coffin, when (aged eight) her brother used to terrify her by dressing up in sheets like a ghost, when (aged nine) she saw her aunt in her coffin and her jaw suddenly dropped, hallucinations she had (aged 19) at the death-bed of her brother and in the same year, coming home and suddenly finding her mother dead, with a distorted face. The sudden death of her husband while she was lying in bed after her second confinement is but the acme of these earlier events. I emphasize this point because I will want to argue that even as hysteria – the illness of the wandering uterus, of imitation, of representation and of reminiscences – stages the body in relation to past trauma and textualizes this enactment, it does so significantly in response to mortality. As Freud obliquely notes in respect to Emmy v. N.'s confessions, 'It has also struck me that amongst all the intimate information given me by the patient there was a complete absence of the sexual element'; for Freud a worrisome admission, given that he seeks to establish sexual disorder as the key to all aetiologies of neurosis (*Hysteria*, p. 103). Yet in fact, his hysteric patient has actually given him another image for that seminal experience 'more liable than any other to provide occasion for traumas', which is why I chose it as the starting point for my discussion of De Quincey's narrative, written some 50 years earlier. For one could read the hysteric, adorning her dead, preserving the taint of death and the grief this calls forth amongst the living, as a meta-representation of hysteria itself.

This brings me to my second quotation, now from De Quincey's *Suspiria de Profundis*, because it illustrates my argument that hysteria be seen not exclusively as a neurotic response to sexuality (as is commonly thought), but perhaps more significantly to experiences of mortality. For as he justifies the technique of digressions that he will employ in his representation of early childhood trauma and its vicissitudes, De Quincey has recourse to an image strikingly similar to that of Emmy v. N.: 'view me, as one ... making verdant, and gay with the life of flowers, murderous spears and halberts – things that express death in their origin ... things that express ruin in their use'. In what follows I will want to argue that, as it welds notions of the origin of trauma, a theory of creativity with a gendered notion of death, De Quincey's autobiography can be read as a hysterical narrative. In view of this, it is interesting to note that De Quincey, the narrator, self-consciously calls himself 'the ruler of the oscillations' (p. 137), so that my focus will be on the way his text enmeshes phantasies of empowerment with a recognition of disempowerment. As Jo McDonagh argues, even as De Quincey's obsessive return to scenes of violence and mortality express a desire for control, 'he can never achieve the control he desires ... despite himself, he constantly celebrates his disempowerment'.[6]

My interest in developing the paradigm of a male hysteric text for De Quincey is both to explore what this celebration of disempowerment, i.e. of mortality, entails as well as to rethink what has so readily been conceived as a misogynist stance. Mary Jacobus, using De Quincey's discussion of style in *The English Mail-Coach* as her example, has rightly noted that 'women in his writing are especially accident-prone', that in a sense 'he must commit (wo)manslaughter if he is to write at all' precisely because he conceives of himself while writing as a 'helpless passenger on an out-of-control vehicle that threatens death to what he holds dear', namely the feminine, the language of feeling.[7] De Quincey thus fashions himself – and in this self-representation I want to locate his hysteria – as someone who functions at once as the 'agent of disaster, its herald, and its witness'. In her discussion of male hysteria as it was reformulated around 1800, Christina von Braun suggests that this rediscovery / invention of masculine femininity need not be seen as a reappraisal of the feminine. Rather, as the male hysteric cultivates his own vulnerability, his loss of control, his disempowerment, he obliterates the concrete feminine completely, so as to carve a discursive space for his own, better Womanness. Her main thesis: the romantic male hysteric undertakes a translation of the living woman's body into a trope of the feminine that serves to express masculine Womanness.[8] In the same counter-intuitional stance with which I want to privilege mortality over sexuality as the origin of hysterical trauma, I will also want to explore not only how De Quincey repeatedly uses images of dead women as the radical Other, onto whom he can displace that which threatens. Rather, I also want to show that within his theory of creativity, the repeated construction of phantasy scenes, where loss, difference, solitude, death are only imperfectly put aside, indeed restored and celebrated in their return, requires the deanimated feminine as a point of identification, i.e. a hysterical acknowledgement of the feminine in himself.

My argument will contain two parts: I will suggest that the scenario of interpersonal influences De Quincey represents in his recollection of his friendship with William Wordsworth – so crucial for his self-fashioning as a poet and for his theory of creativity – has as its lynchpin the strange figure of Dorothy Wordsworth, a hysterical body because she oscillates between the feminine and the masculine, the living and the dead, representing original nature and functioning as the medium for another, notably her brother's voice. As such she emerges as a repositum of difference. The phantasy De Quincey develops as he records his experience of the William, Dorothy and Mary Wordsworth triangle could be called a family romance in Freud's sense of a wish-fulfilling phantasy, by means of which the subject invents a new family for himself, modifies his relationship to the other members of his family and in so doing works out a sort of romance.[9] Crucial for my argument, however, is the fact, that this phantasy of how a brother-sister couple enhances creativity will reappear in a somewhat altered state in the autobiographical writings that centre on what he called an 'affliction of childhood', namely the experience of his sister Elizabeth's death in 1792 when he was six years old. For this encounter with death produces very

similar psychic and somatic symptoms to the ones Freud will trace at the
end of the century in hysterics like Emmy v. N. – loss of consciousness,
hallucinations, a traumatic return of the repressed incident in dreams
and opium-induced visions as well as a reconstruction and restoration
of the experience in the form of an autobiographical text. Significantly
De Quincey likens the brain to a palimpsest, 'everlasting layers of
ideas, images, feelings, have fallen upon your brain softly as light. Each
succession has seemed to bury all that went before. And yet in reality not
one has been extinguished' (p. 144), while the act of dreaming and of
writing counteracts this process, 'effacing all above which [had been]
superscribed; restoring all below which [had been] effaced' (p. 141).
Traced over a central organizing childhood experience that seems to
have faded but that reinserts itself in moments of psychic oscillation, the
text resurrects this 'privileged' (p. 91) agitation, adorns the dead, keeps
the grave open. Indeed, in her discussion of De Quincey's palimpsest
technique Eve Kosofsky Sedgwick notes the remarkable connection not
only between 'what is past and what is written, but between both of
these and live burial'.[10]

The first family romance

In his article on 'William Wordsworth', published 1839 in *Tait's Edinburgh
Magazine*, De Quincey describes his first meeting with Wordsworth and
the two ladies living with him at Grasmere. At this point in his life De
Quincey had constructed Wordsworth as the figure meant to guarantee
the stability of self he had lost with his sister's death, a trauma which
had, furthermore, returned in his opium-dreams in Oxford just previous
to this momentous meeting. In his phantasies the poet Wordsworth,
however, also serves as the embodiment of precisely the pure, celestial
love he thought to have experienced and then lost with Elizabeth.
Immediately striking about William's two feminine companions is, in
turn, the difference, the 'most effective contrast' they seem to represent.
The tall Mary Wordsworth, expressing benignity and a 'sweetness all
but angelic', appears as a paradigm of simplicity and purity of heart. She
strikes De Quincey as one who speaks through her looks, acts and
movements but whose words are few. 'Certainly her intellect was not of
an active order,' he suggests, 'but, in a quiescent, reposing, meditative
way, she appeared always to have a genial enjoyment from her own
thoughts'. Her forte, he concludes, was 'to feel and to enjoy in a luxurious repose of mind'.[11]

Against this figure of mental passivity, seemingly content with the
constraints that conventional notions of feminine behaviour posed for
her, De Quincey presents Dorothy Wordsworth: short, slight, with an

unusually tanned face, her manner warm and ardent, her eyes neither soft nor bold but rather 'wild and startling, and hurried in their motion'. In De Quincey's description she emerges as the classic hysteric, perpetually performing a fundamental 'self-counteraction' and 'self-baffling of her feelings', because oscillating between the desire for masculine activity and the dictum of a feminine passivity. He notes, 'some subtle fire of impassioned intellect apparently burned within her, which being alternately pushed forward into a conspicuous expression by the irrepressible instincts of her temperament, and then immediately checked, in obedience to the decorum of her sex and age, and her maidenly condition, (for she had rejected all offers of marriage, out of pure sisterly regard to her brother and his children,)' finds its expression in 'embarrassment' and utter 'self-conflict' that is 'distressing to witness'. The hysteric symptom for this conflict is a stammer, such that 'her very utterance and enunciation ... generally suffered in point of clearness and steadiness, from the agitation of her excessive organic sensibility, and, perhaps, from some morbid irritability of the nerves' ('Wordsworth', p. 131).

Thus, in this family romance, the idealized, awe-inspiring poet Wordsworth appears positioned between a virtually dumb 'partner and second self' on the one hand and on the other a companion and confidential friend who had 'couched his eye to the sense of beauty', had indeed humanized him by her 'delicate female touch', and endowed his by nature rude genius with graceful loveliness and beauty. But in this transaction the latter had paid the price of becoming a figure of discord – an 'ungraceful, and even an unsexual character' owing to a 'physical quickness of motion' and a 'stooping attitude when outdoors', her remarkable intellectual endowments and her ardent feelings tainted by an 'embarrassment in their utterance' that stemmed from the conflict between innate impulse and 'continual restraint of good sense' ('Wordsworth', p. 155, p. 132 and p. 199).

Mary Jacobus is tempted to view the 'biographical fact of Wordsworth having a sister as ... a necessary fiction for De Quincey ... especially revealing vis-à-vis her function in constituting the poet as masculine'.[12] In this fiction, Dorothy emerges as the perfect midwife for creative genius, even as she does so in a complex manner. She subjects herself completely to the mission of waiting upon the poet, loving him, sympathizing with him, counselling him, cheering and sustaining him, all of which is possible because she ingrafts by her feminine hand 'upon his masculine austerity that delicacy and those graces which else it would not have had' ('Wordsworth', p. 201). Without the support, indeed the domesticating embellishment of the feminine, the masculine poet can neither survive nor create, and one senses that De Quincey in part projects nostalgic desire onto the other poet's sister, that is to say, fashions Dorothy as the repetition of the sister-figure he requires for his

own creative aspirations. As John Beer argues, in the intense affection
William felt for Dorothy, he not only fulfilled the Wordsworthian
program of cultivating intense personal relationships but also recalled
for De Quincey his own fraternal love of the heart which seemed to
transcend conventional sexual desire. At the same time the Wordsworthian family romance seemed to recollect for him his own sense that
at the centre of childish sensibility and pulsing vitality lies a link with the
subliminal source of vision and divine light; 'Wordsworth had, it seems,
become for him a supreme guarantor of the world into which he felt
himself to have been initiated by his early relationship with Elizabeth'.[13]
What is crucial to remember, however, is that such quasi hallucinatory
visions of divinity as an all encompassing force not only required
extreme emotional states one could call hysterical, but were most likely
to be precipitated by events of death. That is to say, this sister, obliquely
recalled in the wish-fulfilling phantasy that the Wordsworths apparently
perform, is both necessarily a maidenly and a dead sister.

Dorothy's enlivening feminine touch is, furthermore, uncultivated,
wild, natural. She is irregular in her education. Bewitching with her
'native freshness of intellect' she seems at the same time deficient in
ordinary female accomplishments, lacking manner and deportment,
leaving the impression of abruptness, rudeness, and unsexual awkwardness – a depiction which resonates with the traits many hysterics will
again display at the end of the century. The paradox De Quincey thus
develops in this phantasy-scenario is such that Dorothy seems almost
too alive – 'the truest, most inevitable, and, at the same time, the
quickest and readiest in her sympathy with either joy or sorrow ... with
the realities of life and the larger realities of the poets' – and at the same
time completely deanimated by virtue of her function as medium for her
brother's self-expression ('Wordsworth', p. 203 and p. 201).

As Simon Wilson notes: 'It is not too far-fetched to claim that De
Quincey sees, in the relationship between William and Dorothy Wordsworth, an image of what unity with his own sister Elizabeth would have
been like if she had miraculously survived into adulthood'.[14] I would,
nevertheless, venture to speculate that even as he in the course of this
family romance thus fashions Dorothy into the perfect sister he has lost,
De Quincey also experienced some uncanny though never directly
articulated empathy for Dorothy, thus himself oscillating between these
two points of identification. He senses this proximity to Dorothy rather
than her brother precisely because her exceeding sensibility – which he
describes as 'constitutionally deep', as 'always ready and always
profound' – is not a sign of quietude but rather poised precariously on
the brink of neurotic illness and a gender-conflict that entangles power
with disempowerment ('Wordsworth', p. 132). Furthermore, Simon
Wilson suggests another point of connection between De Quincey and

the poet's strange sister when he argues 'De Quincey shows that Dorothy Wordsworth is actually "imagined" to death by her brother – or at least into the life-in-death of nervous disease. De Quincey does his best to avoid the same fate.'[15]

Indeed, having transformed the Wordsworths into his phantasy-scenario of familial relations most conducive to the origin and improvement of poetic genius, De Quincey implicitly deconstructs it. Not only in his explicit estrangement from Wordsworth himself, whom in a later article he describes as 'a man so diffused amongst innumerable objects of equal attraction that he had no cells left in his heart for strong individual attachments'.[16] But also when, even as he ranks Dorothy among the most fortunate of women for having chosen virgin seclusion and singleness so as to enjoy the ennobling companionship of her illustrious brother, he admits that after her brother's marriage, when her function to inspire and feminize his poetic work had been superseded by Mary, it would have been 'better for her own happiness if she had been a blue-stocking'. That is to say, she might have been happier if she had caste off the role of Dorothy, the name prefiguring her mission as 'gift of God' to the poet Wordsworth and become more profanely Miss Wordsworth, a professional author. Ironically against his proclivity to phantasize the sister into the image of the origin and agent of male poetic genius, De Quincey recognizes the self-consumption that inhabits Dorothy's remarkable self-effacing dedication: 'Had [professional authorship] been opened for Miss Wordsworth,' he concludes, 'I am satisfied that she would have passed a more cheerful middle-age, and would not, at any period, have yielded to that nervous depression which, I grieve to hear, has clouded her latter days' ('Wordsworth', p. 204 and p. 205). Dorothy emerges as the fatal victim of Williams's intensive, unstructured tutelage as well as the onesidedness in extremity of his reading and writing activity ('Estrangement', p. 381). While he was 'organised and made whole by her love,' thus Wilson, 'Dorothy was gradually trapped'. Like so many hysterics in the 19th century, somatizing the futility of their life through bodily incapacitation, Dorothy seems to have unconsciously realized that she could not go on playing the role of the devoted sister for ever, but with nothing else to do, succumbing to despair and relinquishing her health, she began to lead a kind of 'death-in-life' (Wilson, *Troubled Body*, p. 164 f.). As David Wright notes, after a series of illnesses beginning in 1828 Dorothy Wordsworth's mind gave way in 1835, and she lived on, in a kind of twilight existence, for another twenty years' (*Recollections*, p. 408).

Indeed Dorothy Wordswoth seems not only to have anticipated her anxiety about her brother's wedding in a letter to Mrs. John Marshall, dated September 29th, 1892; 'I look forward with perfect happiness to this connection between us, but, happy as I am, I half dread that concentration of all tender feelings, past, present, and future which will come upon me on the wedding morning'.[17] For she actually seems to have somaticized this sense of psychic depletion. In her journal entry for October 1802 she records her hysterical response to William and Mary's wedding as follows: 'I slept a good deal of the night & rose fresh & well in the morning – at a little after 8 o clock I saw them go down the avenue towards the Church. William had parted from me up stairs. I gave him the wedding ring – with how deep a blessing! I took it from my fore-finger where I had worn it the whole of the night before – he slipped it again onto my finger and blessed me fervently. When they were absent my dear little Sara prepared the breakfast. I kept myself as quiet as I could, but when I saw the two men running up the walk, coming to tell us it was over, I could stand it no longer & threw myself on the bed where I lay in stillness, neither hearing or seeing anything, till Sara came upstairs to me & said 'They are coming'. This forced me from the bed where I lay & I moved I knew not how straight forward, faster than my strength could carry me till I met my beloved William & fell upon his bosom'.[18]

In his family portrait of the Wordsworth, De Quincey obliquely acknowledges what recent critics have deconstructed as the hidden pre-supposition of masculine romantic theories of poetic creativity, namely that the price for the brother's creative power is the incapacitation of the sister. In the poem 'The Sparrow's Nest' Wordsworth records his debt – 'She gave me eyes, she gave me ears', – but being the living agent that restores her brother's imagination entails both a deanimation and a desex-ualization on her part. 'The motif of brother-sister love,' thus Jacobus, 'swiftly assimilates sexual difference to narcissistic identity ... the sister simultaneously figures the repression of sexuality and the refusal of sexual difference' (*Romanticism*, p. 208). Or as Spivak notes, the itinerary of Wordsworth's securing of the imagination involves apostrophizing Dorothy, so that the poet-brother can address himself, and in so doing claim for himself 'an androgynous plenitude which would include within the self an indeterminate role of mother as well as lover'. The logical consequence for this results in rememorating 'through the medi-ation of the figure of Dorothy his own Oedipal accession to the Law, Imagination as the androgyny of Nature and Man – Woman shut out';[19] that is to say precisely the figure of the male hysteric von Braun discerns for the romantic period. Yet even as this is the paradigm typical for romantic poetry, De Quincey argues both in his discussion of Dorothy Wordsworth, and in his return to his own brother-sister constellation, that as sexual difference is assimilated into the body of the hysterical male poet, what is precisely not repressed is mortality.

For when De Quincey some six years later narrates another family romance – the story of his own childhood affliction – the incapacitated feminine body re-emerges, in a sense enmeshing the dumb woman (Mary) with the woman who fatally suffers from her remarkable intellectual gifts because she turns medium to her brother (Dorothy). Having realized that what holds the Wordsworth family romance together is the deanimation of the feminine body, he discovers *qua* invents the same family scenario for his fictional reconstruction of the self in *Suspiria de Profundis*. The itinerary of his argument seems to be: At the centre of the wish-fulfilling phantasy of William, Mary and Dorothy Wordsworth as the family most ideally structured to enhance the brother's poetic creativity, a phantasy which, furthermore, was meant to assuage the traumatic disruption of his sense of plenitude and unity with his beloved sister, which was brought upon him by virtue of her early death, he discovers Dorothy as a living corpse. He responds by writing the ultimate family romance, namely his autobiographical fiction, where the ideal source of inspiration is a sister, now literally dead. This dumb body – recalling the silence of Freud's death drive – emerges as the superlative source for his own creative powers, for his constitutionally deep sensibility that brings him to the brink of neurotic illness. If Wordsworth's apostrophes to Dorothy, in Jacobus' words, 'mirror an aspect of Wordsworth's salvaged poetic identity, serving to reflect back on him the chastened, stemmed, and balanced qualities necessary if he is to confront, not the sublime, but mortality', De Quincey's reformulation of this fraternal relation is precisely not directed toward the image of a salvaged poetic identity, but rather one emerging from and embracing strife (*Romanticism*, p. 181).

Thus the analogy I want to unfold for the two autobiographical texts by the author De Quincey is the following. Dorothy, the living-dead medium is to the brother William Wordsworth as the corpse of Elizabeth is to her brother Thomas De Quincey. In both cases the deanimation of the sister, her apostrophe, engenders the poet's life, his phantasies, his creativity. In the gesture of overdetermination, De Quincey implies that, if Elizabeth had survived, she as his medium might have become the living dead Dorothy seemed to have transformed into, so better to die young. Or, if he is to be the more supreme poet, he requires not a hysterical, living-dead sister, incapacitated, depleted, but rather its superlative, the dead sister, repeatedly restored as such a figure of death returning to life, encroaching upon the living. The crucial distinction resides in the fact that while Wordsworth transcends the difference posed by the feminine, subsuming her into an image of the androgynous poet and obliterating her as source for his memory images, words and phrases,[20] De Quincey returns to the feminine body that threatens and thwarts him – the difference his sister embodies not only through her other sexuality but above all through her death. This is why I want to cast him as a male hysteric – identifying with the deadened feminine body and symptomizing this incapacitation in the form of hallucinations and gaps in consciousness.

The primal scene of mortality

J. Hillis Miller is one of the first critics to point out that the death of Elizabeth De Quincey, troubling all further events in his life with a knowledge of fatality, also forms the scene, to which his writings repeatedly return. Given that she embodied for him the mediator that bound him to the world and to divinity, her loss, thus Miller, provokes a sense that 'what was an indissoluble unity has been fragmented,' that God has become unattainable, 'hidden himself, as if with secret malice' as well as the 'awareness of the self as a solitary point'.[21] The loss of this stabilizing agency could henceforth only be restored through an act of phantasy and memory (Beer, 'Dark sublime', p. 185),[22] casting him – thus my argument – into the role of the hysteric precisely because he fashions himself as one suffering from representations and reminiscences, but above all, in the vein of Emmy v. N.'s dream image, adorning the dead sister, refusing to put the lid on her coffin.

John Barrell has gone further in a sense to argue that all scenes of violence in the writings of De Quincey converge on the domestic violence he experienced at the death of his sister. The psychoanalytic paradigm he develops is the following. The traumatized self reconstitutes itself in relation to an other that is either reassuringly self-consolidating or threateningly other, 'whereby the strategy of self-consolidation, of the recuperation or domestication of the other, always involves the simultaneous constitution of a new threat, or a new version of the old, in the space evacuated by the first. Within this constant perpetuation of narratives of trauma and narratives of reparation, 'haunted by a hateful memory, and actively colluding with the ghost', returning to a primal scene of trauma as much in pleasure as in horror, the personal and the political become mutually interchangeable in such a way that, for Barrell, De Quincey's fear of the oriental is in fact a displaced anxiety about his sister's death.[23]

In these narrative refigurations, De Quincey sketches a complex array of responses to Elizabeth's death that can nevertheless be reduced to two related stories. The first is the story of murder, in which De Quincey feels guilty for having failed to prevent the death of the sister. The second is a story of violation, in which De Quincey feels a diffuse sense of sexual taint and infection connected with his guilt at having kissed his sister's corpse, and in so doing having infected both his and her body. The resurrection of Elizabeth becomes a continual theme (witness the many surrogate women who are endangered or die in his texts) precisely because De Quincey feels himself to have been tainted by this moment of death. That is to say, Elizabeth's deathbed scene is a powerful primal fantasy because it allows the brother to dream his own impotence and to perpetrate narratives of reparation of this psychic wound that involve, thus Barrell 'the sense of guilt as a pollution conse-quent upon an intrusion'. Paradoxically meant to recuperate his sense of integrity, these narrative refigurations continually disturb his self-image in a seemingly endless cycle of resurrection and restoration.

However, while I would agree that Elizabeth's death-bed scene involves the issue of guilt contingent upon impotence and infection, what is at stake – if the scene is read literally – is not just sexual pollution or sexual disempowerment. Rather, what emerges as the crucial taint involved is above all an irrevocable stain of mortality; 'the terrific grief which I passed through, drove a shaft for me into the worlds of death and darkness which never again closed, and through which it might be said that I ascended and descended at will, according to the temper of my spirits' (p. 92). Furthermore, what is negotiated over this primal scene of death is not just the transformation of Elizabeth into an ambivalently assuaging and threatening body of alterity but rather the way De Quincey identifies with both the sister's *feminine* and *dead* body. The aspect I will, therefore, want to highlight in my reading of this scene and its narrative repetitions is the way Elizabeth is fashioned as being a part of De Quincey even as she is other to De Quincey. Thus the impotence invoked in the narrative repetition and restoration of this scene involves not merely his guilt in respect to what death does to Elizabeth, but identifying with her dead body, the question instead becomes, what does a knowledge of death do to him?

Uncannily foreshadowing the line of argument Freud will undertake in his case histories of hysteria at the end of the century, De Quincey sketches three enmeshed temporal events for this privileged case of grief and profound passion: the actual primal scene of mortality in 1792, which functions as a traumatic 'seed' that finds both repetitions and fructifications in the belated opium-induced hallucinations in Oxford some twelve years later and finally a refashioning of these experiences into an autobiographical narrative some forty years later (which itself called forth several textual repetitions). In De Quincey's refiguration of his family romance, the eight year old Elizabeth and her death from a 'predisposition to a brain-complaint' immediately stands out from the other childhood events owing to the fact that he apostrophizes her – 'For thou, dear, noble Elizabeth' (p. 99) – in what de Man has so poignantly called the rhetorical gesture 'by which the dead are made to have a face and a voice which tells the allegory of their demise'. Yet De Man also points out that prosopopeia is inhabited by a 'latent threat … namely that by making the death speak, the symmetrical structure of the trope implies, by the same token, that the living are struck dumb, frozen in their own death'.[24] Addressing the sister in some sense also prefigures the brother's own death and indeed De Quincey isolates two attributes marking Elizabeth as superlative, that confirm this morbid identification; a 'premature intellectual grandeur', which leads De Quincey to phantasize that the superb developments of her intellect fatally outran the capacities of her physical structuring and the fact that she is his introduction to the mortal ambivalence of the human experience – the progenitress of blessing and blight, of memorable love and memorable bereavement, and above all his romantic preference for difference, for the 'heavenly mixed and polluted with the earthly' as opposed to 'a level experience offering neither one nor the other' (p. 100).

The primal scene of mortality itself contains various stages that I want to sketch in detail. Upon hearing that his sister must die, he hysterically imitates her mortified state by ceding to a loss of consciousness; 'mere anarchy and confusion of mind fell upon me. Deaf and blind I was, as I reeled under the revelation'. The illness of reminiscences begins with the proclamation of death, for De Quincey adds 'I wish not to recall the circumstances of that time, when *my* agony was at its height, and *hers* in another sense was approaching' (p. 102. My emphasis) Indeed in so doing, he seems to have anticipated her dissolution psychosomatically before the actual event of death ever occurred.

The next event he describes is his scheme to see Elizabeth's as yet unviolated corpse on the day after her death, a sight that is particularly poignant because he knows an autopsy will be performed on her brain, given that her symptoms had shown anomalies. His sight is, in a sense, meant to supersede the deflorative gaze of the doctors, but again I would emphasize, the knowledge (*qua* experience) at stake is less sexual than morbid. Having clandestinely climbed the staircase around noon to steal into her chamber alone, he, upon seeking his sister's face, significantly finds that the bed has been moved. He is forced instead to confront a blank; 'one large window wide open, through which the sun of midsummer at noonday was showering down torrents of splendour' (p. 103). While this visual void could be read (as Barrell does) as a displaced sign for feminine genitalia I again would argue that it can equally be interpreted as the futility and disempowerment involved in gaining knowledge of mortality. De Quincey's gaze of death is precisely an empty gaze. The dead body initially defies his violation, the knowledge of death he seeks as point of identification, having already imitated it in the form of his own loss of consciousness, recedes from his grasp, forcing him to acknowledge the concrete phenomenon of the outside world as a diffuse source of light. And – equally significant – only after he has intercepted this gaze with a digression about why this experience of death is the privileged, indeed superlative event in his life, can he find his sister's corpse and read it. In this digression he weaves together a series of images that ultimately lead him to a trope for his sister's corpse as well as to a definition of his own poetic practice, which I want to argue is also the strategy of hysterical self-performance. For as he enmeshes a discussion about why death is most profoundly affecting in summer with a remembrance of how in the nursery he and his siblings had read about Jerusalem on Palm Sunday in an illustrated Bible, he justifies his narrative technique by arguing 'our deepest thoughts and feelings pass to us through perplexed combinations of concrete objects, ... in compound experiences incapable of being disentangled, than ever reach us directly, and in their own abstract shapes' (p. 105).

Without going into this point in detail, I want to recall for you that in his *Interpretation of Dreams*, inspired by the language of his hysteric patients, Freud formulates a similar theory of interpretation when he argues that dream representations are constructed on the basis of an interplay between condensation and displacement, at that same time that each one has a navel, a representational knot, that can not be disentangled but remains as a point of contact with the unknown.[25] What is particularly uncanny, is that De Quincey anticipates Freud's rhetoric not only by performing the associative language of hysteria – knotting the nursery reading-scene with that of his sister's deathbed – but that he should also resort to a similar metaphor of the knot when he seeks a trope for Elizabeth's corpse, namely the image of Jerusalem; 'for earth's tenant Jerusalem was the omphalos of mortality ... there it was ... that mortality had been trampled under foot ... there it was that mortality had opened its very gloomiest crater ... that the human had risen on wings from the grave ... that the divine had been swallowed up by the abyss' (p. 105).

In line with a discussion of hysteria as an illness by representation, what is crucial about the digression, then, is that it offers De Quincey the iconographic language to describe death in its relation to the origin and condition of creativity, much as Didi-Huberman has suggested for Charcot's hysterics, that in order to symptomize their traumas, they performed to excess precisely the representations of the possessed and of the feminine body culture ascribed to them.[26] For the irrevocable stain of mortality, De Quincey finds a trope – the omphalos – to suggest both its centrality to human existence and the fact that it knots together all strands of psychic experience into a palimpsest that can repeatedly either be uncovered or traced over. He then performs this rhetoric of the omphalos by tracing how his feelings and images of mortality are entangled with received cultural notions of summer as death's antagonist and with scriptural iconography, and in so doing verbally oscillates between disclosure and revealment. At the same time this particular scene of death translates into the omphalos of all further phantasy work

– his hallucinatory experiences and his writing. Finally, only once he has found this trope for mortality can he return to the actual death-bed chamber, turn from the visionary view of gorgeous sunlight to the corpse, the sweet childish figure, the angel face and scrutinize it for any traces of death, or, more specifically examine it, to see whether it could 'be mistaken for life'.

At this point a further hysteric identity with or imitation of the dead feminine body occurs. For as the brother is about to 'spring to those heavenly lips with tears and never-ending kisses' he becomes himself immobilized, 'I stood checked for a moment; awe, not fear, fell upon me, and, whilst I stood, a solemn wind began to blow' (p. 105). Oscillating in the gesture of the hysteric between the literal and the tropic, his phantasy translates this phenomenon into the 'one sole audible symbol of eternity,' only to in turn perform the metaphor. The brother falls into a trance; 'a vault seemed to open in the zenith of the far blue sky ... I in spirit rose ... the flight seemed to go on for ever ... slowly I recovered my self-possession, and found myself standing, as before, close to my sister's bed' (p. 106). This hysteric performance of disembodiment – 'this wandering or suspension of my perfect mind' – brilliantly stages the knotting of disempowerment before death (Elizabeth) and before creative vision (Thomas), as it fuses the two bodies into one, but also as it turns into the omphalic-scene for all future renditions of hallucinatory loss of consciousness (at this point he anticipates the operation of opium he will experience some ten years later).

I have presented this scene in such detail so as to show how the kiss that finally closes the sequence is indeed preceded and inscribed by hysterical responses – that is to say, by an oscillation between the register of the real body and cultural representations that has transformed the sister's corpse into a trope and the brother's body into an imitation of the sister's death before any sexualization comes into play. What wanders is not the feminine sexual part, but rather the mind. As the brother *fancies* that he hears someone approaching on the stairs he 'kisses the lips that I should kiss no more, and slunk like a guilty thing with stealthy steps from the room' (p. 107). Even though guilt, in the sense of sexual violation, is acted out, what is equally at stake is that this kiss infects De Quincey not only with a forbidden sexual knowledge but also with a knowledge of mortality that will accompany him for the rest of his life; 'when passing for ever from my sister's room ... [the] worm was at my heart ... the worm that could not die'. For even as the sister is transformed into the one signifier that can stabilize an otherwise strife-ridden existence, she is a hysterical signifier – representing death as difference *and* as transcendence. At her corpse the brother has discovered that man though 'doubtless one by some subtle *nexus* that we cannot perceive' (and I would glean that as the omphalos of mortality, that one can only become cognisant of through perplexed combinations), he adds 'as regards many affections and passions incident to his nature at different stages, he is *not* one' (p. 107). The dead Elizabeth has initiated him into the loss of unity, of a love 'altogether holy' even as a phantasy of 'that final experience in my sister's bedroom ... will rise again for me to illuminate the hour of death'. I am calling this scene of mortality omphalic, then, because it radiates forward toward all future scenes of phantasy even as it serves as the retrograde inspiration for his final phantasy, his own death-bed scene. In this family romance, Elizabeth's death serves as the omphalos that certifies that life expands through strife, that 'without a basis of the dreadful there is no perfect rapture' (p. 161).

While the spectacle of her corpse disfigured by the medical examination of her brain is forbidden him (he finds the room locked and the key taken away) he uses his description of the funeral to critique a notion of Christian resurrection that restores the dead, but in a changed aspect, and pleads instead for the hysteric power of reminiscences, that restores the lost beloved with all her 'faults and frailties' rather than in perfect beauty (p. 109) because it is deformity that marks the living body he wishes to recollect. At the grave De Quincey once more acknowledges his affinity with the feminine, rebuking the insult that his tears are girlish by explaining the 'word "*girlish*" had no sting for me, except as a verbal echo to the one eternal thought of my heart – that a girl was the sweetest thing I, in my short life, had known – that a girl it was who had crowned the earth with beauty, and had opened to my thirst fountains of pure celestial love, from which, in this world, I was to drink no more' (p. 111). Again, the dead feminine body serves as the transcendental signifier over which De Quincey could stabilize his incoherent, disparate world, the 'subtle nexus' that makes man *one*, even as it is also a signifier for the futility of any such aspiration for plenitude and divinity during ones mortal existence.

One final hysterical hallucination puts closure to this encounter with death but signals the beginning of his ability to phantasize ['shaping images in the distance out of slight elements, and grouping them after the yearnings of the heart']. Repeatedly during the Sunday service he would practice the kind of auto-hypnosis so often reported by Freud's hysterics. He would raise his tear-filled eyes to the windows of the galleries, to that sublime memorial of apostles, martyrs, saints, and in his 'self-sustained' hallucination these bodies would ultimately transform into a multitude of dying children (in a sense a multiplication of his sister's dead body), until he envisages himself as part of this desired but impossible sphere; 'sometimes I seemed to walk triumphantly upon those clouds which so recently I had looked up to as mementos of prostrate sorrow, and even as ministers of sorrow in its creations' (p. 112).

In a sense the text *Suspiria de Profundis*, seen as a whole, performs the process of psychoanalysis *avant la lettre*. The nursery scene of mortality has been reconstructed as a narrative in part to show that it has the same 'relation to the convulsions of the dreaming faculty' as does the opium and in so doing to mitigate affect by virtue of interpretive representation. The metaphor De Quincey invokes is that of excavation. The hysteric re-enactment of scenes of trauma causes the 'pall, deep as oblivion', that life has thrown over every trace of this past scene to be removed, until 'the whole depths of the theatre are exposed' (p. 145). The narrative repeats this possibility of resurrection, constituting in the act of unfolding the hidden nexus.

At the same time the opium-induced hallucinations in Oxford prove to be not only a symptom of this earlier trauma but precisely in their belatedness, they function as the first conscious experience of this omphalic scene – 'now first the agitations of my childhood reopened in strength, now first they swept in upon the brain with power and the grandeur of recovered life' (p. 138). And, to refer one last time to the dream-image of Emmy v. N. which I have called a meta-representation of hysteria, this belated repetition contains a similar self-reflexive moment. For it is within the trance of opium that De Quincey not only hysterically relives the childhood scene whose reminiscence has haunted him – the death sentence, the corpse, the funeral and burial – but hallucination also forms within hallucination; 'within these Oxford dreams remoulded itself continually the trance in my sister's chamber ... once more I, that wallowed, became he that rose up to the clouds'. In De Quincey's vision, the navel of the dream merely opens up another hallucinatory space that nevertheless signifies a disentangled knot, the omphalos of mortality; 'And now in Oxford, all was bound up into unity; the first state and the last were melted into each other'. The 'truth' that the hysterical delirium reveals is that like the navel, which marks the infant's real severment from the maternal body, the child's separation from his beloved feminine other transforms into a signifier – the omphalos of mortality – as the sign of stain lurking below all other phantasies and self-representations, resilient, urgent and insisting to the end.

It is then only logical, that a final re-enactment of the sister's death scene was to be found in his own death-bed vision, for he seems here to have hysterically performed what in *Suspiria de Profundis* he had designated as 'a remembrance so affecting and revolutionary for my own mind, and one which (if any earthly remembrance) will survive for me in the hour of death' (p. 103). His biographer H. A. Page notes in 1877, 'Twice only was the heavy breathing interrupted by words. He had for hours ceased to recognise any of us, but we heard him murmur, though quite distinctly, "My dear, dear mother. Then I was greatly mistaken." Then as the waves of death rolled faster and faster over him, suddenly out of the abyss we saw him throw up his arms, which to the last retained their strength, and say distinctly, and as if in great surprise, "Sister! sister! sister!" The loud breathing became slower and slower, and as the world of Edinburgh awoke to busy work and life, all that was mortal of my father fell asleep for ever' (Miller, *Disappearance*, p. 79).

Barrell notes that this scene need not only be read as a restorative event, a final reparation of strife and affliction, but rather as 'final nightmare, the final appearance of the terrifying and two faced figure of the woman, at once, or ambiguously mother and sister' (*Infection*, p. 194). I would add, it is the fitting hysterical finale to a hysterical existence, precisely because it straddles the recuperation of a psychic wound with the impossibility of a seamless restoration. The dead sister who had haunted him and sustained his psychic life and his creative genius, whom he had imitated and as such revitalized throughout his earthly existence, is the only body he can phantasize as he moves fully into the realm of death.

Notes

1   Thomas De Quincey, *Suspiria de Profundis*, in *Confessions of an English Opium-Eater and other Writings*, ed. Grevel Lindop (Oxford: Oxford University Press, 1985), p. 146. All further references will be to this edition and included in brackets in the text. I will be using the edition of *Suspiria de Profundis* compiled by Grevel Lindop because it is the entire though unfinished text, rather than the dismembered version De Quincey published in 1845 under the title *Autobiography from 1785–1803*, available as volume one of the *Collected Writings* edited by David Masson. For a discussion of the status of textual editions of De Quincey see Lindop, p. xxiii. One could, of course, see the layering and dislocation of textual bits undertaken by De Quincey as he rewrote and republished this narrative of reminiscences as a hysterical gesture in its own right, but this is not a line of argument I wish to pursue.

2   Sigmund Freud, *Studies in Hysteria*, *The Standard Edition*, II, trans James Strachey (London: Hogarth, 1955), p. 74.

3   G. S. Rousseau, 'A strange pathology: hysteria in the early modern world, 1500–1800', *Hysteria Beyond Freud*, (eds) Sander L. Gilman et al (Berkeley: University of California Press, 1993), p. 102.

4   See Pierre Janet, *L'etat mental des hysteriques* (Paris: Alcan, 1894).

5   See Irvin D. Yallom, *Existential Psychotherapy* (New York: Basic Books, 1980).

6   Josephine McDonagh, 'Do or die: problems of agency and gender in the aesthetics of murder', *New Feminist Discourses*, ed. Isobel Armstrong (London: Routledge, 1992), 222–237, p. 236.

7   Mary Jacobus, 'The art of managing books: Romantic prose and the writing of the past', *Romanticism and Language*, ed. Arden Reed (Ithaca: Cornell University Press, 1984), pp. 221, 223.

8   Christina von Braun, 'Mannliche Hysterie – weibliche Askese. Zum Paradigmenwechsel in den Geschlecterrollen', *Bei Lichte betrachtet wird es finster. FrauenSichten*, ed. Psychoanalytisches Seminar Zurich (Frankfurt am Main: Athenaum, 1987), pp. 41–80.

9   Freud, 'Family romances', *The Standard Edition*, vol. IX.

10   Eve Kosofsky Sedgwick, *The Coherence of Gothic Conventions* (London: Methuen, 1980), p. 89.

11   De Quincey, 'William Wordsworth', *Recollections of the Lakes and the Lake Poets*, ed. David Wright (Harmondsworth: Penguin, 1970), pp. 131, 129.

12   Mary Jacobus, *Romanticism, Writing and Sexual Difference* (Oxford: Oxford University Press, 1989), p. 252.

13   John Beer, 'De Quincey and the dark sublime: the Wordsworth-Coleridge ethos', *Thomas De Quincey*, ed. Robert Lance Snyder (Norman: University of Oaklahoma Press, 1985), p. 178.

14   Simon Wilson, *De Quincey's Troubled Body*, Ph.D Dissertation, University of Hull, 1993.

15   Simon Wilson, Private Correspondence, 1994.

16   De Quincey, 'The Estrangement from Wordsworth' (1840), *Recollections*, p. 79.

17   Dorothy Wordsworth, *The Letters of William and Dorothy Wordsworth I*, ed. Ernest de Selincourt (Oxford: Clarendon, 1967), p. 377.

18   Dorothy Wordsworth, *The Grasmere Journals*, ed. Pamela Woof (Oxford: Oxford University Press, 1991), p. 126.

19   Gayatri Chakravorty Spivak, *In Other Worlds* (London: Routledge, 1987), pp. 55, 57.

20   See Jack Stillinger, *Multiple Authorship and the Myth of Solitary Genius* (Oxford: Oxford University Press, 1991).

21   J. Hillis Miller, *The Disappearance of God* (Cambridge: Harvard University Press, 1963), p. 22.

22   See John Beer, 'Dark sublime', p. 185.

23   John Barrell, *The Infection of Thomas De Quincey* (New Haven: Yale University Press, 1991), pp. 19, 24.

24   Paul de Man, *The Rhetoric of Romanticism* (New York: Columbia University Press, 1984), pp. 122, 78.

25   See my 'Death: the navel of the image', *The Point of Theory*, Mieke Bal and Inge Boer (eds) (Amsterdam: Amsterdam University Press, 1994).

26   Georges Didi-Huberman, *Invention de l'hysterie* (Paris: Macula, 1982).

Naming Places:
Wordsworth and the
Possibilities of Eco-criticism

Tony Pinkney
Lancaster University

The relationship of language to the non-human has long been a central issue for ecologically minded criticism. In what may well be the earliest instance of this critical genre, Thomas J. Lyon's 'The Ecological Vision of Gary Snyder' (1970), Lyon wrestles with the linguistic dilemmas posed by the 'general deceit of naming':

> how to talk about things, especially wild ones, without harming their integrity by language; how to preserve and communicate suchness without falling into an arch aesthetic distance between subject and object, a romantic decoration that destroys the very wholeness, which is wildness, one loved and wanted to convey somehow. The thin line of poetic truth between overstatement and private code requires first of all respect for things, letting them stand free instead of being marshaled into line for a mental performance.[1]

Lyon has here, in effect, run head first into the paradox of any modernist aesthetic premised on an Imagist or Russian Formalist 'resurrection of the word'. For the very defamiliarising violence one has to exercise to break through the automatised clichés of 'ordinary language', far from rendering up the object in its pristine suchness, may further distance the latter, interposing its own ungainly, alienating bulk between the eye and the object of its gaze. Does the defamiliarising style of a Gerard Manley Hopkins, say, truly 'hand over sensations bodily' (T. E. Hulme) and 'make the stone stony' (Viktor Shklovsky), or is it not rather a bizarrely coagulated medium – a Schwarzenegger-like linguistic body sinking beneath the weight of its own knotted muscularity – through which Hopkins's assorted windhovers, skylarks and harvest landscapes can barely any longer be even glimpsed? The sheer energy with which one struggles towards a utopian name plumped full with the 'thusness' of its object, a motivated rather than arbitrary sign, may be self-defeating. The would-be Adamic name, under its own estranging momentum, arguably mutates into its dystopian opposite, and is then dismissed by a later postmodern populism for its self-regarding elitism and difficulty. While Thomas Lyon registers the 'general deceit of naming', this vexing

41

paradox of modernist *over*-naming, he nonetheless believes his hero, Gary Snyder, has successfully avoided it, and therefore does not feel inclined to pursue the issue at length. Snyder's Zen-inspired poetics, in Lyon's view, is both Hopkinsianly strenuous ('tuned so closely to muscular and breath paces' as it breaks up the bleached abstractions of everyday language) *and* Heideggerianly open to things, which it delicately lets be in their Being. In this 'kind of textual Buddhism', poetry achieves 'a form that grows so rightly out of *wild* things' – to the point indeed where, in what will become an embarrassingly naff cliché of eco-criticism, 'the birds and other animals seem almost to have written the poem by themselves'.

The dilemma of poetic naming, or of the general relation between language and the non-human, is taken up intermittently in the pio-neering British work of eco-criticism, Kim Taplin's *Tongues in Trees: Studies in Literature and Ecology* (1989). 'To read with an ecological eye', as Taplin here sets out to, is once again to encounter the problems of modernist aesthetics.[2] In its amiable, untheoretical way, her chapter on Hopkins endorses the Eliotic theory of a 'dissociation of sensibility', or the related Leavisite model of a collapse from the muscular physicality of 'Shakespearian English' into the anaesthetised linguistic abstractions of 'technologico-Benthamite' modernity: 'in the language of the older books we often find words that have life in them, a Hopkins-like specificity and exactness of term that reveals a recognition of other being, of essence. Of course, the liveliness and specificity of language has itself been in decline' (p. 88). That 'of course' shows how deeply this modernist paradigm has taken grip. Not even the muted objection of a Leavisite 'yes, but' is envisaged here; modernist ideology sits too close to the eyeball to be focused as a detached object in its own right. But from the viewpoint of our own postmodern or Bakhtinian present, it is surely clear that all such theories of linguistic degeneration involve an unacceptable homogenising of 'ordinary' or 'practical' language – in opposition to which avantgarde poetic defamiliarisation would indeed be our only hope for the sensory redemption of the word. In an epoch of abundant heteroglossia – both practical, in the postmodern prolif-eration of subcultures and lifestyles, and theoretical, in the Bakhtinian reworking of linguistics and literary theory – we need no longer confine our thinking about language to the frozen modernist binarism of banal 'ordinary language' versus the 'organised violence' (Jakobson's term) of poetic language.

But in an earlier chapter of *Tongues in Trees* Kim Taplin herself problematises the modernist account of language which underpins her Hopkins analysis. Discussing the 'forms of celebration' in the poetry of William Barnes, she broaches that aspect of the relation of language to the non-human which will be my main focus in this essay: the naming of places. 'The naming of places', she had earlier noted, 'can have very contrary effects, including or excluding, depending a good deal on the reader as well as the writer' (p. 49). In the case of Barnes's dialect poetry, 'names, perhaps especially those that have obviously arisen from the nature of the places they belong to, work as Barnes's mind and poetry work, which is one reason why he uses them so lovingly. For his purpose the simple naming of a species was enough, perhaps accompanied by a single unsurprising epithet or fact about it' (p. 62). The epithet 'unsurprising' itself surprises: there is a strong if latent vein of anti-modernism at work here. Barnes's names and adjectives are generic rather than unique, familiar rather than estranging, concerned to situate the object in a known traditional context rather than explosively blast it out so that its breathtaking haecceity might stand forth. He 'celebrates the life of the tree, though as usual its elminess is not dwelt on – everyone knew what an elm was like' (p. 69). 'In assembling the elements of a landscape Barnes is frequently obvious, and often repeats himself' (p. 63); but while there could be no greater sin for the Imagist poet in the grip of a Poundian injunction to 'Make it New', obviousness and repetition are here *favourably* contrasted with the 'twentieth-century quest for strangeness, in phenomena and expression'. This Hopkinsian poetics, endorsed by the author elsewhere, is now unaccountably deemed 'both disturbing and ominous' (p. 63).

As much a poetry anthology as a work of literary criticism and aimed more at a general readership than at the academy, *Tongues in Trees: Studies in Literature and Ecology* is a welcome pioneer, but one which leaves much work to be done in its wake. Simultaneously defending and defaming 'ordinary' names, adjectives and language, both sensitive to and suspicious of the modernist project of over-naming, the book at no point systematically reflects on its contradictions which are, in my view, endemic to an eco-criticism which has not yet come to terms with its (often unconscious) modernist aesthetic inheritance. For a fuller treatment of these matters, we can turn from Kim Taplin to the next significant British eco-critical study, Jonathan Bate's *Romantic Ecology: Wordsworth and the Environmental Tradition* (1991).[3] Bate's book has been much reviewed and certainly, in its slimline hundred-odd pages, opens more issues than it settles. In the long run, surely, the key term of dispute between Bate and his critics will be *pastoral*. His spirited attempt at 'recuperating the Wordsworthian pastoral' (p. 20) which then, on this showing, becomes 'republican pastoral' (p. 33) will require specialist assessment; but, whatever the rights and wrongs of that critical argument, a bigger debate will rumble on too. For it is hard to conceive of any compelling eco-criticism (or even ecological literature at large) which doesn't have some viable concept of pastoral underpinning its operations; but it's equally clear that Marxist, feminist and post-structuralist critiques have

done severe damage to traditional versions and notions of pastoral.
Unless eco-criticism can emerge on the other side of all this, taking the
full weight of ideological critique and yet producing a utopian model
of pastoral, leaner, fitter and postmodern all at once, it probably has no
long-term future in the crowded ranks of literary theories which are
currently battling it out in the academy.

My purpose isn't to produce that concept here. If I aim, in the greater
space available to me, to give fuller treatment to Bate's book than his
reviewers, I intend also to be notably narrower than they were, homing
down on his single chapter on 'The Naming of Places' and aiming to
test out the eco-critical project, not at the level of pure theory, but
through an extended reading of the small group of Wordsworth poems
that is at issue here. To read with an ecological eye, indeed, in Kim
Taplin's appealing slogan; but how closely *can* that eye read? For if the
greening of literary criticism is to take place, it will do so not via general
propositions (after all, we're all ecologists now, in one way or another –
and it hasn't made much difference to our criticism) but by the power
and precision of what eco-criticism can deliver at the level of the 'words
on the page'. Jonathan Bate's chapter, running the big issue of the relation
of language to the non-human through a detailed analysis of Wordsworth's six 'Naming of Places' poems (five in the *Lyrical Ballads* of 1800,
the sixth added to the 1815 edition), can thus provide an admirable test-
case for the possibilities of a compelling practical eco-criticism.

Bate operates in a framework constructed from the categories of
Friedrich Schiller's *Naive and Sentimental Poetry* (1795), and thus
announces of the 'Poems on the Naming of Places' that 'it is their
namings that provide the bridge, the uniting of sentimental and naive,
of poet and nature' (p. 105). A few pages later, discussing a poem from
Housman's *A Shropshire Lad*, he remarks: 'Here, as in Wordsworth, the
recitation of place-names bridges sentimental and naive' (p. 109). Moreover, since, in Bate's view, *Lyrical Ballads* as a whole effects a 'movement
… from sentimental to naive … We begin as spectators *ab extra* and
end with Michael' (p. 105), it is clear that the entire volume for him
constitutes – to stick to his governing metaphor – a kind of bridge. To
cross it, on this showing, is to shift from a position of alienated,
educated self-consciousness to reintegration into the life and work of
field and mountains: 'the process of working through the collection in
sequence reconnects the reader to nature' (p. 105). This reconnection
operates at the micro-level in the act of naming, where language, that
guilty index of our postlapsarian distance from nature, once more hooks
fruitfully on to the specificities of landscape. In the Wordsworthian
name-as-bridge, place gives body and substance to language, rescuing it
from 'the gaudiness and inane phraseology of many modern writers'
(1798 Advertisement), while language redeems place from the silence of

brute materiality. Naming is, in Bate's phrase, Wordsworth's 'way of spiritualizing his places' (p. 87).

I admire Jonathan Bate's attempt to bring a group of intriguing but relatively neglected poems back into critical visibility, and one can't but be attracted by his imagery of bridging, his generous sense of naming in *Lyrical Ballads* as 'a mediation … resolving the tension that exists between the "lived, illiterate and unconscious" and the "learned, literate and conscious"' (p. 88). If only the world – and poems – did work like that! However, a preliminary shot across the bows of this happy reconciliation of opposites is afforded by the fate of its underlying metaphor, the bridge, in *Lyrical Ballads* itself. The volume may or may not *be* a bridge in Bate's terms, but it certainly features bridges – and seems to have scant confidence in them. Bridges are for crossing from A to B – from sentimental to naive, if you will – but in *Lyrical Ballads* they seem (even at best) to make for stasis rather than movement, magnetising you to the spot rather than mediating your passage. Four lines into 'The Nightingale' the speaker declares to his companions: 'Come, we will rest on this old mossy Bridge!', and they never do move on thereafter.[4] All the energy in the poem belongs to the nightingale, who 'crowds, and hurries … his delicious notes', rather than to the human body; the latter would optimally 'better far have stretch'd [its] limbs / Beside a brook in mossy forest dell', rather than purposefully striding across bridges. A more spirited effort to make a bridge function as a bridge, i.e. to let you get across, is made in 'The Idle Shepherd-Boys': 'Into a chasm a mighty Block / Hath fallen, and made a bridge of rock'. Challenged by Walter, James, 'all eyes and feet, hath gain'd / The middle of the arch'. So far, so good; but then this bridge too fails as the two boys hear the forlorn cry of the lamb below and 'gladly now deferr'd their task', i.e. abandon the attempt to cross over their makeshift bridge.

In his *Guide to the Lakes* Wordsworth notes the 'daring and graceful neglect of danger and accommodation' which characterises traditional Lakeland bridges.[5] In 'Lucy Gray' this cavalier attitude to bridges becomes positively lethal. As Lucy's parents desperately follow the footsteps of their lost child:

> They track'd them on, nor ever lost,
> And to the Bridge they came.
>
> They follow'd from the snowy bank
> The footmarks, one by one,
> Into the middle of the plank,
> And further there were none.

If the bridges of *Lyrical Ballads* don't seem very efficient – seem, indeed, to do anything but mediate from one bank to another – nor, on the other hand, do the bodies of the volume seem particularly well qualified to use bridges, even if they had safer ones at hand than the poems actually offer. For either these bodies are so hyper-active that they don't need bridges in the first place, as with the phenomenal bounds of the Hart in 'Hart-Leap Well', or they are so sluggish or crippled – William on his old gray stone, the lolling Poet in the outhouse on Grasmere Island, the preternatural slowness of the Old Man Travelling, the ruined legs of Simon Lee and of the sick Angler in 'A narrow girdle of rough stones and crags' – that they probably couldn't get across a bridge even if miraculously parachuted down into the middle of one. Mediation of opposites, whether it's a question of bridges or of the bodies that use them, can come to seem the very last thing of which *Lyrical Ballads* is capable. The volume's most characteristic mode of 'rural architecture' is not, after all, a Batesian bridge but rather a broken pile of stones.

But if the image of the bridge runs into difficulties, does Jonathan Bate's general case – that the 'Poems on the Naming of Places' serve a vital function 'in Wordsworth's establishment of himself as a "dweller"' (p. 101), and in so doing institute 'an ecological tradition of English place-poetry' (p. 91) that runs through to Clare, Hardy and Edward Thomas – necessarily collapse with it? There is, as I have suggested, much that is attractive about this case. Indeed, I don't believe Jonathan Bate does adequate justice to its attractiveness, since he states it in terms which in the end become damagingly parochial, a celebration (through Thomas) of a faded Georgian nostalgia; and before testing out his detailed account of the 'Naming of Places' sequence, we might first restate the general argument in more forceful, fully twentieth-century terms.

Bate himself refers us back to Geoffrey Hartman's seminal essay on 'Wordsworth, Inscriptions, and Romantic Nature Poetry' in *Beyond Formalism* (1970), which demonstrates the poet's debt to and transformation of the genre of poetic inscription, including, crucially, the epitaph. If an inscription is, in Hartman's terms, 'anything conscious of the place on which it was written' (cited *RE*, 90), then epitaphs, perhaps more than other forms of the genre, benefit from this physical locatedness. As Wordsworth contemplates the classical practice of roadside burial in his first 'Essay upon Epitaphs' (1810), he reflects upon:

> the beauty which the monuments, thus placed, must have borrowed from the surrounding images of nature – from the trees, the wild flowers, from a stream running perhaps within sight or hearing, from the beaten road stretching its weary length hard by … These, and similar suggestions, must have given, formerly, to the language of the senseless stone a voice enforced and endeared by the benignity of that nature with which it was in unison.[6]

Even in a contemporary English churchyard, some of these advantages are preserved. The epitaph for Wordsworth, clearly enough, is not just one genre among others but rather, in its democratic accessibility and physical locatedness in nature, a utopian possibility for poetry as a whole:

> an epitaph is not a proud writing shut up for the studious: it is exposed to all ... the stooping old man cons the engraven record like a second horn-book; – the child is proud that he can read it ... it is concerning all, and for all: – in the church-yard it is open to the day; the sun looks down upon the stone, and the rains of heaven beat against it.   (*SP*, 334)

The sluggish bodies of *Lyrical Ballads* may not get about very much, but if they did, they would find poems everywhere around them: left upon seats in yew-trees, written upon tablets in schools, inscribed upon spots where hermitages stood, written with slate-pencils upon stones near island quarries, inscribed upon outhouses, even being carried around by little boys at small distances from houses. The 491 lines of 'Michael' are one vast epitaph for which the technology for carving it upon the 'straggling heap of unhewn stones' which is his monument hasn't been invented yet; and if the Wordsworthian stationary body is well on its way to metamorphosing back towards the mineral (the 'jutting crag' that Martha Ray has virtually become), then it is already in effect the 'speaking corpse' of the epitaphic tradition.

Lyrical Ballads, then, is in one aspect a bold attempt to break beyond the confines of the written book, whether its underlying model for this be the rural epitaph or the 'files of ballads' dangling from London walls in *The Prelude*. The volume dots poems up and down the countryside with something of the spatial opportunism of the modern graffiti artist – Wordsworth's slate pencil being a cumbrous version of the latter's spraycan. The daring of this venture puts it on a par with the attempts of the early twentieth-century avant-garde, as described by Peter Bürger in his *Theory of the Avant-Garde*,[7] to break out of the sealed realm of aestheticism and reintegrate art with the praxis of everyday life; and what it would achieve, if successful, is that dissolution of the high art/ popular culture binarism, that 'aestheticisation of everyday life', which we have come to see as characteristic of the postmodern. In one of Words- worth's 'Poems on the Naming of Places', graffiti is precisely the point as the poet metamorphoses, for an unsettling moment, into an inner- city teenage hooligan being taken to task by his social betters:

> He with grave looks demanded, for what cause,
> Reviving obsolete Idolatry,
> I like a Runic Priest, in characters

> Of formidable size, had chisel'd out
> Some uncouth name upon the native rock.

In his attempt to elucidate Wordsworth's 'theology of place' (*RE*, 92), Jonathan Bate finds this poem, 'To Joanna', to be a key text; for it seems to provide an encyclopedia of all the possible modes of naming at work in this group of poems. It contains the one literal act of inscription in the group, even if Wordsworth's workmanship with the chisel is so poor that the Vicar has been unable to decipher Joanna's name on the rockface. It also features that act of naming within the immediate circle of family and friends which for Bate (borrowing a phrase from Hugh Sykes Davies) establishes the 'Grasmere ecolect' (p. 91): 'And I, and all who dwell by my fireside / Have call'd that lovely rock, Joanna's Rock'. And finally it contains the grand roster of Lakeland names – Helm-crag, Hammar-Scar, Silver-How, Loughrigg, Fairfield, Helvellyn, Skiddaw, Glaramara, Kirkstone – which, as Coleridge first noted, echoes Michael Drayton's *Poly-Olbion* (1622). 'In the act of incantation', Jonathan Bate argues, 'the poet takes possession of the place-names' (p. 98), effecting on a grander scale the spatial mapping of the 'geographic Labourer' of 'Written with a Slate Pencil on a Stone, on the side of the Mountain of Black Comb'.

Let us then turn in detail to the Poems on the Naming of Places which play so important a role in Bate's version of Romantic Ecology. They are indeed fascinating poems and Bate's account of the 'ecological holiness' (a phrase he borrows from Karl Kroeber) of such acts of naming certainly has an initial plausibility. Yet, as with the founding metaphor of his theoretical framework, it seems to me that in his analyses of the poems he too often takes the ecological will for the actual poetic deed. Wordsworthian naming, even at its best, is a more complex process than the eco-critic allows, and often shot through with purposes less benign than his own. 'It was an April morning', the first of the poems in this group, is perhaps the most attractive of them in its evocation of that pastoral *locus amoenus* which will at last be named 'Emma's dell'. The poem evokes a moment in nature which is itself a kind of Batesian 'bridge', mediating apparent opposites:

> It was an April Morning: fresh and clear
> The Rivulet, delighting in its strength,
> Ran with a young man's speed, and yet the voice
> Of waters which the winter had supplied
> Was soften'd down into a vernal tone.

'And yet' (a construction repeated ten lines later) bespeaks the limits of rational thought, whose rigid binary categories break down in the face of what Wordsworth elsewhere terms 'the subtle progress by which, both in the natural and the moral world, qualities pass insensibly into their opposites, and things revolve upon each other' (*SP*, 326). Strength and softness, dynamic eagerness and wise passiveness, the visible and the audible, benignly coexist and interact; and the poet himself, 'Alive to all things and forgetting all', also participates in this Eden beyond worldly dualisms. But other impulses are at work here too. A young man's speed is 'soften'd down' into something presumably more feminine, silently laying the groundwork for that female naming – Emma's dell – in which the poem culminates. We are thus already alerted in this muted way to the issues of gender which are so prominent in the Poems on the Naming of Places and which remain so absent from Jonathan Bate's eco-critical study of them.

The opening stretch of the poem is, we realize, governed by a low-level, highly tentative mode of interpretation of natural objects. Overt simile – 'Went circling, like a multitude of sounds' – is itself 'soften'd down' to a gentler hermeneutic:

> The budding groves *appear'd as if* in haste
> To spur the steps of June; *as if* their shades
> Of various green were hindrances ...
>
> That every naked ash, and tardy tree
> Yet leafless, *seem'd as though* ... (my emphases)

In one sense, these are interpretations foisted on to mute natural objects. Yet, delicately tentative as they are, they seek rather to elicit a latent significance *from* the object rather than write it imperiously into the poet's own script. We are in the presence, I suggest, of a process of 'sub-naming', the very opposite of flamboyant modernist over-naming, which aims to seed the ground for the decisive act of poetic naming which follows thirty lines later. Human commentary supervenes upon the natural object from outside, to be sure; but a sufficiently reverent mode of commentary might, in the poem's view, be midwife to significances that were already present in the object. Interpretation begins as it were *ex nihilo*, from a realm of culture beyond the landscape; but it must then, retrospectively, be found to be motivated *by* that landscape and its features, to have 'always-already' inhered in them. This would be a fusion or bridging of signifier and referent as utopian as that already effected between energy and contemplation in the spring weather itself.

Enjoying the sounds of beast, bird and waterfall, the narrator remarks that they:

made a song
Which, while I listen'd, seem'd like the wild growth
Or like some natural produce of the air
That could not cease to be.

The last two lines offer a stirring image of the utopian name, which should seem to crystallise out of nature itself rather than be imposed by fiat; it is ideally delivered over into the human realm with full motivation from its object. The question the poem then poses for us, having set up such rigorous criteria, is whether 'Emma's Dell' is truly a name of this kind, whether it possesses such plenitude of motivation, to the point where it might (in the words of 'The Nightingale') 'share in nature's immortality, / A venerable thing!' Other poems in the series certainly seek to give a clinching logical force to the act of naming:

– And *hence*, long afterwards …
I chisel'd out in those rude characters
                    ('To Joanna', my emphasis)

And, *therefore*, my sweet MARY, this still nook
With all its beeches we have named from You
                    ('To M. H.', my emphasis)

I leave aside for the moment the question of whether such gestures are actually convincing, but clearly they denote a strong impulse towards motivation. A similar drive is at work in the Advertisement to this sequence of texts, which announces that 'Names have been given to Places by the Author and some of his Friends'; the passive construction mutes deliberate human agency and intervention, softening it down towards a natural produce of the air.

A related but stronger strategy is at work in the remarkable poem to his brother John which Wordsworth added to the series in 1815. Celebrating the 'stately Fir-Grove' in which, he claims, he and his brother have spent many hours, Wordsworth writes:

– Back to the joyless Ocean thou art gone;
Nor from this vestige of thy musing hours
Could I withhold thy honoured name.[8]

The negative construction implies that the poet might modestly *want* to withhold the name, that it is virtually wrung out of him by nature itself. Moreover, since the name isn't actually given in the poem, the reader must supply the gap for him or herself. It's true that a certain instability thereby enters the text (Jonathan Bate takes the name to be 'John's Grove', while I'd be inclined to go for a stricter reading of the 'vestige of thy musing hours' and plump for 'John's Path'), but none the less if the reader *can* supply the name at this point, its motivation has been narratively secured. It is wrung out of rather than handed on a plate to the reader, just as it is for the poet himself. In any event, the name is particularly strongly motivated in this case by the natural object. Returning to the fir-grove in Spring, the narrator discovers 'A hoary pathway traced between the trees' which hadn't been there the previous winter; it was, he concludes, worn by his brother's pacing up and down 'In that habitual restlessness of foot / That haunts the sailor'. The path is thus taken to be, in effect, his brother's inscription on the landscape, a human marking of the natural object. Since John Wordsworth is, in the poem's phrase, 'a *silent* Poet', it is appropriate that his inscription should take non-linguistic form rather than being written with a slate-pencil or carved with a chisel. The Wordsworthian act of naming is then offered as maieutically articulating a significance already marked mutely in the object rather than as violently imposing itself from without. It's true that one can raise questions about this version of the poem if, like the straggling sheep in the grove, one 'watches [the poet's] motions with suspicious stare'; what it actually does may well not coincide with its official image of itself. Crucially, there is no guarantee that the path in the grove *was* actually worn by John. The 'pleasant conviction' that it is is based upon a set of unconfirmed hypotheses, and since the poet is characterised throughout by his blindness to the obvious (he had failed to note a possible route for a path in the first place), one feels no particular confidence in the detective work he thereafter carries out. The powerful male bonding that the poem effects may be based on an incorrect surmise; the act of naming may be utterly wrong. Yet even so, the poem works harder than the others in the sequence, at least at its official level, to motivate the name. For what we have here is not a bold confrontation of name and thing, culture and nature, but a gentler transition involving three terms rather than two: object (grove), marked object (path), name.

A name that isn't motivated would be simply arbitrary, a temporary private imposition rather than an enduring natural inherence. Such arbitrariness already, famously, troubles Wordsworth in the Preface to *Lyrical Ballads*:

> I am sensible that my associations must have sometimes been particular instead of general, and that, consequently, giving to things a false importance, sometimes from diseased impulses I may have written upon unworthy subjects; but I am less apprehensive on this account, than that my language may frequently have suffered from those arbitrary connections of feelings and ideas with particular words, from which no man can altogether protect himself.
>
> (*LB*, 268)

Similar anxieties make themselves felt in the brief Advertisement to the Poems on the Naming of Places. These texts aim to memorialize places 'where little Incidents will have occurred, or feelings been experienced, which will have given to such places a private and peculiar interest' (*LB*, 217). 'Little Incidents' is perhaps already nudging towards 'unworthy subjects'; certainly in 'To Joanna' Wordsworth has to work hard to persuade himself that his addressee will 'gladly listen to discourse / However trivial'. 'Private and peculiar interest', in turn, may not be that far removed from 'particular', 'diseased' and 'arbitrary' in the Preface. While one can offer a defence of the private associations in terms of a 'Grasmere ecolect', it is significant that the one poem which actually does locate itself on 'the eastern shore / Of Grasmere safe in its own privacy' (the fourth in the sequence) quite clearly shows the poet and his inner circle in the grip of 'diseased' class impulses which thoroughly denature their grasp of both natural setting and its human inhabitants.

Naming places, then, may begin as a private act, but it ideally shouldn't remain so: the utopian name should be motivated both diachronically and synchronically, justified both by the narrative from which it emerges and the natural object in which it inheres. Is 'Emma's Dell', to return to that key instance, a name of this kind, 'ecologically holy' in Jonathan Bate's terms? One minimal reason why 'Joanna's Rock' gets called what it does is that Joanna accompanies the poet on the walk during which they encounter it, just as Dorothy names the 'Eminence' after Wordsworth in the third poem partly because he is always at her side when *they* behold it. But Emma is *not* present on the walk that culminates in the naming of her dell, just as 'my sweet MARY' is not part of the excursion that names the 'calm recess' after her. Nor has Emma at some previous time left traces of her physical presence in the dell, as John Wordsworth had in his fir-grove. So without even this minimal narrative motivation, how can the act of naming be justified? Perhaps we might next try motivation-by-similitude, which seems most clearly at work in 'There is an Eminence'. A further Wordsworthian instance of proleptic sub-naming gives the game away here: the cliff 'often seems to send / Its own deep quiet to restore our thoughts', which of course is precisely what William's own poetry ideally does – and thus Dorothy names the peak after him. Other qualities thicken the texture of the implied comparison: the Eminence is grand, sublime, beyond influence, powerfully detached ('so distant in its height') from the trivialities of the everyday – and Dorothy's big brother would like to think himself all of these things too. We may not much care for the poet ventriloquising quite so much self-praise through his sister's supposed act of naming (even Jonathan Bate, otherwise so friendly to these poems, baulks at this), but it does nonetheless adequately motivate the naming of place in this instance.

Some such argument by similitude can also be elaborated for 'To M. H.'. Within a stereotypical imagination of the feminine, there's a taken-for-granted appropriateness about naming calm and self-effacing places – 'This glade of water and this one green field' – after placid and modest women. This equation is made in the convergent adjectives of the penultimate line which, as I have already noted, seeks to forcefully motivate the naming: 'And, therefore, my *sweet* MARY, this *still* nook ... we have named from You' (my emphasis). This broad metaphorical linkage is given more specific biographical point elsewhere in the poem. Discovering the beautiful recess, Wordsworth begins to speculate on what it would be like to dwell in such an Edenic spot, after which, in a process of free association whose motivation is now clear, thoughts of the woman with whom *he* may dwell for the rest of his life enter his mind. Moreover, the 'therefore' of the closing line refers specifically to the speculation that, if anyone *did* dwell in such an idyllic spot, 'in his death-hour / Its image would survive among his thoughts'. Wordsworth presumably believes that Mary Hutchinson's image would endure and sustain in this manner too; and this forges another link in the chain of resemblances between her and the 'still nook'. In this single instance in the entire sequence, the motivation is based on a speculative future – 'if a man ... He would ... And, therefore ... ' – rather than a past incident. Whether we're dealing with conventional gender associations or the details of the author's own emotional life, Mary's entry into the poem, the 'therefore' of the penultimate line, is sufficiently worked for and justified.

No such delicacy of suggestion prepares us for Emma's entry into her poem. Her appearance, rather, constitutes for the reader exactly the kind of 'sudden turning' which the poet had earlier experienced in the formerly 'continuous' glen:

> I gaz'd and gaz'd, and to myself I said,
> 'Our thoughts at least are ours; and this wild nook,
> My EMMA, I will dedicate to thee'.

Motivation-by-similitude, along the lines of 'There is an Eminence' or 'To M. H.', does not hold up here. Wordsworth has just spotted a 'single mountain cottage' and this may evoke the theme of dwelling by which, in a chain of association, the name of the woman he dwells with enters his thoughts. But the cottage is 'beyond the dell'; and it is the dell, which may well have no connection of *any* kind with the cottage, that he dedicates to Emma. If it is only a movement of sight or thought *beyond* the dell which gets Emma's name into the text in the first place, then the dell itself would seem to have peculiarly little to do with her, to have no power of evoking her by analogy. Moreover, since we learn absolutely nothing of Emma's personal qualities in the poem, there is no basis for building metaphorical equivalences (sweet/still) between her and the dell. Nor can a conventional gender equation – placid woman/placid place – be evoked: first because we have *no* epithet for Emma, and second because the dell is expressly 'wild' (an adjective repeated twice).

The enigmatic claim that 'our thoughts at least are ours' brings a quite new note into the poem. What, then, *isn't* ours? To which the answer is, presumably, the land itself. The dell may or may not belong to anyone (the inhabitants of the cottage? the 'Shepherds who have seen me there'?); but even if it does, Wordsworth can name it in the freedom of thought or imagination, thereby making himself – to borrow Jonathan Bate's borrowing from Edward Thomas – 'lord of that he does not possess' (*RE*, 112). True enough; but I should want to insist that such claims to the unfettered autonomy of imagination are in profound contradiction with the previous forty lines of the poem. Having begun in utopian mood, demonstrating how qualities which appear antagonistic to dualist thinking pass seamlessly into and out of each other, the text can hardly endorse an act of 'thought' which defines itself in opposition to landownership or, let us say, materiality in general without betraying its own opening impulse, without taking a disabling 'sudden turning' into dualism in its own right. The poem itself, to its credit, begins to acknowledge as much five lines later, when it concedes that the dedication to Emma was a 'fancy'; the noun, linked even here with 'idle talk', passes wholly into the realm of negative connotation in the fourth poem, in which the poet and his companions are 'Feeding unthinking fancies' and cruelly misinterpret real human suffering. The idle talk of the Emma poem is with 'the Shepherds who have seen me' in the dell, and leads to the hope that

> two or three, perhaps,
> Years after we are gone and in our graves,
> When they have cause to speak of this wild place,
> May call it by the name of EMMA'S DELL.

With this exchange between educated narrator and working shepherds, we do indeed return to the terrain of Jonathan Bate's version of Schiller's 'naive' and 'sentimental'. But this is hardly a successful 'bridge'. Having veered off into an ungrounded flight of fanciful naming, the poem now bends the stick too far back in the opposite direction, desperately oscillating from pole to pole after its early utopian fusions. Wordsworth now hopes to motivate his individual act of naming through the anonymous and collective practice whereby country people give names to local places (about which I shall have more to say at the end of this essay).

Since this can apparently only occur after the deaths of himself and Emma (which in his case took place fifty years after the composition of the poem in 1800), we're witnessing some impressively long-term planning here – which thoroughly contradicts that dissolution of anxious self into present pleasure ('forgetting all') which characterised the poem's opening. The place name would then effectively have become an epitaph, achieving the desirable impersonality that Wordsworth usually associates with that genre. Yet this would-be synthesis of naive and sentimental remains at best small-scale ('two or three') and at worst entirely speculative ('perhaps', 'May call it'). The poem acknowledges the need for 'bridges', and even defines the criteria for successful naming in its early lines; but it is not, *pace* Jonathan Bate, anything like a workable bridge in its own right. The act of naming goes sadly askew as the name 'Emma' is dragged unmotivated into the text; Wordsworthian nomination in this poem fails to meet its own internally self-defined criteria and never really puts itself to rights thereafter. It seems likely that the bemused local shepherds will be as unfruitful an audience for the narrator as the 'hoary-headed Swain' is in Gray's *Elegy*; indeed, my hunch is that they'd be more likely to call it Wordsworth's Dell or Poet's Dell (or perhaps something altogether ruder) rather than Emma's. And in Wordsworth's poem, unlike Gray's, no saving 'kindred Spirit' turns up.

If you can't readily motivate the name, the next best thing may be to ward off criticism of its arbitrariness by disabling the critics in advance, building a sceptical Solitary into your text as in *The Excursion* precisely in order to contain and ultimately outmanoeuvre all his best points. In *The English Poetic Epitaph*, Joshua Scodel has demonstrated how the late eighteenth-century epitaph is increasingly concerned to define the qualified reader who alone is competent to appreciate it, and a poet as powerfully committed as Wordsworth to the 'epitaphic mode' certainly shares this concern. As Scodel notes of the one poem in *Lyrical Ballads* which is formally an epitaph, Wordsworth's 'A Poet's Epitaph' actually 'neglects to describe the deceased in order to concentrate wholly on the reaction of readers, good and bad'; the poem then becomes, in effect, 'a meta-epitaph that dramatizes the confrontation between the expectations of his imagined readers and the traditional values that he believes are embodied in the genre at its best'.[9] In similar vein, one might term 'To Joanna' a meta-inscription, a wide-ranging meditation on the motives of inscription which is much concerned with ruling out the responses of incompetent readers. And just as several of the disqualified readers of 'A Poet's Epitaph' turn out to be urban professionals – statesmen, lawyers, doctors – so we realise, with a gentle shock of mild surprise, that having spent her youth 'amid the smoke of cities' Joanna is actually an incompetent reader of her own poem:

> your heart
> Is slow towards the sympathies of them
> Who look upon the hills with tenderness.

The reader of *Lyrical Ballads* too, struggling with 'feelings of strangeness
and aukwardness' (*LB*, 7), is no doubt included in this indictment of
urban literacy. In 'A Poet's Epitaph' the ideal reader is the withdrawn
rural figure 'clad in homely russet brown', who seems happily to cross
traits of both the kindred spirit and the hoary-headed swain of Gray's
Elegy; but in 'To Joanna' rural readers seem to inspire as little confidence
as urban ones. The vicar, emerging from his 'gloomy house', could hardly
be further removed from that ideal decoder of graves and mounds, the
Pastor of *The Excursion*. He has already failed to decipher the chiselled
inscription; and while we might take this as a sign of Wordsworth's
dismal craftsmanship, the poem certainly views it as a sign of the vicar's
readerly obtuseness. Nor does he fare any better as a reader/auditor of
the text's central narrative, proving a particularly dim-witted Wedding
Guest to the poet's Ancient Mariner: at the key point of the story, with
the echoes circulating from mountain to mountain, the vicar can exhibit
only a baffled 'hey-day of astonishment'.

To be afflicted with readers as dull as this might try any poet's
patience. It certainly does Wordsworth's, who admits that he answers
the Vicar in a distinctly double-edged spirit, 'those dear immunities of
heart / Engender'd betwixt malice and true love'. The same tight-lipped
hostility can be felt again forty lines later, in the barbed reference to the
uncomprehending Vicar as 'our cordial Friend'. With the word 'malice'
something quite new has entered the Poems on the Naming of Places,
a tacit acknowledgement that the impulse to name or inscribe may be
aggressive rather than utopian, or perhaps inextricably both at the same
time. The local 'malice' towards the Vicar is, I would suggest, a mask or
decoy for a deeper malice towards Joanna, just as the poem's opening
antagonism between city and country is a decoy leading our attention
away from the more radical conflict of the sexes that it works through
later; but we ought even so to linger on the hapless Vicar for a moment
before turning to Joanna herself. How does the Vicar *know* that
Wordsworth carved the indecipherable 'runic' characters on the rock,
since he presumably didn't catch the poet red-handed with his hammer
and chisel? It seems that a report has reached him at secondhand from
one or more people who did actually witness the act of carving. If we ask
who they are, the Emma poem has already given us an answer; the
'witnesses' to the act of naming in that earlier poem are 'the Shepherds
who have seen me there'. These sharp-eyed shepherds or, perhaps better,
local people in general have caught the poet at it again and reported
him back to the local thought-police. If Wordsworth welcomed the

shepherds' intervention in the Emma poem, creating a benign fantasy of the achieved impersonality and endurance of his act of naming around them, here the social truth of the relationship between 'sentimental' poet and 'naive' countryfolk is more clearly spoken. They form a network of spies rather than Jonathan Bate's 'bridge', regarding the poet's 'sentimental' antics as so bizarre that they deserve reporting to the local authorities. Wordsworth then responds in kind, with 'malice' towards their chosen investigator – all of which is very different indeed from the genial 'idle talk' with the yokels which closed 'It was an April morning'. One thinks rather of D. H. Lawrence's embittered relations with his Cornish neighbours in Zennor during the Great War.

If the peculiar emotional field of this poem is 'engender'd betwixt malice and true love', then one must assume that official protestations of regard for Joanna – 'we love you well' – entail subtextual malice too. The Vicar, as I have suggested, is ultimately a decoy; Joanna is the real target here. At the very core of this intensely self-conscious poem is Joanna's reading of Wordsworthian 'reading' and the extraordinary traumatic consequences this triggers off in the poet. Inscribing the rock with her name is then, I will argue, an aggressive stratagem to close this disturbance down rather than an ecologically holy Batesian bridge. As the couple stroll at break of day along the banks of the Rotha, they arrive 'in front of that tall rock / Which looks towards the East'. The rock is experienced here as an absolute obstruction, severing both pedestrian and poetic continuity; it is a 'lofty barrier', at which 'I here stopp'd short'. If the budding groves of Emma's poem only *seemed* to encounter 'hindrances that stood / Between them and their object', Wordsworth now actually runs full tilt into one. Undaunted, the poet then proceeds to 'read' the object: 'I ... trac'd the lofty barrier with my eye / From base to summit', just as brother John 'traced' a pathway between the trees in the fir-grove poem. In both cases, a radical obstruction is dissolved, turned into literal path or metaphorical bridge:

> such delight I found
> To note in shrub and tree, in stone and flower
> That intermixture of delicious hues,
> Along so vast a surface, all at once
> In one impression, by connecting force
> Of their own beauty, imag'd in the heart.

It is Wordsworthian vision itself here which exercises 'connecting force', reducing an awesome object that threatens to exceed the very limits of human perception to a manageable organic unity; the prodigious barrier is dissolved into characteristic intermixtures, connections and blendings. But though two minutes' intent contemplation suffices to

quell the sublime object, Joanna's 'incompetent' response to the poet's
reading throws everything into crisis again:

> Joanna, looking in my eyes, beheld
> That ravishment of mine, and laugh'd aloud.
> The rock, like something starting from a sleep,
> Took up the Lady's voice, and laugh'd again:
> That ancient Woman seated on Helm-crag
> Was ready with her cavern ...

That hint of oppressive physical closeness in the first line, which is
picked up again later when the Vicar 'smil'd in my face', might give
us cause to look across to the close of 'There is an Eminence'. With
Dorothy's love and company, 'no place on earth / Can ever be a solitude
to me'; this sounds at least as claustrophobic as it does comforting, and
might well make you want to be perched (linguistically at least) on top
of a distant, lonesome Peak as far away from the woman as you could
get. Joanna here, however, is a far more formidable female, not just
physically close but spiritually challenging too; it is as if the Solitary in
The Excursion, in one great snort of satirical energy, had blown away
all the mildly consoling doctrines of the Pastor and the Wanderer. But
the sceptic here is a woman. In this, the one great moment of female
laughter in *Lyrical Ballads*, Joanna shakes and shatters the poet's hard-
won equanimity; she has roughly the effect on him that Goody Blake's
curse does on Harry Gill elsewhere in the volume. At this instant of
textual subversion, all the mad mothers, female vagrants and forsaken
Indian women of *Lyrical Ballads* take their revenge on their author.
The rock too throws off its subjection, and Joanna's laughter resounds
throughout and 'feminises' an entire landscape. If female bodies elsewhere in Wordsworth are often metamorphosing back towards the
mineral or vegetable, here the mineral 'starts from sleep' and incarnates
an alarming femaleness: that 'ancient woman seated on Helm-crag'
brings Martha Ray of 'The Thorn' forcefully into Joanna's poem, and
even when we've grasped from the footnote that we're dealing with
'a Rock which from most points of view bears a striking resemblance to
an Old Woman cowering', the intertextual power of the reference isn't
lost. True, the poem then works hard to contain this laughter and re-
masculinize its landscapes: 'Skiddaw blew / His speaking trumpet', 'the
brotherhood of ancient mountains'. But on the other hand the power
of female laughter is such that it infects even figures of patriarchal
authority like the Vicar, who smiles in the poet's face in astonishment
in a gesture that echoes Joanna's own. 'Ancient' is a key-word in this
poem, used three times (and again in the 'ancient trees' of 'To M. H.').
And what seems to be unleashed here is some primordial, precultural

female laughter, riotous and carnivalesque, for which the nearest poetic analogue I can think of is T. S. Eliot's prose-poem 'Hysteria'.[10] Even Joanna seems taken aback by the monstrous energies she has liberated, switching from a rampant Bertha Mason to a timorous Jane Eyre, 'as if she wish'd / To shelter from some object of her fear'.

Jonathan Bate notes that Wordsworth's listing and chanting of Lakeland names – Helm-crag, Hammar-Scar, and so on – is 'act of incantation' which 'personalises' Drayton's systematic mapping of the whole of England in *Poly-Olbion* (*RE*, 99). But 'incantation' gives the wrong emphasis here. We are in the presence of a sorcerer's apprentice, buffeted by forces far beyond his command, rather than of an assured mage chanting his powerful spells. The very lines that Bate takes as evidence of ecological dwelling and holiness are shot through with gender politics and violence, with Wordsworth for once in *Lyrical Ballads* on the receiving end; a 'romantic ecology' that is gender-blind to this extent is no ecology at all. We must then extend this account to the Wordsworthian naming or inscribing which, as I've noted earlier, the poem seeks strongly to motivate: 'And *hence*, long afterwards … '. Far from effecting a bridge between Schiller's naive and sentimental, the inscription surely continues the sexual *agon*. To carve Joanna's name in the rock is partly to acknowledge her disturbing power, but it is also to localize and delimit it, confining it like a genie in a bottle rather than having it run riot across the entire landscape. If the inscription is a kind of scar, then scars testify to the fact that the wound has healed as well as the fact that it was deep. Moreover, Joanna's name is defaced to the point where even her acquaintances can't make it out; in this arguably aggressive gesture, its power is surely dissipated as well as memorialized. Affectionate remembrance at the official level, sexual-political stratagem in the subtext, the inscription, like the poet's answers to the Vicar, is engendered betwixt malice and true love. In the end, however, the turbulent female laughter that resounds throughout this poem is successfully contained. The reference to 'your own fire-side' in line four is written out by the shift to 'all who dwell by my fire-side' in the penultimate line, the dissident voice being effaced in favour of the confirming Grasmere ecolect. And at the level of the sequence as a whole, Joanna's Rock is thoroughly displaced by its successor poem, which sets up (erects, dare one say?) a powerfully patriarchal Peak or Eminence which bears the name William Wordsworth. The poem added to the group in 1815 may also be regarded as closing down some of the troubling impulses raised by its predecessors. No Emmas or Joannas here; for women are altogether banished from a text which celebrates a place which forcefully bonds brother to brother.

In his account of the place-naming poems in *Romantic Ecology*, Jonathan Bate does at one point 'confront the possibility that the poet is so busy identifying with the place that he ignores the inhabitants' (p. 100), and he recognises that the fourth poem, 'A narrow girdle of rough stones ... ', is a key text for addressing this issue. No longer are we in the *locus amoenus* of Emma's dell or 'To M. H.'; rather does the landscape gather to itself all the 'hindrances' and 'barriers' of the earlier poems, being composed of 'rough stones and crags', a 'rude and natural causeway', a 'retir'd and difficult way'. This is a terrain of resistance, not soft green turf and glades of water, and one cannot but read its physical obstructiveness prophetically, as a hint of a challenge to that project of naming which governs its counterparts in the series. Such resistance also features in the poem to brother John, where the 'thickly planted' fir trees, 'in such perplexed and intricate array', eventually drive the poet out of the grove (though, oddly, the grove was first valued precisely for having an 'unincumbered floor'). But natural resistance, in this powerful poem of male bonding, is subsequently overcome, with John's pacings to and fro wearing 'an easy line / Along a natural opening'. Subdued back down into Wordsworthian mildness, the terrain is ready for that second act of inscription which is the poet's naming it.

True, the rugged terrain of the fourth poem doesn't initially hold back the poet and his companions; their trivial 'unthinking fancies' seem to 'skim' lightly above it much as the dandelion seed or thistle's beard does across the surface of the lake. We are in the world of radical dualisms that was announced late in the Emma poem by the declaration that 'Our thoughts at least are ours': autonomous imaginings versus a brutely material landscape or 'dead unfeeling lake'. The flimsy attempt of that earlier poem to ground the sentimental back in the naive, to reinforce individualist naming with the collective authority of the shepherds, is here abandoned from the start. The labourers are hard at work with the harvest, but the 'busy mirth / Of Reapers' is mere background here; it is as pleasurable as the 'sallies of glad sound' from birds and beasts in Emma's dell, but no more humanly meaningful than that. The breakthrough in this poem is that the dichotomy is here identified, as it was not in 'It was an April Morning', as a class dualism by means of the encounter with the peasant fishing on the bank. The 'ready comments' on an angler who is not participating in the work of harvest constitute a kind of extended though low-level naming, one which is laden with complacent class-prejudice and woefully out of touch with the named object as it actually exists, 'a man worn down / By sickness, gaunt and lean ... Too weak to labour in the harvest field'. Physical resistance here mutates into moral 'admonishment', and a second full act of geographical naming cancels out the first rudimentary human one: 'POINT RASH-JUDGEMENT is the name it bears'. This gesture seems to put the whole project of Wordsworthian naming under erasure. The only name that sticks (rather than 'skims') is one which announces a necessary *mis*-naming, a name that is not so much a bridge as an anti-bridge, marking an insuperable distance between Schillerian naive and sentimental. If the poem's opening image of a 'rude and natural causeway' gives some succour to the Batesian image of the bridge, such metaphorical hopes are dashed when we encounter the most spectacularly useless and unbridgeworthy pair of legs in the whole of Wordsworth:

> wasted limbs, his legs so long and lean
> That for my single self I look'd at them,
> Forgetful of the body they sustain'd.

Since the chastening lesson afforded by the sick peasant is 'What need there is to be reserv'd in speech', this presumably applies also to every impulse one has to open one's mouth and name a place; it threatens the whole project of this sequence of poems.

Or rather, one kind of naming is put into crisis – which allows the outlines of a quite different practice to be faintly discerned. While the first sixty lines of the poem are mostly frivolous leisured fancy, they aren't quite entirely that. At one key moment, in terms reminiscent of the Emma poem, they sketch the theoretical criteria of successful naming, and then offer a little-noticed instance thereof. In the midst of superficial fancies the poem suddenly rounds on such fancies, preferring the rough terrain and hardy plants of Grasmere to Grecian Naiads or romantic Ladies of the Mere. The local flowers and water-weeds are

> too fair
> Either to be divided from the place
> On which it grew, or to be left alone
> To its own beauty.

Here again is an oblique evocation of the utopian name. Coming from elsewhere, from the realm of culture, it doesn't merely 'leave alone' the mute natural object; but once given, it seems, in its benign organic appropriacy, as if it never could 'be divided from the place' or object which it names. Ideal names superficially disturb but more fundamentally participate *in* that which they name, just as a man might '*plant* his cottage' in the peaceful nook of 'To M. H.'. This is by now familiar theory, but the practical instance of it is not the poet's own final act of naming but rather the continuation of the lines I have been citing:

> Many such there are,
> Fair ferns and flowers, and chiefly that tall plant
> So stately, of the Queen Osmunda nam'd.

Named *of* Queen Osmunda not named *by* her: the passive seems to denote a name whose origins are lost in the mists of history or legend, running all the way back in fact to the *osmund* of Old Danish. The name is perhaps motivated by similitude; this 'stately' fern with its very large fronds is aptly named after a noteworthy royal figure. But it is a popular and collective term, unlike the esoteric labels doled out elsewhere in this sequence of poems; whoever coined it in the first instance is now lost in the anonymity of time and distance, at the maximum remove from the fresh-minted neologisms of the place-naming poems, each bearing the distinctive stamp of the 'Grasmere ecolect' on its face. The Emma poem tried tentatively to move from self-conscious coinage to shepherdly impersonality; its Point Rash-Judgement successor shows that these two things cannot be bridged and, at this crucial if marginal moment, seems to plump for the latter rather than the former.

And it may be that, if we stand back from Poems on the Naming of Places and survey *Lyrical Ballads* as a whole, an anonymous and collective model of naming wins out, and proves more 'ecologically holy' than its Wordsworthian counterpart. A key text here is 'Hart-Leap Well', a poem as centrally concerned with the naming of place as any of those I have discussed above:

> And they, who do make mention of the same,
> From this day forth, shall call it Hart-Leap Well.

Sir Walter's exuberant private naming of the place does successfully enter the collective local memory; the shepherds who were merely wished for in 'It was an April Morning' actually turn up in 'Hart-Leap Well' in the form of that 'grey-headed Shepherd' who, long years later, explains the origin of the place name to the poet. However, this is far from being any sort of desirable bridging of naive and sentimental. For the human naming of place is at one with the violence that has hunted the Hart to its death; and the name, far from benevolently inhering in the landscape, blights the very spot to which it is attached: 'More doleful place did never eye survey'. If names can thus vandalize nature, so we must think of aggressive vandalism as a kind of naming or inscription; such, surely, is the import of 'Nutting' with its 'ungracious *sign* / Of devastation' (my emphasis). Historically distanced as it is, 'Hart-Leap Well' can afford to come clean about the individualist violence of names in a way that the formal naming sequence in *Lyrical Ballads* on the whole cannot.

In *Romantic Ecology* Jonathan Bate makes much of the fact that the Naming of Places sequence immediately precedes 'Michael' which, in his view, 'recovers the Schillerian "naive" for the English poetic tradition':

it is here that the ordering of *Lyrical Ballads* is even more suggestive, for immediately before 'Michael' the reader encounters the five 'Poems on the Naming of Places'. It is their namings that provide the bridge, the uniting of sentimental and naive, of poet and nature.

(p. 105)

Yet it seems to me that the relation between the Naming sequence and 'Michael' is not one of preparation or symbiosis but rather, on this all-important issue of names, one of direct contradiction. For the acts of naming highlighted in 'Michael' operate on altogether different principles from those of the previous group:

> And from this constant light so regular
> And so far seen, the House itself by all
> Who dwelt within the limit of the vale,
> Both old and young, was nam'd The Evening Star.

> that large Oak, which near their door
> Stood, and from its enormous breadth of shade
> Chosen for the Shearer's covert from the sun,
> Thence in our rustic dialect was call'd
> The CLIPPING TREE, a name which yet it bears.

These instances thoroughly contradict Bate's assertion that 'the people who know places best, who are most rooted in them, tend not to be those who give them names ... They are not likely to articulate, to make a meal of, their bond with place' (p. 87). 'Make a meal of it' perhaps they don't, but the dwellers in the vale certainly articulate the significance of place and local object. Anonymous and collective, modestly local but also stoutly enduring, such names must be evoked in the passive – 'was nam'd', 'was call'd' – not as an imperious 'I name' or Sir Walter's 'shall be called'; their punctual origin cannot be located, though their aptness can be enjoyed. These names are true bridges, yoking human work and natural object as with the Clipping Tree, but also poet and shepherds in their joint use of '*our* rustic dialect'. But they achieve this unity from the ground up, not the top down – which was the model for the transmission of names from poet to shepherd in Emma's dell. Far from being benignly led up to by the place-naming sequence, the 'Michael' names highlight, by contrast, how far short the poems of that grouping fall of the optimal criteria for naming which they evoke *en route*.

And the fact, that, on the evidence of 'Michael', local names are already in place on such a wide-spread basis can take us back to an important hesitation in the Advertisement to the naming sequence. It begins: 'By Persons resident in the country and attached to rural

objects, many places will be found unnamed or of unknown names ... '
Well, *which*? If these places are indeed unnamed, then perhaps we might
feel inclined to endorse the project of Wordsworthian naming, which
would have all the freedom of Adam labelling the birds and beasts for
the very first time. But what if these places are rather 'of unknown
names', already, that is, have local names which poetic naming could
only in effect displace? The concluding image of the Point Rash-
Judgement poem throws up the very same issue. The poet and his
friends call the place

> By a memorial name, uncouth indeed
> As e'er by Mariner was giv'n to Bay
> Or Foreland on a new-discover'd coast.

'New-discovered' from the mariner's viewpoint, perhaps, but it seems
likely that that coast is already mapped out by names bestowed by its
native inhabitants, its own equivalents of the Clipping Tree and the
Evening Star; one doesn't happen upon the 'virgin scenes' of 'Nutting'
or 'To M. H.' all that often. The assumption that places are unnamed
and open to Wordsworthian inscription may be simply *pres*umption.
And if there is even a possibility that they are of 'unknown names' rather
than no names, then one would have thought that some humble research
into local maps, work practices, dialect forms, history and customs,
might be the 'ecologically holy' thing to do.

Such, at any rate, is surely the import of 'Home at Grasmere', which
makes it the very opposite of the 'addition to and summation of' the
Naming sequence which Jonathan Bate has argued it to be (*RE*, 102).
A fir-grove which you and your brother assume the right to loiter in and
inscribe with paths and names turns out, in 'Home at Grasmere', to be
the product of another's labour and the site of her fond personal memories. Planted by the young Grasmere couple to afford a 'friendly covert'
to their sheep, the 'grove of Firs' is now, many years later, haunted for
the elderly widow by memories of her dead husband. One could hardly,
without bad faith and arrogance, venture to re-baptize a place that is
already so richly and poignantly 'named'; the task of verse here, rather,
is to 'preserve / Some portion of its human history / As gathered from
the Matron's lips'. The poem then generalizes from this instance,
looking out over a landscape so fully worked and humanly 'written' over
that an Adamic naming of places seems entirely out of place:

> Look where we will, some human hand has been
> Before us with its offering; not a tree
> Sprinkles these little pastures but the same
> Hath furnished matter for a thought.

'We do not tend a lamp', Wordsworth informs his sister, 'which we alone participate'; yet the Naming poems, generating new names from within the enclosed fireside ecolect, had tried to do just that. 'Home at Grasmere', on the other hand, is governed by nominative modesty ('but I cannot name it') and a turn, as in 'Michael', to local naming practices: 'The Owl that gives the name to Owlet-Crag'. The latter then govern *The Excursion*, with its Joyful Tree ('named … from dateless usage'), its Path of Perseverance, and its ideal Priest nicknamed the Wonderful by 'our simple shepherds, speaking from the heart' – instances which are implicitly but favourably contrasted with the Solitary's merely wilful naming of the individual rocks in his recess ('that I gravely style / My theban obelisk'). By which time, surely, the early Wordsworthian project of place-naming is well and truly over.

What, then, are the consequences of all this for ecologically minded criticism? First, surely, we must conclude that Thomas J. Lyon's anxiety over the 'general deceit of naming' and Kim Taplin's hard-nosed sense that 'the naming of places can have very contradictory effects' are both much truer to the overall thrust of Wordsworth's Poems on the Naming of Places than Jonathan Bate's genial confidence that the Wordsworthian name bridges naive and sentimental, restoring to us in miniature the Leavisite organic community from which these two dissociated terms ages ago split off. In fact, Taplin's ambivalence between strenuous Hopkinsian over-naming and William Barnes's traditional, generic names captures something of the movement I have been tracing in Wordsworth himself between the 'I name' of the *Lyrical Ballads* sequence and the 'is named' of 'Michael', 'Home at Grasmere' and *The Excursion*. Eco-criticism must certainly sustain the utopian buoyancy that Bate often eloquently expresses, but it must also deploy the 'hermeneutics of suspicion' for which both Lyon and Taplin speak; the best readers of Wordsworth's Naming poems remain, as I noted above, those sheep in John's fir-grove who 'watch my motions with suspicious stare'. And a reinvented or postmodern version of 'pastoral' will have to incorporate both impulses, welding utopian projection and critique of ideology into a difficult but formidable (non-)synthesis. The limits of Bate's account of the Naming poems can be cast in theoretical terms, as an absence of Marxist, feminist or poststructuralist concerns; but might also be put more empirically, as a weakness in *reading*. He simply doesn't read these six poems closely enough; he too often takes the will for the deed, reversing the terms of D. H. Lawrence's great dictum by trusting the artist rather than the tale. The poems' official self-image is taken as pretty well the last word there is to be said about them, whereas the texts themselves bear enough overt marks of conflictual impulses –

'Engender'd betwixt malice and true love', 'Huddling together from *two fears*' (my emphasis) – to warrant a minute, frame-by-frame analysis which will do full justice to the tangled subtexts at work here as well as the level of official intentionality. Eco-criticism will have to learn to read *harder* if it is to persuade, and for a while at least forgo that 'wise passiveness' which confines it to overt authorial intention. Utopian bridges between language and the non-human or the sentimental and the naive will have to be built (if indeed they can) on the *other* side of that textual complexity, that slow and disturbing task of deep reading, which Marxism, feminism and poststructuralism enjoin upon us. Wordsworth's Poems on the Naming of Places are a signal instance of how *not* to build such bridges – which the poet, to his credit, fully recognizes in other aspects of his work.

Notes

1   Thomas J. Lyon, 'The Ecological Vision of Gary Snyder', *Kansas Quarterly* 2 (Spring 1970), pp. 117–24.

2   Kim Taplin, *Tongues in Trees: Studies in Literature and Ecology* (Bideford, Devon: Green Books, 1989), p. 26. Page references are hereafter given in my text.

3   Jonathan Bate, *Romantic Ecology: Wordsworth and the Environmental Tradition* (London: Routledge, 1991). Hereafter abbreviated in my text as *RE*.

4   Quotations from *Lyrical Ballads* are from R. L. Brett and A. R. Jones (eds), *Lyrical Ballads*, second edition (London: Routledge, 1991). I have not given page references to individual poems.

5   William Wordsworth, *Guide to the Lakes*, ed. Ernest de Selincourt (Oxford: Oxford University Press, 1977), p. 64.

6   William Wordsworth, *Selected Prose* (Harmondsworth: Penguin, 1988), p. 327. Hereafter cited as *SP*.

7   Peter Bürger, *Theory of the Avant-Garde*, trans. Michael Shaw (Manchester: Manchester University Press, 1984).

8   Cited from William Wordsworth, *The Poems: Volume One* (Harmondsworth: Penguin, 1977), pp. 448–51.

9   Joshua Scodel, *The English Poetic Epitaph: Commemoration and Conflict from Jonson to Wordsworth* (Ithaca: Cornell University Press, 1991), p. 387.

10 See Tony Pinkney, *Women in Poetry of T. S. Eliot: A Psychoanalytic Approach* (London: Macmillan, 1984), pp. 18–23.

Keeping Mum:
Wordsworth's Woman in White

Keith Hanley
Lancaster University

I

The most vivid of Wordsworth's recollections of his mother from the Cockermouth days, before she died when he was seven, are included in his 'Autobiographical Memoranda', dictated at Rydal Mount in 1847:

> I remember my mother only in some few situations, one of which was her pinning a nosegay to my breast when I was going to say the catechism in the church, as was customary before Easter. I remember also telling her on one week day that I had been at church, for our school stood by the churchyard, and we had frequent opportunities of seeing what was going on there. The occasion was, a woman doing penance in the church in a white sheet. My mother commended my having been present, expressing a hope that I should remember the circumstance for the rest of my life. 'But,' said I, 'Mama, they did not give me a penny, as I had been told they would.' 'Oh,' said she, recanting her praises, 'if that was your motive, you were very properly disappointed.'[1]

This second event – seeing the woman doing penance ... in a white sheet' – which took place in the parish church some time before the death of Wordsworth's mother in 1778 was extraordinary.

Cases of public penance, nearly always for breaches of the seventh commandment, had long been rare enough to attract particular attention in the press. *Fogg's Weekly Journal*, for example, gives an account in 1733:

> On Sunday last a Woman did Penance in the Parish Church of St. Bride's, by standing in a white Sheet, with a Wand in her Hand, on a Stool in the middle Isle during the time of Divine Service for Adultery and Fornication, and having a Bastard Child in the Absence of her Husband.[2]

The church historian who provides the above instance disputes the evidence of another who writes that

Stephen Hales, the famous physiologist and chaplain to the prince afterwards King George the Third, died in 1761. He is said to have been the last of the clergy who made his female parishioners do penance.[3]

But he himself is able to refer specifically to only four other examples of this form of 'Discipline and Penance' up to 1813, including the one he cites from Wordsworth's account, two in Durham and North Yorkshire in 1770, the year of Wordsworth's birth, and one recorded by Augustus J. C. Hare, a member of the influential Anglican clan, in describing his grandmother, Mrs Hare-Naylor's life at Hurstmonceaux in the early 1800s. This last is recorded in a Proustian sketch from Hare's *Memorials of a Quiet Life* (1872–6):

> Mrs Hare-Naylor's life at Hurstmonceaux must have astonished her rustic neighbours, and still more her neighbours in her own rank of life ... Not only, when within the house, was she always occupied in the deep study of Greek authors, but during her walks in the park and shrubberies she was always seen dressed in white, and she was always accompanied by a beautiful tame white doe, which used to walk by her side, even when she went to church. Her foreign life led her to regard Sunday merely as a fête day, and she used frequently to scandalize the church-going population by sitting at a window looking out upon the road, working at her tambour-frame, when they were going to church. Her impetuosity in liking and disliking often led her to make friends with persons beneath her, or to take them into her service when they were of a character which rendered her notice exceedingly undesirable. The two women she took most notice of in the parish were the last persons who ever did public penance at Hurstmonceaux, having both to stand in a white sheet in the churchyard for their 'Various offspring,' so that people said, 'There are Mrs Hare-Naylor's friends doing penance.' And it was long remembered with amusement that when one of her maids was afterwards found to have misbehaved herself, she said, 'Poor thing, she cannot help it; I really believe it must be *something in the air!*'[4]

Hare's grandmother appears outlandishly exempted from the moral regime to which her acquaintances are subjected. Though she doubles the other transgressive mothers, *her* white dress affirms her odd social and cultural apartness that, in its premonition of Emily in Wordsworth's *White Doe of Rylstone*, lays claim also to symbolic spotlessness and the innocence of 'nature'. The split between these women in white serves to point up the implication of Wordsworth's own mother in the penitential figure of his reminiscence, her emancipation from a guilt in which she is involved relies too on habituation – on its having become 'something in the air'. But in the case of Wordsworth's mother, the habituation is to a discourse of self-discipline that she is inaugurating for her son.

Clearly, Wordsworth's Woman in White represented a subjection, whereby his (the good) mother introduced her son (according to Lacan) to the Name of the Father, and the institution of moral law. 'My mother', writes Wordsworth, 'commended my having been present, expressing a hope that I should remember the circumstance for the rest of my life', and it is obviously appropriate that the accompanying recollection should have been one of his mother's proudly preparing him for being catechised, as he was again to recall in his sonnet, 'Catechising', from *Ecclesiastical Sonnets*:

> From Little down to Least, in due degree,
> Around the Pastor, each in new-wrought vest,
> Each with a vernal posy at his breast,
> We stood, a trembling, earnest Company!
> With low soft murmur, like a distant bee,
> Some spake, by thought-perplexing fears betrayed;
> And some a bold unerring answer made:
> How fluttered then thy anxious heart for me,
> Belovèd Mother! Thou whose happy hand
> Had bound the flowers I wore, with faithful tie:
> Sweet flowers! at whose inaudible command
> Her countenance, phantom-like, doth reappear.[5]

His mother's spectral surveillance pins down signifieds that she helps happily naturalise ('With low soft murmur, like a distant bee'), binding flowers into ritual expression ('with a faithful tie'), and mediating an authorisation that remains a *silent* corroboration within the symbolic word of the father – issuing an 'inaudible command', as the injunction to remember the Woman in White makes memory itself a penitential rite converting difference and change into a structure of pious constancy.

'Penance', according to Robert Phillimore, the most notable of all authorities on English canon law, quoting previous authorities,

> is said to be an ecclesiastical punishment used in the discipline of the church, which effects the body of the penitent; by which he is obliged to give a public satisfaction to the church for the scandal he has given by his evil example. So in the primitive times they were to give testimonies of their reformation, before they were re-admitted to partake of the mysteries of the church. In the case of incest, or incontinency, the sinner is usually enjoined to do a public penance in the cathedral or parish church, or public market, barelegged and bareheaded, in a

white sheet, and to make an open confession of his crime in a prescribed form of words; which is augmented or moderated according
to the quality of the fault, and the discretion of the judge.[6]

Primitively, it had been a corporal punishment, that was accompanied
by 'thrusting [the culprit] into a monastery, branding, fustigation [i.e.
beating], and imprisonment'.[7] But by Wordsworth's day its punitive
function had in effect become outmoded, little more than a customary
practice like donning a nosegay for being catechised, and, as in the case
of Mrs Hare-Naylor's acquaintances, wherever it had anomalously
survived, its punitive function of spectacular warning had become
ineffective (following Foucault's argument in *Discipline and Punish*).
What Wordsworth's Woman in White represents is in effect an historical hang-over, a provincialism that provides an exceptional exhibition
of ritual humiliation and purification that was becoming part of, as it
disappeared into, a disciplinary moral regime. The sight was marked
vestigially by the violent inscription of power on the body of the culprit,
though the chief focus of concern, which was effecting the abolition of
the practice, had become 'technologies of power'.[8] What Wordsworth
had witnessed was the cusp of the passage of institutional violence into
invisibility, or 'nature'.

Discipline, naturalisation, is, of course, Urizenic. Wordsworth's trem-
bling company of schoolchildren awaiting interrogation, 'From Little
down to Least, in due degree, / Around the Pastor, each in new-wrought
vest', is not far removed from Blake's charity orphans in the 'innocent'
version of 'Holy Thursday', 'walking two & two in red & blue & green',
'these flowers of London town; / Seated in companies they sit with
radiance all their own'[9] There is the same impression of regimentation
(in the word 'company'), and the contrivance of a ceremony in which
law is imposed by institutionally domesticated instruments of authority:
'Grey headed beadles walk before with wands as white as snow, / Till
into the high dome of Paul's they like Thames waters flow.' (ll. 3–4)
In Blake's poem, the 'lambs' (l. 7) are being trained in the process of self-
sacrifice, whereby their subservience constitutes the economic and
religious discourse of charity, which occludes injustices of social and economic division by using its victims to represent its illusory magnanimity.

In Wordsworth's autobiographical anecdote a similar move is negotiated by his (good) mother, who sacrifices another version of herself, the
sexually transgressive penitent, as the *other* of the regime of moral law
that also constitutes her presence within the disciplinary discourse she is
endorsing. In this way, the Lacanian good mother resembles the Blakean
abusive parent, concealing while enforcing an alienated precocity. But
the Wordsworthian *penitent* mother figures other and more complicated
investments in the mechanics of disciplinary discourse. In her case, the

taking on herself an act of suffering, representing the acceptance of her transgression as the necessary origin of the disciplinary regime, is bound up with a private psychological predisposition in Wordsworth that compulsively evades the oedipal struggle that Lacan has retold as the violent origin of language itself. The figure of conversion is preformative and exemplary of the personal history that may be recovered from all the key discourses into which his poetry enters. It led him to *remember her* by courting self-chastisement throughout his adolescence, whether at the hands of his domestic disciplinarian, uncle Kit Cookson: 'But possibly, from some want of judgement in punishments inflicted, I had become perverse and obstinate in defying chastisement, and rather proud of it than otherwise' (*Memoirs*, I, 9); or in welcoming his father's deflected revenge after Wordsworth had seemed to conspire in his death as is revealed by the horse-waiting episode of *The Prelude*: 'The event, / With all the sorrow which it brought, appeared / A chastisement … / And I do not doubt … / The workings of my spirit thence are brought';[10] or in internalising its moral institutionalisation by becoming the 'Bondman' (*PW*, IV, p. 86, l. 64) of 'duty' in '[t]he spirit of self-sacrifice' (l. 62). The victimhood of his Woman in White is the empowering of a protective as well as a deceptive device that constantly brings about that denial of oedipal initiative so dear to the redemptive maternal scheme, the fortunate fall, of the Wordsworthian imagination.

II

Despite the disciplinary tendency of Wordsworth's Woman in White – and the white dress is, of course, the uniform of institutionalisation – there is something uncanny about her, something that resists as well as facilitates naturalisation in her marking of a point of origin. Wordsworth had not got the point of seeing her – he was only in it for the money – until his mother made it: she was to be an unforgettable marker that was to control his future history, and it seemed to him that his mother's adjuration was peculiarly necessary for him. In another recollection he claimed that she was intimately cognisant of the nature of his originality: 'the only one of her five children about whose future life she was anxious, was William; and he, she said, would be remarkable either for good or for evil' (*Memoirs*, I, 9). The Woman returns as a recurrent spectral figure throughout his works, obsessively repressing and transmuting the power of the father, and the story of its potentially lethal oedipal origin. Her apparition insistently enables and presides over the algorithm of his desires – a symbolic passage that denies or apologises for its violent implications.

The figuration can be at least partly 'busted'. Following his mother's death, Wordsworth was sent away to school at Hawkshead, in the Vale of Esthwaite. No less than many other northern rural communities, Hawkshead has its local wraiths, such as the 'tall, white-robed female' which, by local report, was often seen to '[walk] regularly on the road between Belmont avenue and Hawkshead Hall, or in Scarhouse Lane.'[11] The author of the *History of Hawkshead* records a late example of 'the oldest inhabitant of Satterthwaite ... [who] ... when working at Hawkshead, as a lad, about 1825, ... was riding in a cart from Hawkshead Hall towards Gallow-barrow, when he saw a tall female figure, dressed well but old-fashionedly, suddenly leave the highway and rapidly ascend into the air, finally disappearing from sight' (*Hawkshead*, p. 328). Wordsworth moved in this local atmosphere and was of course spooked during those formative experiences of his childhood in the vale recounted in Books 1 and 2 of *The Prelude*. There, gigantesque and blanched forms are described as pursuing his guilty retreat following the consciousness of transgression, as when, in the fantasy that is the aftermath of his stealing the shepherd's skiff:

> no familiar shapes
> Of hourly objects, images of trees,
> Of sea and sky, no colours of green fields,
> But huge and mighty forms that do not live
> Like living men moved slowly through my mind
> By day, and were the trouble of my dreams.
>
> (ll. 422–6)

Or when, in that exemplary oedipal situation, 'the bird / Which was the captive of another's toils / Became my prey' (ll. 326–8):

> I heard among the solitary hills
> Low breathings coming after me, and sounds
> Of undistinguishable motion, steps
> Almost as silent as the turf they trod.
>
> (ll. 329–32)

Wordsworth seems in all these episodes to have been haunted by a disturbed memory that, though it looked like threatening punishment, after all turns into the suggestion of an encompassing disciplinary regime with peculiar attractions for himself.

Disciplinary discourse is assumed by way of transgression – by virtue, that is, of seeking to deny it. The equivocal anxiety that, replaying the process of language acquisition, announced that of inscription into specific discourses extended throughout his youth. He records a crucial discursive passage in 'Tintern Abbey': 'The sounding cataract / Haunted me like a passion' (*PW*, II, p. 261, ll. 76–7). The way in which he had formerly felt confirmed by a comforting shift in the aesthetics of 'nature', from a sense of challenge (the sublime) producing a more congenial disciplinary discourse (the picturesque): 'more like a man / Flying from something that he dreads than one / Who sought the thing he loved' (ll. 70–2), provided a template for containing the castrative threats of the specifically non-reflective Revolutionary discourse into which he had erroneously entered. At the same time, Wordsworth recuperated the earlier childhood experiences as prized moments of self-building, because they suggested to him how the guilt of transgression had been alternatively transformed into disciplinary discourse that managed the rebellion of oedipal struggle into a moderated inscription in the law.

Throughout his works the familiar sense of the numinous that is attached to evanescent vision, especially through mists and vapourous veils, fades typically into the act of imagination that effectively legitimises a chosen discourse, often and increasingly associated with the ecclesiastical associations of its Cockermouth source. The unearthly phantom, for Wordsworth, is usually close to institutionalisation. As Wordsworth writes in Book 4 of *The Prelude*, the whole Vale of Esthwaite was presided over by the church:

> I saw the snow-white church upon its hill
> Sit like a thronèd lady, sending out
> A gracious look all over its domain.
>
> (ll. 13–15)

In *The White Doe of Rylstone*, Emily and the doe, though participants in the very bloody Rising of the North, appear resiliently pure and undefiled by their historical context and rather mediate an aura of Anglican spirituality. The child-woman Lucy disintegrates into a pantheistic theology rather than material things, and all those dead mothers, who return throughout his work, become increasingly explicit representations of redemptive promise.

Overt or implied, the narratives that relate to this figuration are gratefully received, however chastening. The personification of the disciplinary regime is most exemplarily that of Pallas (offspring of power and wisdom) in 'Ode to Duty', where the held taper, after the penitent's, has become a phallic rod with a difference, vindicating an inner battle that has become satisfactorily resolved – a commanding voice that has been feminised:

> Stern Daughter of the Voice of God!
> O Duty! if that name thou love
> Who art a light to guide, a rod
> To check the erring, and reprove;

Thou, who art victory and law
When empty terrors overawe;
From vain temptations dost set free;
And calm'st the weary strife of frail humanity!
                               (*PW*, IV, p. 83, ll. 1–8)

The phallic mother, allegorising the naturalisation of institutional
violence, is welcomed as presenting a moral discourse which elides
violent struggle and celebrates victory without acknowledging strife.

By his 'Ode, 1814', actually written in 1816 to commemorate the
final overthrow of Napoleon at Waterloo, Wordsworth envisions his
own version of a French Revolutionary festival in terms of the elective
discourse of a defensive nationalism. Wordsworth 'took an active
part in [the] patriotic celebration' of Waterloo, ascending Skiddaw to
attend the 'scene of festivity' round Southey's bonfire.[12] The second
stanza legitimises British triumphalism in images of an undifferentiated
imaginary family:

And lo! with crimson banners proudly streaming,
And upright weapons innocently gleaming,
Along the surface of a spacious plain
Advance in order the redoubted Bands,
And there receive green chaplets from the hands
Of a fair female train –
Maids and matrons, dight
In robes of dazzling white;
While from the crowd bursts forth a rapturous noise
By the cloud-capt hills retorted;
And a throng of rosy boys
In loose fashion tell their joys;
And grey-haired sires, on staffs supported,
Look round, and by their smiling seem to say,
'Thus strives a grateful Country to display
The mighty debt which nothing can repay!'
                               (*PW*, III, pp. 145–6, ll. 53–68)

To Shelley, who parodied it in 'The Mask of Anarchy', it is a delusive
facade for institutional power. But Wordsworth sees the 'innocent'
'upright weapons' as predictably dis- and re-empowered, sanctioned by
women in white. The regalia seems inseparable from the natural scene,
discourse coming in aid of discourse, and the feminised images of aged
power recall Burke's representation of the immemorial organic nation in
Reflections on the Revolution in France and Britain's gentle mightiness.[13]

'The mighty debt which nothing can repay' is not, though it may cross the mind, the national debt created by sustaining the Napoleonic Wars, but rather a later manifestation of that 'mighty debt of grief' that in his juvenile poem, 'The Vale of Esthwaite', written when he was seventeen, Wordsworth acknowledged was fundamentally to a kind of parentalism whose loss has effectively enabled a peculiarly mild passage into the symbolic order. There he recognises a relation that protected him from anything other than repentant discourses that lament the passing in which they are implicated:

> For much it gives my heart relief
> To pay the mighty debt of grief,
> With sighs repeated o'er and o'er,
> I mourn because I mourn no more.
> (I, p. 280, ll. 430–3)

In the later poem, the debt has been incurred by those whose deaths have protected the nation from violence, including the knowledge of its own inner violence. Their sacrifice has legitimised the British war effort, making it an unquestionable good, by which the enemy is constituted as the necessarily defining victim. So, in the companion 'Ode 1815', Wordsworth can hail a beneficent image of what he calls the 'pure intent' of 'carnage' as the feminised offspring of a disciplinary nationalism:

> But Thy most dreaded instrument, [Almighty God]
> In working out a pure intent,
> Is Man – arrayed for mutual slaughter,
> – Yea, Carnage is thy daughter!
> (*PW*, III, p. 155, *apparatus*)

As with Pallas, so with Wordsworth's Valkyrie: the deflection of filiation to the daughter side-steps the issue of oedipal rivalry.

III

In the Penrith Beacon episode in Book 11, the story of the Hawkshead wife-poisoner, Thomas Lancaster, who killed eight people in all with white arsenic and was hanged in 1672 in Colthouse meadows, (adjacent to the house where Wordsworth boarded during his schooldays), becomes involved with that of the later Penrith robber-murderer, Thomas Nicholson. Wordsworth evokes their composite crime when he describes his having become lost as a five-year old:

I ... at length
Came to a bottom where in former times
A murderer had been hung in iron chains.
The gibbet-mast was mouldered down, the bones
And iron case were gone, but on the turf
Hard by, soon after that fell deed was wrought,
Some unknown hand had carv'd the murderer's name.
...
Faltering, and ignorant where I was, at length
I chanced to espy those characters inscribed
On the green sod.

(ll. 287–301)

Though the last recorded use of the gibbet in the Hawkshead Parish
Register is 1672, the stump of the gallows-post remained until about
1860, and the local writer of a common-place book 'records [at so late
a date] the popular dread of approaching the site even by daylight.'
(*Hawkshead*, p. 44) The place where the murderer was hung up in chains
at Pool Stang was known as Gibbet Moss, and according to the local
historian, Henry Swainson Cowper, was 'thoroughly haunted' (ibid.).
In Wordsworth's account of his childhood trauma, he recognises in the
'ordinary sight' of what he feels to be a distressed female one of the most
formative moments of his life:

forthwith I left the spot,
And, reascending the bare common, saw
A naked pool that lay beneath the hills,
The beacon on the summit, and more near,
A girl who bore a pitcher on her head
And seemed with difficult steps to force her way
Against the blowing wind.

(ll. 301–7)

A bleached supernaturalism surrounding a suffering woman, here par-
tially a revenant of the murder victim, again features in the experience:

I should need
Colours and words that are unknown to man
To paint the visionary dreariness
Which, while I looked all round for my lost guide,
Did at that time invest the naked pool,
The beacon on the lonely eminence,
The woman, and her garments vexed and tossed
By the strong wind.

(ll. 308–15)

There is an obvious ambiguity about the figure, as about the letters written on the grass that Wordsworth writes are those of the killer, though they were in fact those of the victim. Though disturbingly, the woman is the object of (male) violence, haunting the site of the gallows, she is also the unstoppable subject of legal retribution. She offers a particular memory, as she had already done in 'The Vale of Esthwaite', where she had already been involved in reinforcing the poet's awareness of violence, pointing out the iron case and gallow-chains which he is being compelled to confront:

> Now did I love the dismal gloom
> Of haunted Castle's pannel'd room
> Listening the wild wind's wailing song
> Whistling the rattling doors among;
> When as I heard a rustling sound
> My haggard eyes would turn around,
> Which strait a female form survey'd
> Tall, and in silken vest array'd.
> Her face of wan and ashy hue
> And in one hand a taper blue;
> Fix'd at the door she seem'd to stand
> And beckoning slowly wav'd her hand.
> I rose, above my head a bell
> The mansion shook with solemn knell.
> Through aisles that shuddered as we pass'd
> By doors [?] flapping [?] the blast
> And green damp windings dark and steep,
> She brought me to a dungeon deep,
> Then stopp'd, and thrice her head she shook,
> More pale and ghastly seem'd her look.
> [   ] shew'd
> An iron coffer mark'd with blood.
> The taper turned from blue to red
> Flash'd out – and with a shriek she fled.
> With arms in horror spread around
> I mov'd – a form unseen I found
> Twist round my hand an icy chain
> And drag me to the spot again.
>
>   (*PW*, I, p. 275–6, 240–67)

The dragging is a repetition compulsion that characterises all the 'spots of time' through which Wordsworth was conducted into the symbolic. The Woman in White is not spotless: she is invested with a fall into (human) time through language, but she requires a special kind of spotting to overcome her spots. If she is at bottom a figuration for what Lacan describes as the phase of language-acquisition, as the ultimate encounter with the carved initials 'inscribed / On the green sod' reveals, she nonetheless offers a glimpse of a kind of saving foreclosure, through the memory of a prior relation with the mother, 'the discipline of love' (l. 251), which in Book 2 he theorises that for the peculiarly '[b]lessed ... infant babe' (l. 237) will remain '[p]reeminent till death' (l. 280). The original, prelinguistic relation, it is suggested, *may* be carried through into the symbolic order in a correspondent relation with disciplinary discourse symbolised by the Woman in White. Such a symbolisation of structural continuity denies a fall, no sooner than it has been acknowledged.

In the process, as the maternal relation predominates, the Woman comes to represent a version of parentalism that is complicated by her investment of the absent *father's* ghost. Margaret Homans and others have argued that the Romantic construction of subjectivity generally excludes femininity, but in Wordsworth's case it relies on the primacy of femininity in order to legitimise his version of Romantic masculinity.[14] Bogeys that personify the latent guilt and fear of oedipal victory in Wordsworth's juvenile poetry, such as the fifteen foot giant buried in St Andrew's churchyard at Penrith (reputed to have 'killed four wild boars in the neighbouring forest of Inglewood'[15] and the skeletal woodcuts from Foxe's *The Book of Martyrs*, 'Strange and uncouth, dire faces, figures dire / Sharp-kneed, sharp-elbowed, and lean-ankled too, / With long and ghostly shanks, forms which once seen / Could never be forgotten',[16] coalesce with this other, stronger presence of a maternal metaphor that mourns and moderates the fact of transgression to the extent of aggressive protectiveness, even infanticide. Insisting on the continuity of her union with pre-symbolic being, the phallic mother, like Martha Ray or Betty Foy, threatens a benign kind of castration. It turns out to be oddly self-enhancing by virtue of originating an alluringly alternative discourse of self-subjugation, as the betrayed mothers fight shy of the greater brutality of patriarchal law. In 'The Vale of Esthwaite', the 'brooding Superstition' (*PW*, I, p. 270, l. 27), that culminates in the first version of recollection of Wordsworth's father's death, plays around his relation with the beneficent horrors of this progenitor, taking the form of a spectral androgyny. More particularly, it figures the terms in which his predicament might achieve appropriate expression in lyrical poetry, giving him his voice by becoming the subject of Gothic and sentimental poetic discourses.

The poem's self-conscious Gothicism picks up on local legend. In his *Guide to the Lakes*, Thomas West records of the ruined Calgarth Hall, on the east bank of Windermere, which features centrally in this poem, 'spectres still are seen'.[17] The local accordingly serves to domesticate an established literary vogue, enabling its assumption as a personal poetic voice. Though the only Gothic novel to have preceded it is Walpole's *Castle of Otranto*, it is saturated with echoes of Gothic poetry, especially Helen Maria Williams's 'Part of an Irregular Fragment, Found in the Dark Passage of a Tower', from her *Poems*, 1786. The episode quoted above that describes an encounter with a pale woman bearing a taper through 'shuddering' aisles who conducts him to a 'spot' of ancient violence, '[dragging him] to the spot again', has assimilated the local lore of the 'white wiven' to the literary models. Scott's White Lady in *The Monastery* emanates from the same popular superstition to fulfil a similar role as both bugbear and guide.

In his poem, Wordsworth is fascinated by a form that is exaggerated, particularly in height, and that looked 'pale and ghastly' and 'slowly wav'd her hand'. Later on, he encounters in a complementary white-shrouded male spectre a terrifying poet-figure, who bears on his arm a lyre:

> On tiptoe, as I lean'd aghast
> Listening the hollow-howling blast
> I started back – when at my hand
> A tall thin spectre seemed to stand
>
>   . . . .
>
> And on one branded arm he bore
> What seem'd the poet's harp of yore;
> One hand he wav'd, and would have spoke,
> But from his trembling shadow broke
> Faint murmuring – sad and hollow moans
> As if the wind sigh'd through his bones.
> He wav'd again, we entered slow
> A passage narrow damp and low;
> I heard the mountain heave a sigh
> Nodding its rocky helm on high,
> And on we journey'd many a mile
> While all was black as night the while,
> Save his tall form before my sight
> Seen by the wan pale dismal light
> Around his bones so [   ] shed
> Like a white shroud that wraps the dead.
> Now as we wander'd through the gloom
> In black Helvellyn's inmost womb
> The spectre made a solemn stand,
> Slow round my head thrice wav'd his hand,
> And [?] mine ear—then swept his [? lyre]
> That shriek'd terrific shrill and [? dire]

Shudder'd the fiend: the vault among
Echoed the loud and dismal song.
(I, pp. 277–8, ll. 325–8, 334–57)

The mountain's nodding crest of Helm Crag is an allusion to the vast
enchanted helmet of Otranto, but it is also more intimately associated
with Wordsworth's privately overdetermined oedipal spots. Carol Landon
has shown that the rough drafts at this stage compare Helm Crag to the
mountain that uprears its head in the stolen boat episode of *The Prelude*:

As when by solemn moonlight
The shepherd rows his skiff
From the dark rock that overhangs
the dock, he [?kens] the top of a tall
rock – at every measur[ed] stroke ...
Taller & taller [till*del.*] he drops his oars
appalled.[18]

Radically, it is his poetic voice, his 'loud and dismal song', that so
horrifies the young initiate. But though the discourse of the Gothic
awakens for Wordsworth some fearful intimation of the violent and
cryptic origin of language itself, its appropriation is being effectively
regulated by a deeply familiar white-robed figure holding a phallus in its
hand. As Wordsworth gets hold of his poetic voice, it is the convention-
ality that facilitates his presumption. The poem, that is, is being written
in a discourse that after all is mediated by the figuration of a peculiar
relation to the word of the father so as to make it a disciplinary one.

                                    IV

Behind both these encounters in 'The Vale of Esthwaite' lies the text of
Hamlet's meeting with his father's ghost, who commands Hamlet to
'[m]ark'[19] him and who is 'Doom'd for a certain term to walk the night'
(I. v. 10). These resonances constantly recrudesce when Wordsworth
revisits the scene of language-acquisition, highlighting his oedipalism
while (in his case) also indicating a deflection of the vengeful return.
The Shakespearean echoes in Wordsworth's androgynous parent pick
up on the embarrassment of Hamlet's predicament—poised between
two guilts: that of retaining the primary relation with the mother against
the father, and that of disrupting that relation by identifying with the
(violent) word of the father.

    This dilemma is particularly evident in the passage on the Discharged
Soldier in Book 4 of *The Prelude*, where the apparitions from 'The Vale
of Esthwaite' reappear, exciting oscillations between horror and pity:

It chanced a sudden turning of the road
Presented to my view an uncouth shape,

· · · · · · ·

... He was of stature tall,
A foot above man's common measure tall,
Stiff in his form, and upright, lank and lean –

· · · · · · ·

His arms were long, and bare his hands; his mouth
Shewed ghastly in the moonlight ...
... He was alone,

· · · · · · ·

... in his very dress appeared
A desolation, a simplicity
That seemed akin to solitude. Long time
Did I peruse him with a mingled sense
Of fear and sorrow. From his lips meanwhile
There issued murmuring sounds, as if of pain
Or of uneasy thought ...

· · · · · · ·

... In a glen
Hard by, a village stood ...

· · · · · · ·

Scarce distant fom the spot an arrow's flight.
I wished to see him move, but he remained
Fixed to his place, and still from time to time
Sent forth a murmuring voice of dead complaint,
Groans scarcely audible. Without self-blame
I had not thus prolonged my watch; and now,

· · · · · · ·

I left the shady nook where I had stood
And hailed him. Slowly from his resting-place
He rose, and with a lean and wasted arm
In measured gesture lifted to his head
Returned my salutation, then resumed
His station as before.

(ll. 401 ff.)

There are several resemblances between old Hamlet's ghost and the 'ghastly mildness' (l. 493) of the soldier. Both are 'clad in military garb' (l. 414), are suffering pitiably, carry themselves in a 'slow and stately' (I. ii. 202) manner ('with / A stately air' (ll. 443–4)), and gesture with hallucinatory politeness ('with what courteous action / It waves you to a more removed ground' (I. iv. 60–1)):

> Slowly from his resting-place
> He rose, and with a lean and wasted arm
> In measured gesture lifted to his head
> Returned my salutation.
>
> (4, ll. 437–40)

But the *rising* of this father-figure, though one from the dead, is after all unthreatening, as with all those others that are contained by an encompassing imaginary formation: when, for example, the mists '[a]dvanced in such indisputable shapes' (11, l. 381) during the Waiting for the Horses episode, or when the imagination manifested itself on the Alps, '[l]ike an unfathered vapour' (6, l. 527), or when the drowned schoolmaster surfaced:

> At length, the dead man, 'mid that beauteous scene
> Of trees and hills and water, bolt upright
> Rose with ghastly face, a spectre shape –
> Of terror even
>
> (5, ll. 470–3)

– an apparition that is "[hallowed] … / With decoration and ideal grace" (ll. 478–9). And yet the meeting is filled with lingering anxiety and uneasiness on Wordsworth's part that seems to stem particularly from his nervous assumption of authority over this other figure, whose impressiveness resides surprisingly in his deeper passivity, based on scriptural literalism:

> I entreated that henceforth
> He would not linger in the public ways,
> But ask for timely furtherance, and help
> Such as his state required. At this reproof,
> With the same ghastly mildness in his look,
> He said, 'My trust is in the God of Heaven,
> And in the eye of him that passes me.'
>
> (ll. 489–95)

Hamlet says after the appearance of his father's ghost, 'Foul deeds will rise, / Though all the earth o'erwhelm them to men's eyes,' (I. ii. 257–8) and what both he and Wordsworth fear is not so much a punitive visitation as the image of their own murderous fantasy ('Without self-blame / I had not thus prolonged my watch' (IV, 433–4)). He is both disturbed and curiously attracted by seeing himself implicated in the disempowering of the figure before him. What fascinates him in their conversation is something wanting in the soldier's meekness – a

discontinuity between *this* apparition's revelation of the violence done to
him and his refusal of Hamlet's father's call to revenge ('a quiet uncom-
plaining voice, / A stately air of mild indifference'):

> He all the while was in demeanor calm,
> Concise in answer. Solemn and sublime
> He might have seemed, but that in all he said
> There was a strange half-absence, and a tone
> Of weakness and indifference, as of one
> Remembering the importance of his theme
> But feeling it no longer. We advanced
> Slowly, and ere we to the wood were come
> Discourse had ceased. Together we passed
> In silence through the shades, gloomy and dark.
>
> (ll. 472–81)

The original fragmentary version elaborates the soldier's impotent self-
alienation:

> He appeared
> Forlorn and desolate, a man cut off
> From all his kind, and more than half detached
> From his own nature.
>
> (*BWS*, p. 434, ll. 57–60)

Wordsworth is embarrassed by patronising a father-figure to whom
he does not securely feel superior. He sees himself as gaining maturity
by becoming inscribed in a hollow language of social patronage
that assumes authority over the soldier as it has deprived the soldier of
any effective voice in what has happened to him in the past, and
that obscurely turns out to be complicit with the governing rhetoric of
warfare and social neglect that have resulted in the soldier's victim-
isation. In the upshot, Wordsworth is drawn to the other's refusal to
communicate, since his desired subject-formation is filiated to a figure
who offers no resistance and relinquishes the initiative in verbal exchange.
But what worries Wordsworth is the possible incongruity between the
soldier's quietism and his own uncomfortable self-assertion that fails
adequately to mask the negotiations of power in disciplinary discourse.
The soldier's deathly silence and empty speech remain distinctly
unsatisfactory in failing to provide the heroic discourse that Wordsworth requires to incorporate and elide the fact of the violence the
other has undergone. Instead, the difficult identification is attempted
as Wordsworth himself assimilates the emotions of Hamlet's father as
victim. When he writes

> Long time
> Did I peruse him with a mingled sense
> Of fear and sorrow
>
> (ll. 419–21)

Wordsworth is echoing Horatio's description of the ghost:

> *Horatio*. A countenance more in sorrow than in anger.
>
> . . . .
>
> *Hamlet*.   And fixed his eyes upon you?
> *Horatio*. Most constantly.
>
> (I. ii. 232–4)

What arrests Wordsworth's spotting is the soldier's affinity with a familiar looking presence that usually helps him to enter into a regime by which he would otherwise be traumatised. Though the process of identification is painfully protracted, Wordsworth does represent it as an important memory that in the end is socially and linguistically empowering, and this is enabled here through the evocation of a kind of inner resource in the soldier's fatalism that alters the effect of his oppression. The distressing evidence of the soldier's victimhood appeals to traces of another kind of victorious discourse that carries over from the parodic association of Christ's resurrection that were already imminent in Hamlet's father's ghost: the *rising* followed by the ascension that represents the ultimate atonement with the father. Hamlet adjures the ghost:

> tell
> Why thy canoniz'd bones, hearsed in death,
> Have burst their cerements, why the sepulchre
> Wherein we saw thee quietly interred
> Hath oped his ponderous and marble jaws
> To cast thee up again
>
> (I. iv. 46–51)

and the ghost, echoing Jesus resisting but obeying his mother's behest at the marriage in Cana (John, II, 4), tells him

> *My hour is almost come*,
> When I to sulph'rous and tormenting flames
> Must render up myself.
>
> (My emphasis. I. v. 2–4)

A complicating sense of the self-reproach that lies behind Wordsworth's meeting with the soldier is also engaged in his description in Book 10 of

the wounds of Christ that he sees reflected in the butchery of the
September Massacres on his way back to England via Paris in October
1792. That passage is also shaped by another noted *Hamlet* allusion
juxtaposed with one to the Biblical narrative of Christ's resurrection
from the dead. The latter offers a reading of signs of Wordsworth's
inculpation in the bloody Revolution, but also of an unlooked-for
intimation of that violence as the origin of a valued discourse:

> The fear gone by
> Pressed on me almost like a fear to come.
> I thought of those September massacres,
> Divided from me by a little month,
> And felt and touched them, a substantial dread
>   (10, ll. 62–6)

The doubt of Thomas Didimus is directed by Wordsworth not only to
a questioning as to whether the Revolution as he had conceived of it
could indeed have survived its implication in such atrocity, but also to
the suggestion that its bloodletting might, almost unbelievably, be seen
transformatively as productive of redemptive promise.

Wordsworth's account of his attempt at self-recognition in the soldier
similarly recalls the gospels' description of the disciples' fearful hope of
Christ's rising from the dead and their fascination with his reanimated
body-parts, particularly his limbs and 'lean' hands. This immanent
allusion hints at a possibly adequate discursive representation for the
structure of reconciliation with the ghost of the father, the triumphant
structure of the redemptive scheme that underwrites the marks of
violence and suffering Wordsworth actually saw.

V

As Elizabeth Bronfen has argued in *Over Her Dead Body*, the body is
feminised by signs of suffering, but Wordsworth identifies with the
feminised body not so much as the site of male violence as of female
empowering in the *selection* of disciplinary discourses that can contain
violence. For Wordsworth, spotting the feminine body enables a
difficult symbolic passage that forecloses the imaginary structure from a
totally alienated switching into the symbolic. His celebrated solitaries,
like the Discharged Soldier, typically disown the phallus, which is often
detachable and unwillingly assumed:

> At this he stooped,
> And from the ground took up an oaken staff
> By me yet unobserved, a traveller's staff

> Which I suppose from his slack hand had dropped,
> And lain till now neglected in the grass.
> (4, ll. 459–63)

The phallus can only be confidently assumed when it is directed towards the inscription in an appropriate discourse.

Other tall white-robed figures in 'The Vale of Esthwaite' point the way:

> And hark! the ringing harp I hear
> And lo! her druid sons appear.
> Why roll on me your glaring eyes?
> Why fix on me for sacrifice?
> But he, the stream's loud genius, seen
> The black-arch'd boughs and rocks between
> That brood o'er one eternal night,
> Shoots from the cliff in robes of white.
> So oft in castle moated round
> In black damp dungeon underground,
> Strange forms are seen that, white and tall,
> Stand straight against the coal-black wall.
> (*PW*, I, p. 270, ll. 31–42)

This is an ambiguous spotting of the poet, through which an abrupt resolution into natural forms mysteriously escapes the horror of Gothic discourse, relieving the threatening call of minstrel-music that is viewed as a sacrificial demand made by surrounding Druidic forms. In Book 12 of *The Prelude*, a similarly mediating evocation of the Druids was to rise from the nightmare vision of gigantic primitivism that had invested Salisbury Plain in the 1794–5 poems located there:

> I had a reverie and saw the past,
> Saw multitudes of men, and here and there
> A single Briton in his wolf-skin vest,
> With shield and stone-ax, stride across the wold;
> The voice of spears was heard, the rattling spear
> Shaken by arms of mighty bone, in strength
> Long-mouldered, of barabaric majesty.
> (12, ll. 320–6)

This displacement of the Terror and aggressive British nationalism is transformed into the pursuit of enlightened civilisation by a description of the Druids' burning of a vast wickerwork man filled with living men:

                              and lo, again
          The desart visible by dismal flames!
          It is the sacrificial altar, fed
          With living men – how deep the groans – the voice
          Of those in the gigantic wicker thrills
          Throughout the region far and near, pervades
          The monumental hillocks, and the pomp
          Is for both worlds, the living and the dead.
                                                    (ll. 329–36)

The 'pomp' is transitional, as Wordsworth becomes drawn to the institutionalisation of sacrifice while he is at the same time repelled by its
horrors. Echoes of Burke's vision of the organic society as 'a partnership'
which 'cannot be obtained in many generations, it becomes a partnership not only between those who are living, but between those who are
living, those who are dead, and those who are to be born' (*Reflections*,
p. 120) control a scene of violence into a phase in the vaster canvas of
historical inevitability. But that move is itself conditioned by a more
archeological one to coming to terms with representation as such:

          At other moments ...
          ... when 'twas my chance
          To have before me on the downy plain
          Lines, circles, mounts, a mystery of shapes
          Such as in many quarters still survive,
          With intricate profusion figuring o'er
          The untilled ground (the work, as some divine,
          Of infant science, imitative forms
          By which the Druids covertly expressed
          Their knowledge of the heavens, and imaged forth
          The constellations), I was gently charmed,
          Albeit with an antiquarian's dream,
          And saw the bearded teachers, with white wands
          Uplifted, pointing to the starry sky,
          Alternately, and plain below, while breath
          Of music seemed to guide them, and the waste
          Was cheared with stillness and a pleasant sound.
                                                    (ll. 337–53)

Here, the figures on the turf, indicated by a metonymic 'white wand',
negotiate the conversion of 'deep groans' into 'pleasant sounds'. The
translation, between power and ceremony, is precarious, and its phan-
tasmal origins remain elusive: 'But who shall parcel out / His intellect
by geometric rules, / Split like a province into round and square? ...

Who that shall point as with a wand, and say / "This portion of the river
of my mind / Came from yon fountain"?' (2, 208–15) The movement
of Wordsworth's mind, of course, is characteristically less conclusive,
more *wandering*, between foreclosure and representation, as the whole
movement of *The Prelude* and the growth of the *the* Wanderer's mind
from 'The Ruined Cottage' to *The Excursion* divulges.

The structure of Wordsworthian discipline is that of a deepened and
prolonged emphasis on the imaginary as a stage and register that directs
passage into the symbolic, and his adherence to the mirror stage recurs
as a fascination with derealising images of natural reflection in which
the not yet completely divided imaginary subject is represented. The
fragmentary draft (intended for *The Prelude* but included finally in Book
9 of *The Excursion*), 'Whether the whistling kite', contains his most
fixated reduplication: the 'snow-white ram' with its reflection of 'Another
and the same.' Metonymically, it is a startling image of maternalised
virility, and the passage is replete with other images of moderated
power. '[T]he mountain's voice'[20] is, after all, that of a bleating lamb, and
it is where 'A mountain torrent … was becalmed' (l. 16) that, he writes,

> at a glance I saw
> A two-fold image; on the grassy bank
> A snow-white ram and in the peaceful flood
> Another and the same. Most beautiful
> The breathing creature was, as beautiful
> Beneath him with his shadowy counterpart;
> Each had his glowing mountains, each his sky,
> And each seemed centre of his own fair world.
> (ll. 17–24)

Wordsworth's obvious need for this kind of detention is crucial to his
commemorative art, by which the present can only be acceptably
realised when it refigures what has gone before. Grandly, in 'Intimations
of Immortality' Wordsworth makes an explicit claim for this 'Presence
which is not to be put by' (*PW*, IV, p. 282, l. 121) from the protracted
infancy that is his reading of childhood. There the almost impersonal
state preceding language-acquisition is addressed in terms of an uneasy
theism, and the child is seen as 'Haunted for ever by the eternal mind'
(l. 114). But this slippery fit between the imaginary and disciplinary
discourses is a private project that informs what might otherwise seem
bathetically pointless and elusive in many slighter poems.

The end-piece to *Benjamin the Waggoner*, for example, plays a light-
hearted reprise of his familiar positioning. The description of Benjamin's
slow, unrupturing progress through the vale expresses Wordsworth's
sense of a commanding presence that he has enjoyed seeing harnessed

to imaginary discipline – mildly pompous, and recalling those simple shepherd-fathers in Book 8 of *The Prelude* who are made marvellously gigantic by atmospheric effects:

> – Yes, I, and all about me here,
> Through all the changes of the year,
> Had seen him through the mountains go,
> In pomp of mist or pomp of snow:
> Or with a milder grace adorning
> The landscape of a summer's morning;
> While Grasmere smoothed her liquid plain
> The moving image to detain.
> <div align="right">(<i>PW</i>, II, p. 204, ll. 225–33)</div>

But Benjamin's absence deprives him of what is more radically a maternal presence. The later fleet of vehicles that has replaced Benjamin's waggon exposes its cargo to the elements, as the waggon had never done:

> And oft, as they pass slowly on,
> Beneath my windows, one by one,
> See, perched upon the naked height
> The summit of a cumbrous freight,
> A single traveller – and there
> Another; then perhaps a pair –
> The lame, the sickly, and the old;
> Men, women, heartless with the cold;
> And babes in wet and starveling plight;
> Which once, be weather as it might,
> Had still a nest within a nest,
> Thy shelter – and their mother's breast!
> (ll. 252–63)

Regret for this loss, and insistence on the re-expression of its object, are what Wordsworth invariably demands of his poetry:

> Then most of all, then far the most,
> Do I regret what we have lost;
> Am grieved for that unhappy sin
> Which robbed us of good Benjamin; –
> And of his stately Charge, which none
> Could keep alive when He was gone!

For Wordsworth, this episode of local history has somehow served to dramatise the peculiar terms on which he desires to repay the 'mighty

debt of grief' he owes to his dead parents: a way of keeping his father's
word while denying his own forcible appropriation of it. In this way, his
commemorative poetic discourse comes as a revenant from the past, like
Hamlet's father's ghost, to insist on its particular form of expression in
the kind of poetry he feels compelled to write:

> Nor is it I who play the part,
> But a shy spirit in my heart,
> That comes and goes – will sometimes leap
> From hiding-places ten years deep;
> And haunts me with familiar face,
> Returning like a ghost unlaid,
> Until the debt I owe be paid.
>
> (ll. 209–15)

Such oedipal interplay also provides the model for Wordsworth's
interest in the ghosts of intertextual naming, particularly in the later
poems. In 'At Vallombrosa', for example, from 'Memorials of a Tour
in Italy, 1837', Milton is the shade that supplies the requisite poetic
discourse to vent a transhistorical religious awe:

> And now, ye Miltonian shades! under you
> I repose, nor am forced from sweet fancy to part,
> While your leaves I behold and the brooks they will strew,
> And the realised vision is clasped to my heart.
>
> (*PW*, III, p. 224, ll. 29–32)

But Wordsworth's dependence involves, as his Fenwick note on the
poem makes clear, an endorsement of Milton that is also a revision.
There he writes that

> many will think that in this poem and elsewhere I have spoken of the
> author of 'Paradise Lost' in a strain of panegyric scarcely justifiable
> by the tenor of some of his opinions, whether theological or political,
> and by the temper he carried into public affairs in which, unfortu-
> nately for his genius, he was so much concerned. (p. 499)

Wordsworth accordingly argues that 'the poetic mind' should be 'chiefly
exercised in works of fiction' because 'the poet can then follow wherever
the spirit of admiration leads him, unchecked by such suggestions as will
be too apt to cross his way if all that he is prompted to utter is to be
tested by fact' (ibid.). Like the spirit that Horatio tries to block: 'I'll
cross it though it blast me. Stay illusion! / If thou hast any sound or use

of voice, / Speak to me' (I. i. 127–9), that leads Hamlet so irresistibly to follow it, the spirit of the Wordsworthian imagination rises to the occasion. Wordsworth, confronted by the stultification of fact on the Alps as he describes it in Book 6 of *The Prelude*, had formerly realised that the 'strength' of his own 'usurpation' (ll. 532–3) derived from the towering invulnerability that Marcellus acknowledges: 'We do it wrong, being so majestical, / To offer it the show of violence, / For it is as the air invulnerable, / And our vain blows malicious mockery' (I. ii. 143–5). Wordsworth had later appreciated that the spirit of his own poetry could after all side-step a castrative encounter with literalism by affirming its appropriation of heroic discourse ('crossing the Alps') to represent the definitive manoeuvre of his creative imagination. An uncontested passage into the symbolic turned out to be the kind of conquest that was all along most deeply desired, and that accordingly re-authenticated as it redefined what had formerly seemed a failed triumphalism:

> Imagination! – lifting up itself
> Before the eye and progress of my song
> Like an unfathered vapour, here that power,
> In all the might of its endowments, came
> Athwart me. I was lost as in a cloud,
> Halted without a struggle to break through,
> And now, recovering, to my soul I say
> 'I recognise thy glory'.
>
> (ll. 525–32)[21]

The Fenwick note refers to another note attached to the sonnet, 'The King of Sweden' ('The Voice of song from distant lands shall call'), also written 'in this spirit' (p. 499), that claims to see the anti-Napoleonic stance of Gustavus IV as 'embodying moral truths' (ibid.). In the poem, 'the crowned Youth' (*PW*, III, p. 112, l. 3), who 'is raised *above* / All consequences' (ll. 10–11), is seen as the representative of legitimate succession, 'The heroes bless him, him their rightful son' (l. 14), just as in 'At Vallombrosa' Wordsworth's echo of Milton's echo of Dante serves to construct a traditionalist religious discourse, suppressing the trace of controversy and division, in order to seal the jarring of church and national reform at home in Britain that disturbingly preoccupied Wordsworth at that time.

Many later poems likewise revolve around the aptness of expression by more local and less prestigious place-names, as does a sonnet from the 'Yarrow Revisited' sequence, 'Composed … During a Tour in Scotland, and on the English Borders, in the Autumn of 1831'. The poem is titled 'Suggested by a View from an Eminence in Inglewood Forest':

> The forest huge of ancient Caledon
> Is but a name, no more is Inglewood,
> That swept from hill to hill, from flood to flood:
> On her last thorn the nightly moon has shone;
> Yet still, though unappropriate Wild be none,
> Fair parks spread wide where Adam Bell might deign
> With Clym o' the Clough, were they alive again,
> To kill for merry feast their venison.
> Nor wants the holy Abbot's gliding Shade
> His church with monumental wreck bestrown;
> The feudal Warrior Chief, a Ghost unlaid,
> Hath still his castle, though a skeleton,
> That he may watch by night, and lessons con
> Of power that perishes, and rights that fade.
>   (*PW*, III, pp. 276–7)

The border outlaws Adam Bell and Clym of the Clough, celebrated in a popular ballad collected in Percy's *Reliques of Ancient English Poetry*, had saved William of Cloudesley from the gallows at Carlisle and obtained the King's pardon for their crimes. Less specifically, the now enclosed border forest is visited by accustomed evocations of still immanent ancient warfare and religious history, and Wordsworth approvingly hears the signifier 'Inglewood' standing for a continuing history, though of muted power. Altogether, the spectres of literary medievalism return with contemporary force, and their survival bespeaks Wordsworth's piety. A bloody past has faded, but it has now become converted into a revised traditionalist discourse of feudalism, whose pacific political efficacy he would like to see prolonged.

VI

In Wordsworth's family romance, the voices he dutifully assumes are those of a more readily mother-identified daughter, however 'stern' or implacable. His symbiosis with his own sister, Dorothy, obviously points the way to the substitution he desires, not only through her daughterly example, but also because their own relation dates back to a pre-gendered indeterminacy. Together, they can recapture something of their life together before their parents died. This is the implication of his address to Dorothy in 'The Vale of Esthwaite' with its interpretation of the kind of compensation she has provided:

> Sister, for whom I feel a love
> What warms a brother far above,
> On you, as sad she marks the scene,

Why does my heart so fondly lean?
Why but because in you is given
All, all, my soul could wish from Heaven?
Why but because I fondly view
All, all that Heaven has claimed, in you?
(*PW*, I, p. 282, ll. 528–35)

Ostensibly, his relation to Dorothy helps assuage the experience of loss to which he nonetheless remains bound:

What from the social chain can tear
This bosom link'd for ever there,
Which feels, whene'er the hand of pain
Touches this heav'n connected chain,
Feels quick as thought the electric thrill,
Feels it ah me – and shudders still?
(ll. 536–41)

Within this idiom of sentimental melancholy a complication of thought finds indirect expression: that Dorothy links him with both his sense of loss and its relief – with a relation that postdates though it seems to precede its disruption. The particular alleviation she represents, if it can occur, would have to come with a disconnecting from the 'social [signifying] chain' of language that in reality has inescapably proceeded from being chained (as on the gallows) to a primal oedipal guilt. His sister, that is, stands for the sublation of one empowering parental relation over the pain and terror associated, by Wordsworth, with the other.

But though Dorothy offers a diminution of traumatic loss, she does not voice any saving discourse that has survived the unavoidable oedipal passage into the symbolic order. On the one hand, she remains, like her poetic avatar, Lucy, beyond the 'human fears' (*PW*, II, p. 216, l. 2) of violation; but on the other, 'among the untrodden ways' (p. 30, l. 1), she denies communication with 'the difference' (l. 12) that constitutes the poet's world. Ultimately, and with whatever moderation, the poet Wordsworth had to identify with the language of the phallic mother as ghostly father. Harkening to that voice entailed a seemingly culpable separation from his sister-identified subject, as De Quincey's version of the Lucy poems reveals. In his autobiography, De Quincey, who sees himself as a life-long sharer in the love of children, nonetheless finds himself retreating from the bedroom of his dead sister 'like a guilty thing, with stealthy steps from the room'.[22] The *Hamlet* allusion ('it started like a guilty thing / Upon a fearful summons' (I. i. 148–9)) places the writer beyond the experience of the dead child: the ghost may be an innocent victim, yet he is summoning to violence, and De Quincey knows that the out-of-body experience that he undergoes at the site of his dead sister's body is the beginning of a conversion of loss into literature – the originating memory from which his writing career proceeds. For Wordsworth, too, the fantasised body of his dead sister is the founding site of Romantic autobiography, of writing the self. To him, Lucy represents what in 'Intimations of Immortality' he describes as 'the fountain light of all our day, / ... the master light of all our seeing' (*PW*, IV, p. 283, ll. 152–3), and yet, as he realises in the course of composing that poem, that illumination has to become subjected to a 'more habitual sway' (p. 285, l. 192): the 'visionary gleam' that has 'fled' (p. 280, l. 56) can only hope to be matched with consolatory disciplinary discourses that bespeak the ghost of the father. There Wordsworth '[raises] / The song of thanks and praise / ... for ... / High instincts before which our mortal Nature / Did tremble like a guilty Thing surprised' (p. 283, ll. 140–8).

Whenever Wordsworth did absorb a consolatory discourse, he was able to identify with the ghost of the father and offer his passage as cautionary for those (and they included finally all his readers), whom he felt sure would wish to make their cultural insertion on the same terms. 'Tintern Abbey', for example, presents his sister with the same discipline for survival that he had learned, even as it at the time urges a specific discourse – the pantheistic one life – into which Wordsworth had gratefully translated his own exposure to the retraumatisation of language acquisition in his Revolutionary involvement. The offer is made in a voice very similar to that of his mother ('expressing a hope that I should remember the circumstance for the rest of my life') – a voice that itself resonates with that of Hamlet's father's ghost enjoining his son to 'remember me' (I. v. 91):

> Oh! then,
> If solitude, or fear, or pain, or grief,
> Should be thy portion, with what healing thoughts
> Of tender joy wilt thou remember me,
> And these my exhortations!
>
> (*PW*, II, p. 263, ll. 143–7)

Notes

1 Christopher Wordsworth, *Memoirs of William Wordsworth*, 2 vols. (London: Moxon, 1851), I, 9. Further references are in the text thus: *Memoirs*.

2 Saturday 15 Dec., No. 267; quoted by J. Wickham Legg in *English Church Life: From the Restoration to the Tractarian Movement, considered in some of its neglected or forgotten features* (London: Longmans, Green and Co, 1914), p. 259.

3 Quoted in Legg, p. 104.

4 2 vols. (London: Strahan and Co, 1873), I, pp. 142–3.

5   *The Poetical Works of William Wordsworth*, ed. Ernest de Selincourt, rev. Helen Darbishire, 5 vols. (Oxford: Clarendon Press, 1952–9), III, p. 395. Further references are in the text thus: *PW*.

6   *The Ecclesiastical Law of the Church of England*, 2 vols. (London: Henry Sweet, Stevens and Sons, 1873), II, pp. 1367–8.

7   Richard Burn, *The Ecclesiastical Law*, 4 vols. (London: S. Sweet; V. and R. Stevens and G. S. Norton, 1842), III, p. 103.

8   Michel Foucault, *Discipline and Punish*, translated by Alan Sheridan (New York: Vintage Books, 1979), p. 23.

9   *Blake's Poetry and Designs*, ed. Mary Lynn Johnson and John E. Grant (New York and London: Norton, 1979), p. 32, ll. 2 and 5–6.

10 Book 11, ll. 367–9, 384, 388. All references to this work are to the 1805 version in the Norton Critical Edition, ed. Jonathan Wordsworth, M. H. Abrams, and Stephen Gill (New York and London, 1979).

11 Henry Swainson Cowper, *Hawkshead: (The Northernmost Parish of Lancashire) Its History, Archaeology, Industries, Folklore, Dialect, Etc, Etc*, (London: Bemrose and Sons, 1899), p. 327. Further references are in the text thus: *Hawkshead*.

12 *Observer*, 3 September 1815, quoted in *News from the Past 1805–1887*, ed. Yvonne French (London: Gollanz, n.d.), p. 108.

13 See Burke's 'reverence' for the British 'world of reason, and order, and peace, and virtue' opposed to 'those … who are prompt rashly to hack [their] aged parent to pieces', in *Reflections on the Revolution in France*, ed. Conor Cruise O'Brien (Harmondsworth: Penguin, 1968), pp. 195, 194. Further references in the text thus: *Reflections*.

14 See Margaret Homans, *Bearing the Word: language and female experience in nineteenth-century women's writing* (Chicago: Chicago University Press, 1980) and Marlon Ross, *The Contours of Masculine Desire* (New York: Oxford University Press, 1989).

15 T. F. Bulmer, *History, Topography and Directory of East Cumberland* (Manchester: T. Bulmer and Co, 1884), p. 625.

16 The Pedlar', in Jonathan Wordsworth, *The Music of Humanity* (London: Nelson, 1969), p. 175, ll. 73–6.

17 *A Guide to the Lakes in Cumberland, Westmorland and Lancashire*, 3rd edn. (London: Richardson and Urquhart, 1784), pp. 63–4.

18 See 'Some Sidelights of *The Prelude*', in *Bicentenary Studies*, ed. Jonathan Wordsworth (Ithaca and London: Cornell University Press, 1970) pp. 359–62. Further references in the text thus: *BWS*. I owe these associations with Helm Crag to some unpublished notes by Jonathan Wordsworth.

19 *The Riverside Shakespeare*, ed. G. Blakemore Evans (Boston: Houghton Mifflin Co., 1974), I. v. 2. Further references in the text are in this style.

20 The Norton *Prelude*, p. 506, l. 7.

21 See this point elaborated in Keith Hanley, 'Crossings Out: the Problem of Textual Passage in *The Prelude*', in *Romantic Revisions*, ed. Robert Brinkley and Keith Hanley (Cambridge: Cambridge University Press, 1992).

22 *Autobiographic Sketches, The Works of Thomas De Quincey*, 3rd edition, 16 vols. (Edinburgh: Adam and Charles Black, 1862–71), XIV, p. 17.

Resisting Arrest: The National Constitution of Picturesque and Gothic in Radcliffe's Romances

Angela Keane
University of Salford

Novels are like nations. They are narratives of modernity, whose subjects progress through recognizable landscapes and whose anonymous readers are bound through their pages in the imagined community of the secular, capitalist state. This now familiar formulation, abstracted from Benedict Anderson's much fuller, if flawed thesis on the imagining of nation, underpins a number of powerful readings of eighteenth century British fiction and the construction of modern national identity.[1] Some of the more influential theorists of the fiction of the period have been preoccupied with the triumvirate of Defoe, Fielding and Richardson and debates around the classic realist form of the novel.[2] Analyses which look beyond fiction to the imagining of community in other texts of the period follow a similar trajectory. They argue convincingly that the writings of what has been coined the civil Imaginary – the mimetic, ethical representations of journalism and prose fiction, served to legitimate the power of an emerging bureaucratic state and to participate in the construction of its modern subjects.[3] After Habermas, the Whig construction of the 'public sphere' has assumed hegemonic status in our vision of eighteenth-century prose writing.[4]

Post-structuralist and particularly feminist analyses of eighteenth-century fiction have signalled the contested nature of this 'public sphere' and its representations.[5] This paper joins such a project, in an exploration of a form of fiction – Gothic romance – whose representations lie apparently beyond the domain of the civil Imaginary, but which undoubtedly participate in the narration of nation in the 1790s. In an approach to three of the most well-read romances of Ann Radcliffe *The Romance of the Forest* (1791), *The Mysteries of Udolpho* (1794), and *The Italian* (1797) I want to point to the unstable generic and epistemological foundations of the project of narrating the nation.[6] I shall suggest that the ambivalence of Radcliffe's Gothic in national terms is exacerbated by her deployment of the picturesque – an aesthetic which itself has been read recently in terms of the imagining of nation. In the first part of this paper I shall delineate the national significance of picturesque description and of Gothic romance in the 1790s. I shall go on to illustrate the intersection of picturesque and Gothic narrative, reading Radcliffe's romances as narratives of a nation which lacks a hegemonic form or is, at least, uncertain in its modes of self-legitimation.

Reading the National Landscape

Outside of narrative, the British nation has perhaps been imagined most persistently in representations of rural landscape. The myth of a continuous British identity, inscribed in the land, is now reified in the burgeoning and, at least ideologically, state supported heritage industry. It is inscribed in the image of partitioned, cultivated fields; in the landscaped gardens of stately homes; in the regionally inflected, uncultivated topography of the national parks, lakes, lochs, dales, moors, glens. These spaces are varied but familiar signs of Britishness. They are accessible to the public but protected by state and private ownership. They are continuous with the past but change with the march of progress.

It is only too easy to read in this landscape a trope of the British political constitution. Under the pressure of this ready analogy, however, the rural landscape becomes an ideological garden, a fallen Eden. The balanced epithets variation and familiarity, access and protection, continuity and change become sites of rhetorical contest for those who want to be seen to represent the best interests of the nation. Each term yields a subset of others, some privileged, some indicting: tools for self promotion and brushes with which to tar a political opponent. The familiar image of the national landscape can bring comfort but breed contempt. The variety, the regional diversity of landscape, is both a sign of national union and a case for devolution. Access to rural space can be prefaced by 'open', 'limited', or 'strictly no'. Protected land is secure, but monopolized. For continuity read stability and stagnation; for change, improvement or decay.

The privileged image of the British rural landscape, then, is motivated by the contests of the urban centre and the rival claims of its politicians to represent constitutional liberty. The rural landscape is the imaginary space which the people's representatives preserve for and as 'the nation'. It is figured as the idyllic other to urban complexity and as the authentic British space, untainted by the babel of ethnic diversity which marks the cityscape.

It has been well documented that cultural representations of the British landscape are motivated by such political agendas or inflected with ideological signs. Literary and art historians have powerfully accounted for the idealization of rural landscape in the eighteenth century in such terms.[7] The rustic landscape painting, for instance, is figured variously as a mythmaking response to the attenuation of uncultivated land

during the process of enclosure; or as the partial, class-marked perspective of the painter or patron, which occludes the figure of the rural
labourer. Readings of the landscaped garden, or at least of the plans of
its designers, yield an image of the garden as the non-productive partner
of enclosed land, a pleasurable confusion of wilderness and cultivation.
As enclosed land is increasingly partitioned and regulated, the cultivated
space of the garden, the epitome of landscape as private property,
becomes 'more natural'. As Ann Bermingham suggests, the increasingly
close alignment between 'nature' and property throughout the eighteenth
century ushers in new attitudes towards private ownership.[8] A natural
landscape, she argues, 'became the prerogative of the estate, allowing
for a conveniently ambiguous signification, so that nature was the sign
of property and property the sign of nature' (p. 14).

   The dominant aesthetic of these ambivalently natural, class-marked
signs of British identity in the eighteenth century was the picturesque.[9]
Various commentators have traced the political charge of picturesque
theory and its relation to the shifting signification of eighteenth-century
landscape.[10] An awareness of the politics of the picturesque, and of the
motivations of its aestheticians, have recently informed readings of landscape painting, representations of the garden, and the rhetoric of the
rural tourist or the traveller.

   Picturesque theory describes the effect and prescribes the arrangement of objects before the eye; the intricate, rough, shaded, contrasting
picturesque scene engenders curiosity, delight, diversion in the spectator.
It is an experience which leaves the viewer somewhere between the
sublime and the beautiful. A sensitivity to the political motivations
and ideological inflections of picturesque theory has provided recent
criticism with a way to comprehend, to rationalize that which is described
in terms of sensation, and to look beyond and behind the arrangement
of objects in the picturesque frame. Such readings have provided
narrative motivation for the aesthetic gaze and its apparently arrested
objects; they have suggested that structures of desire, of power, of
resistance are endemic to picturesque discourse.[11] Approaches to the
gendering of picturesque discourse have been the most suggestive in
this context. For instance, in an essay on the deployment of picturesque
effect in prose fiction by women in the 1790s, Vivien Jones has explored
the gendering of the picturesque gaze and its objects – landscape,
property, woman.[12] In this essay I want to elaborate on Jones's gendered
reading of the picturesque in narrative in an approach to some of Ann
Radcliffe's Gothic romances of the 1790s. I shall illustrate that the
way in which Radcliffe deploys picturesque description simultaneously
objectifies her heroines and enables them to resist the arrest of the
picturesque gaze; that aspects of narrative progress in her texts can themselves be described as picturesque effects and gendered as feminine; and

that the tensions within narrative picturesque echo the ideological hybridity of the Gothic romance. Further, I shall argue that Gothic and picturesque are ambivalent signs of British national identity. In literary terms, ideological ambivalence often reads as generic incongruity. I shall argue that the wavering gender and national politics of Radcliffe's romances account in part for her exclusion from a Leavisite line of English literary history, which demands a more consistent epistemological frame of reference in which to situate the politics of the English novel.

In a reading of the picturesque in Ann Radcliffe's Gothic, I want to suggest that narrative picturesque betrays the tensions which are latent within the visual aesthetic. Radcliffe's fictions bring the picturesque aesthetic into the realm of romance, where its idealizing function becomes more and less transparent. That is, the picturesque is brought into the service of a form of romance which announces its author's attachment to a particular narrative of national history whilst it diverts attention from the contemporary scene.

Romance and the picturesque have both an idealizing and a self-historicizing function in Radcliffe's texts. In national and political terms, the picturesque and the Gothic romance are to some degree representative of a particular 'constitutional' form of the British nation. Tapping into this range of association, Radcliffe deploys the picturesque both as a strategy of narrative movement (as the mechanism of scenic contrast which transports the reader temporally and spatially through the text towards comedic closure) and as a static cultural sign. It is a sign of familiarity, protection, continuity and improvement – that is, it mobilizes the privileged image of the British landscape. The landscape extends metonymically in Radcliffe's fictions to take in the female protagonists and the property which they inherit, so that they too become signs of a constitutional order. However, these fictions also portray unruly, counter or unconstitutional forces. In the domain of Gothic fiction where the dominant aesthetic is the sublime, the picturesque signs are contested by alienation, threat, discontinuity and degeneration. The mechanisms of scenic movement and narrative progress struggle with those of arrest. This arrest takes the form of the purely sensational, non-narrative aspects of Gothic romance. In the context of the 1790s, it is difficult not to read this struggle in terms of a battle between English and French revolutionary tropes.

Before reading this narrative, constitutional contest in Radcliffe's texts in more detail, I want to trace the status of the picturesque aesthetic and Gothic romance in the context of the eighteenth-century British national imagination and the tensions placed upon it in the decade of the French Revolution – at least as far as this context has been understood in recent criticism.

The Institution of Picturesque and the Arrest of Narrative

One of the most suggestive emplotments of the politics of the picturesque in the eighteenth century is Alan Liu's reading of Wordsworth's 'An Evening Walk'. For Liu, the experience of the picturesque described by the poet is that of the tourist before the landscape. In the face of the aesthetic's intricacy, the tourist's gaze apprehends a fetishized, fixated beauty; the landscape's roughness pushes the observer close to the violence of the sublime. The sensation of this experience is one of erotic arrest – arrested desire and arrested violence. According to Liu, this two-pronged arrest inhibits the picturesque tourist's progress, and formally elides his narrative motivation elides it in form.

In political terms, the picturesque is, for Liu, the aesthetic of Anglican institution, of Reformation. It is less a religious aesthetic than the aesthetic of nationalism, for the 'meaning of Reformation in England was also … nationalism. It was state' (p. 88). Significantly, Liu talks about 'nationalism' as the imagining of nation which is prescribed in and as the formal institutions of state. The picturesque viewer is mindful of old national (Catholic) forms, but forgetful of their significance; he is an inhabitant of the modern nation state which, for Liu, begins with the Reformation. In this scheme, the 1790s picturesque as state, or as a prescribed imagining of national institution, encompasses its relation to 'property, local government, and national politics' (p. 91).[13] It is a landscape version of the Panopticon, 'the late-eighteenth and early-nineteenth-century idea of bureaucracy as "natural"' (p. 100).

For Liu, then, the imagining of nation in the 1790s is synonymous with the spatial imagining of the bureaucratic state and the epistemology of post-Reformation culture. In narrative terms, I would suggest that this formulation is consistent with the mimetic, state – legitimating narratives of the Whig civil Imaginary. However, alongside and within such imaginings, sometimes collusive with and sometimes counter to them, there exist non-mimetic, 'romantic' narratives of nationhood. In Liu's drive to assert the institutional force of picturesque form, he loses sight of the aesthetic's narrative address, the political range of this address, and its less certain ideological significance. To think in these terms it is necessary to introduce the dynamic of narrative into the picturesque scene; to consider the possibility of resistant agency within the panopticon; to catch the movement within the frame. As Stephen Copley and Peter Garside have recently commented, '[i]f pictorial Picturesque representation suppresses narrative for decorative effect, this possibility is altogether more difficult to contrive in written narrative' (p. 6).[14]

To explore the picturesque's intersection with Gothic narrative is to uncover the more dynamic aspect and the ambivalent nationalism of the aesthetic. This intersection also yields an insight into the gender politics of the picturesque aesthetic – a politics which, as Vivien Jones has noted, Liu does not interrogate even as he defines the picturesque in sexualized terms as a 'lamination of eroticism and sadism, intricacy and roughness' (Liu, 64). As Jones's argument suggests, Liu's exploration of the picturesque's institutional import, its control over landscape and property, its imagining of the nation in new class and party political terms, does not fully incorporate an approach to the status of 'woman' in / as these picturesque spaces.

I want to pursue Radcliffe's ambivalent investment in the picturesque narrative of national institution and her collusion with a discourse which arrests the agency of the 'feminine' to assert a certain political power. The political significance of these investments becomes more explicit when the picturesque is contextualized in terms of the various political inflections of 'Gothic' in the 1790s.

The Gothic Constitution and the Origins of Romance

In the most simple aesthetic terms, picturesque description provides ornament for Radcliffe's fictions; it gives visual form to her landscapes and architecture, and signals their Gothic provenance. As Uvedale Price suggests in his *Essay*, the picturesque is what distinguishes Gothic from Grecian architecture (pp. 63–4):

> Gothic architecture is generally considered as more picturesque, though less beautiful, than Grecian, and, upon the same principle that a ruin is more so than a new edifice. The first thing that strikes the eye in approaching any building is the general outline against the sky (or whatever it may be opposed to) and the effect of the openings: in Grecian buildings the general lines of the roof are strait, and even when varied and adorned by a dome or a pediment, the whole has a character of symmetry and regularity.

Beyond this set of tautological distinctions between the Gothic and the Grecian, the picturesque and the beautiful, lies a cultural map, a national genealogy of the term 'Gothic': Gothic as an aesthetic; as a historical moment; as an ethnic denomination; and as a narrative mode.

This range of association which springs from the term Gothic frequently manifests itself in explorations of Romance. In the 'romance revival' of the late eighteenth century, the provenance and the representational province of these terms were variously reimagined.[15] British 'Romance' a term which signified the demotic languages of Europe and their fictions was traced in various histories (literary and non-literary) to

'Gothic', Anglo-Saxon origins and to a culture which was lost or attenuated under the Norman Yoke. 'Gothic Romance' is variously distanced
from and compared to 'Classical' and 'Saracen' romances, as a means of
explaining and describing the cultural origins of the 'native' Briton.
These genealogies trace the racial origins of a native British culture.
Further, they come to underpin class distinctions which are described in
the eighteenth century in terms of ethnicity.

Explorations of native British culture collapse into two political
trajectories, which, as Ian Duncan has suggested, were founded on 'two
myths of national constitutional foundation, and two different attitudes
toward the modern revolutionary settlement' (p. 21). On the one hand,
Gothic culture was claimed by radical Whigs as 'the ancient constitutional source of British liberties usurped by the Norman Conquest
and subsequent aristocratic rule including the present Whig landlord
establishment' (p. 21). On the other, a Whig establishment view 'held
that the 1689 Constitution marked the final defeat of Gothic barbarism,
represented by contending forces of royalist absolutism and popular
anarchy, and secured the liberty of the subject in private property-
ownership' (p. 23). 'Gothic', then, is both the nature of a stolen British
liberty and of the barbaric culture out of which a native neoclassicism
triumphantly arose.

Theories of Gothic fiction speak of ancient and modern romance.
According to Horace Walpole in the preface to the second edition of *The
Castle of Otranto*, the two are distinguished as the fictions of different
historical moments, divided by the revolutionary settlement of 1689.
Other versions of the modern romance suggest that its aesthetic is
explicitly and dangerously extrapolitical, or, at least opposed to the
order of public life. Gothic theory of the 1760s and 1770s, as Harriet
Guest has pointed out, defines its aesthetic in terms of a 'lack of classical
unity, of a visible plan of action, and thus by its proliferation of occa-
sional detail, circumscribed by specificity of place and historical time'
(p. 119).[16] Although the specific places and times are variable, critics all
describe locations which are opposed to any 'classical or republican
ideal' and which are governed by arbitrary power. Consequently, Guest
argues, contemporary theorists read the political charge of Gothic
fictions ambivalently. Such fictions they suggest (p. 119):

> are the means by which the popular imagination apprehends the
> mystified operations of arbitrary power, and by which the popular
> subjection to that power is maintained, through the manipulation of
> prejudices and superstitions.

According to such theory, to read contemporary Gothic fiction, the
modern romance, is to enter a sensualised and feminised space.

The pleasures of this place are problematically derived from its 'furtive and feminine opposition to the social and fraternal virtue of public life' (p. 19).

Richard Hurd's *Letters*, which trace the congruence of Gothic and Heroic Romance, condemn the furtive extrapolitical frisson of modern romance, even as they celebrate the seduction of England's and Italy's national poets by the 'barbarities' of Gothic (p. 81):

> The greatest geniuses of our own and foreign countries, such as Ariosto and Tasso in Italy, and Spenser [sic] and Milton in England, were seduced by these barbarities of their forefathers; were even charmed by the Gothic Romances. Was this caprice and absurdity in them? Or, may there not be something in the Gothic Romance peculiarly suited to the views of a genius, and to the ends of poetry? And may not the philosophic moderns have gone too far, in their perpetual ridicule and contempt of it?

According to Hurd, the dawn of reason and a pious modernity put to flight 'the portentous spectres of the imagination', and forced Milton to relinquish 'his long-projected design of Prince Arthur ... for that of Paradise Lost' (p. 153). Romance survives only in the poetically attenuated form of allegory (p. 154):

> Under this form the tales of faery kept their ground, and even made their fortune at court; where they became, for two or three reigns, the ordinary entertainment of our princes. But reason, in the end (assisted however by party, and religious prejudices) drove them off the scene, and would endure these lying wonders, neither in their own proper shape, nor as masked in figures.
>
> Henceforth, the taste of wit and poetry took a new turn: And fancy, that had wantoned it so long in the world of fiction, was now constrained, against her will, to ally herself with strict truth, if she would gain admittance into reasonable company.

Perhaps what underwrites this lament for 'fancy' is a nostalgia for the epistemological foundations of a pre-Civil War nation; the nation which, he imagines, could collectively decipher through faith the fancies of Milton's projected Arthurian romance. Instead, Milton constructs a Biblical epic for the modern emergent state and its subjects who must rationally, individually interpret the truths of his text. As Robert Miles has argued, this sort of 'Gothic nostalgia registers an anxious wish to recoup the last moment in Western history when the supernatural was knowable, when metaphysical presence lay behind words, emblems, events, behind human and natural signs' (p. 41).[17]

This epistemological anxiety, Miles suggests, is expressed discursively in the 1760s and 1770s as 'fear of cultural dislocation', displayed in a 'fashion for "primitivism"' and a distaste for 'luxury' (p. 41). The over-determined Gothic, it seems, evokes the primitive and the luxurious, and its theorists find it hard to embrace one without the other.

The characterisations of Gothic fiction and aesthetic theory of the 1760s and 1770s, then, depict modern romance as unfit for reasonable company. Gothic is wanton and fanciful, nothing more than the prolif-eration of particularity and detail, the incongruous sign the premodern imagination detached from premodern culture. Unlike the ancient poetic form, the modern prose romance does not speak to a nation, but appeals to what Guest has called the 'irresponsible and extrapolitical' spaces; the irrational sites which are antagonistic to classical epistemology and public order. These prose fictions are the signs of degenerative, luxurious cultural present, counter to what Miles has described as the Gothic aestheticians' 'desire for chaste origins, impeccable genealogies and patriotic paths of descent' (p. 42).

The somewhat unstable cultural, national significance of Gothic and its fictions alters again in the 1790s, with a shift in political semiotics. In the wake of the French Revolution, the property-owning subject, the reasonable, common sensical neo-classicist faced new threats. His version of native British liberty is no longer defined in opposition to the values of radical, demotic romancers, but of barbaric, imported rationalism. Conversely, counter-revolutionaries come to be tarred with the brush of Gothic romancers, who are seen by radicals to be clinging on to outmoded, feudal, chivalric values.[18]

In broad political terms, and despite her affinities with Dissent, Radcliffe's texts speak for a continuum of Whig sensibility which runs from Shaftesbury to Burke. Her narratives transpose the British pic-turesque, the aesthetic sign of a modern, liberal, British (Protestant) constitution, into Mediterranean medieval locations, which bear the signs of premodern, Catholic superstition and tyranny. Versions of national character and descriptions of foreign locations in Radcliffe's texts are all to some degree recognisable quotations from other texts, tapping into an available lexicon of cultural difference. In *The Mysteries of Udolpho*, Radcliffe quotes from the seventeenth-century Italian painter Salvator Rosa, her picturesque descriptions putting into narra-tive his representations of landscape. Radcliffe's texts domesticate the exotic by their English perspective, with their literary stereotype or traveller's version of a wild southern Europe. These 'other' places, with their mysterious natures are mediated and made safe not only by their representation in these texts, but by the repetition of their repre-sentation in other texts. Quotation serves not only to establish a literary genealogy (poetry and ancient romance rather than modern romance or novel), and to evoke a mood of place through the established literary and visual types.

The confrontation of different epistemological registers – the premodern and the modern – is echoed at the level of genre. Although Radcliffe's fictions stand on the threshold of 'the real' and 'the imaginary', they are proclaimed unambiguously as 'romance'. Her fictions proclaim a genealogy with the national, poetic romancers of Britain, Milton and Spenser, and of Italy, Tasso and Ariosto. To this extent they self-consciously distinguish themselves from that 'species' of modern prose romance which troubled Hurd's nationalist imagination.

Radcliffe lays claim to this lineage by virtue of her use of the picturesque. Picturesque description ostensibly corrects, elevates and universalizes the circumscribed particularity, the proliferation of detail which marks the Gothic aesthetic. Theories of picturesque description claim that it transcends such circumscription, and that it universalises the rude particulars of nature which are associated with a dangerous and degraded Gothicism. For instance, Uvedale Price, writing in 1796, sees that the value of the picturesque is its capacity to represent and preserve 'what is of such great moment in all arts and sciences, the accumulated experience of past ages' (p. 5). In literary terms, Price suggests that in the study of the works of Shakespeare and Fielding (which, by virtue of their combination of incident and variety of composition, constitute picturesque subjects) 'common observers' are given 'more enlarged views of human nature in general, as well as a more intimate acquaintance with particular characters, than he would have had from the observation of nature only' (p. 60).

Radcliffe strives for such universalising effect. Her fictions transform morally ambivalent particulars into prescriptive generalities; by means of picturesque description her readers are asked not to wallow in the wanton pleasures of the Gothic aesthetic.

Daughter's Plots and Father's Archetypes

Radcliffe's modern prose romances, then, are culturally and generically ambivalent. For epistemological reasons they assert a poetic genealogy; in their mode of representation they exist on the threshold of 'the real'. They constantly threaten to collapse into the mimetic realm of the contemporary novel, which is itself an ambiguous domain. This ambiguity is evident in the attempts to distinguish the novel from the romance throughout the eighteenth century and since; as generic categories they repeatedly merge. As Duncan suggests, the romance never quite leaves the mimetic domain, just as the novel, even as it comes to theorise its own range of reference, asserts fiction, more particularly plot, as its governing critical principle.[19] Indeed, George Canning, writing in *The Microcosm* makes a broad comparison between the contemporary novel, and the nebulously defined romance.[20] He ironically draws attention to the archetypal elements of novelistic plot, and the conventional adherence to chivalric values, transferred to a bourgeois setting (p. 342):

> we shall find that the novel is but a more modern modification of the same ingredients which constitute the romance; and that a recipe for the one may be equally serviceable for the composition of the other.
> A Romance (generally speaking) consists of a number of strange elements, with a hero in the middle of them; who, being an adventurous knight, wades through them to one grand design, namely the emancipation of some captive princess, from the oppression of a merciless giant, for the accomplishment of which purpose he must set at naught the incantations of the caitiff magician; must scale the ramparts of his castle; and baffle the vigilance of the female dragon, to whose custody his heroine is committed.
> Foreign as they may be at first sight seem from the purposes of a novel, we shall find, upon a little examination, that these are in fact the very circumstances upon which the generality of them are built; modernized indeed in some degree, by the transformations of merciless giants into austere guardians, and of she-dragons into maiden aunts. We must be contented also that the heroine, though retaining her tenderness, be divested of her royalty; and in the hero we must give up the knight-errant for the accomplished fine gentleman.

Whilst Canning's playful comparison does little to distinguish generically between the novel and the romance, it provides an apt summary of the archetypal plots of contemporary fictions. To follow Nancy Armstrong, it is possible to see that such plots figure and prescribe the subjectivity of the modern individual through the deployment of sexual and gendered archetypes.[21] By the 1790s, as Ian Duncan has suggested, the novel is the 'dominant genre of "private history"', replaying the 'domestic archetype of patriarchal tyranny' which was put in place by Richardson's *Clarissa* (p. 36):

> the persecution of a maiden, involving rape in the worst, literal case, or the invasion, appropriation, education of a cultural space of feminine privacy, in sublimated, rationalized, benevolent versions that claim the status of legitimate persuasion.

This plot is available for appropriation by Burke in his depiction of the violation of Marie-Antoinette's bedroom and his critique of revolutionary tyranny. Radcliffe's enactment of the plot is, like Burke's, a 'dialectic of privacy and persecution' (p. 37).

Patricia Meyer Spacks, in an account of the historically and culturally inflected variations of plot in eighteenth and early-nineteenth-century fiction, characterizes plot itself in gender terms.[22] The Gothic fictions of Walpole and Lewis, she argues, 'recapitulate, with fresh trimmings, the structure of novels by Richardson, Fielding and early Smollett', their action derived from 'struggles of power' and versions of 'male conflict'. Conversely, Radcliffe's Gothic, she suggests, develops the kind of plot introduced by Fanny Burney (p. 148):

> 'daughters' plots' – not simply because they originate in a female consciousness, but because they establish internal principles of action by giving due weight to the psychology and morality traditionally associated with daughters as well as to the assumptions of sons.

Radcliffe's fictions, like their novelistic contemporaries and predecessors, figure the fate of the middle-class subject in the moral and psychic progress of its heroines. The sovereignty of this subject is also preserved in the chastity of her body and the safety of her home. Radcliffe's texts, which place their heroines in Gothic contexts, play out the sexualized and politicised menace to this multiply sovereign and private site. Libidinous, aristocratic tyrants and the dangerous energy of the populace (troped as roving banditti) threaten to force entry into the home, the body and the mind of the heroine. More ambivalently, they arouse this middle-class subject's illicit desire. Radcliffe's fictions imagine, then, a dual assault on the liberty and chastity of the middle-class heroine who, in the modern Chivalric romance, is the standard bearer of the national constitution.

Home Improvements and Sentimental Journeys

It is possible to suggest that Radcliffe's texts stand, as Liu might argue, in the service of a post-Reformation nation state; that, in their ambivalent conflation of British picturesque with their Mediterranean settings, they wilfully forget the institutional significance of the British Catholic past. The description of Gothic architecture and Catholic ritual pays only aesthetic homage to the forms, evacuating them of liturgical significance. In the context of the French Revolution, the evocation of Catholic tyranny plays ambivalently into the hands of pro-revolutionary sentiment. In these texts, however, liberty is restored not by popular revolution nor the declamations of rights and rationality, but under the agency of sensibility and improvement. This individuated agency is, I would suggest, synonymous with the agency of the picturesque aesthetic.

The historically progressive dynamic which underwrites the picturesque aesthetic, the dynamic of 'improvement', depends on troping
the picturesque object as 'property'. As Vivien Jones suggests in her
reading of the politics of the picturesque in this period, 'woman / estate /
nature / nation' provide a set of 'flexibly analogous signifiers'; signifiers
which come to be naturalized as property; property which is threatened
by political instability. A range of fictions mobilize these signifiers.
Their plots, as Jones suggests, are variations on that of the 'socially
marginal heroine, discovered in an isolated rural house, subjected
metonymically to "improvement" and eventually revealed as true heir
... to the estate' (p. 120). Once the heroine's genealogy is secured,
liberty and property are secured.

In Radcliffe's versions of this plot, the estate to which each heroine is
restored offers ostensibly unbounded prospects of the surrounding
landscape.[23] Ownership, however, provides a boundary, and creates an
enclosure and a refuge for the previously exiled protagonists. In aesthetic
terms, it is the boundary which defines the picturesque scene. As
Uvedale Price suggests, the effect of the picturesque is dependent on the
provision of literal and figurative enclosure of the sketching in of a
boundary and of the sight of a horizon. It is this 'frame' which distinguishes the picturesque from the sublime (p. 100):

> – Infinity is one of the most efficient causes of the sublime; the
> boundless ocean, for that reason, inspires awful sensations: to give it
> picturesqueness, you must destroy that cause of its sublimity; for it is
> on the shape and disposition of its boundaries, that the picturesque
> must, in a great measure, depend.

To follow Liu's argument, it is the enclosure, the boundary, which
facilitates the panoptic gaze of the modern bureaucratic state. This is
not, of course, how the picturesque enclosure is figured in Radcliffe's
texts. Rather, like Burke's configuration of the civil Imaginary in his
Reflections on the Revolution in France, refuge from the sublime regime of
absolutist power is not to be found in the rational, bureaucratic nation
state, but in the local, affective sites of familial connection and private
property. In the Burkean – and Radcliffean imagination – these domestic zones are figured as the natural sites of constitutional order.

The progress of the constitutional subject, then, is figured in the
'improvement' of the daughter, who is schooled to be fit for her inheritance of the picturesque estate. Her education is monitored by
benevolent, surrogate fathers who are sensitive practitioners of the
picturesque aesthetic, and tasteful improvers of its objects. For them,
the landscape is less ornamental than a reminder of native, familial
attachments. 'Patriots' and 'citizens of the world', these enlightened and

virtuous inhabitants of Radcliffe's fictions guide the education of the heroine and move the texts towards the fulfilment of a benign, providential order.

In the course of the narratives, this progress – the improvement of estate, woman, nature and nation – is disrupted by the grand designs of Machiavellian and Satanic tyrants: the Marquis de Montalt, Montoni and Schedoni. Each is characterized by his lack of true picturesque sensibility. They are unpatriotic opportunists, a trait which is epitomised by Montoni's mercenary exploitation of internal unrest in Italy. This absence of native regard extends to filial inadequacies: they expose surrogate daughters to threats of abduction, sexual harassment and death. These are the covetous imperialists of the picturesque. The nouveaux riches, the vulgar improvers, are its conspicuous consumers. The clash of the sympathetic and the vulgar improver is epitomised in *The Mysteries of Udolpho* when the Quesnels plan to cut down an old chestnut tree at La Vallee to make room to plant a more ornamental variety. St. Aubert voices the appropriately sentimental, perhaps Burkean, objection (p. 13):

> 'Good God,' exclaimed St. Aubert, 'you surely will not destroy that noble chestnut, which has flourished for centuries, the glory of the estate. It was in its maturity when the present mansion was built. How often, in my youth, have I climbed among its broad branches, and sat embowered amidst a world of leaves .. I am talking of times and feelings as old-fashioned as the taste that would spare that venerable old tree'.

The enlightened bourgeoisie are the sensitive media of the picturesque, expressing the aesthetic, neither desiring to possess nor display its objects, but to guide the heroine and all that rests on her through a proper education.

Despite the privileged place which these texts assign to such an education, and to the force of historical and cultural process, the orphaned heroine can only secure her escape from the malign forces which surround her by means of a romance trope. She must be restored to a chaste, patriotic line and discover her true identity. Such discoveries displace the ambiguity of mistaken relationships and bogus parentage, and facilitate the restoration of natural order and the reclamation of the estate. In *The Romance of the Forest*, for instance, the origins of the heroine Adeline are to be discovered in a decaying manuscript. In a scene which is loaded with picturesque effect, designed to arouse curiosity, Adeline reads the faded manuscript in feeble light (p. 128):

> Adeline's light was now expiring in the socket, and the paleness of the ink, so feebly shone upon, baffled her efforts to discriminate the

letters … Thus compelled to suspend the inquiry, which so many attendant circumstances had rendered awfully interesting, she retired to her humble bed.

The decaying manuscript, which is itself a picturesque object, is a fragile appeal to the truths of the past (Adeline's true parentage). Ultimately, Radcliffe asserts the verifiable content of the manuscript as a type of archetypal inscription; it exists for Adeline as a myth of origin, fixing her identity, affirming her virtue and guaranteeing her inheritance. As an aesthetic artefact, however, the decaying form of the manuscript bears literal testament to its susceptibility to historical change.

The objects of picturesque description are inherently vulnerable sites on which to base an appeal to origin. The picturesque is an aesthetic which privileges decay, ruin and the effects of time on its objects. It is a peculiarly contingent aesthetic, reaching its fullest moment as its stops being 'the picturesque'. In some respects, it is an aesthetic discourse which contains the seeds of the destruction of its own artifacts. The picturesque is always in the process of becoming more picturesque, something other, or nothing at all. To be too picturesque is not only to lapse into deformity, but to be on the verge of annihilation. The presence in time of its objects is both the source of, and the elegy for, their aesthetic status.

Correcting the Sublime

A vulnerable bearer of historical progress, the picturesque is also an ambivalent guarantor of improvement. Even as they move their protagonists and readers towards familial safety, the realm of the beautiful, Radcliffe's fictions and their picturesque transformations expose them to the sexualized thrill, an erotic fantasy of the sublime. The narrative dynamic moves towards the 'correction' and 'domestication' of the sublime; in the process, however, it produces an eroticized frisson. In Radcliffe's fictions, this dynamic is figured repeatedly in encounters between heroine and tyrant. In *The Italian*, for instance, a cliff-top confrontation between Ellena and the villain Schedoni catches the heroine somewhere between terror and ecstasy, and the scene yields an erotic frisson (p. 222):

'Poor insect!' added Schedoni, 'who would crush thee?'
Ellena made no reply; she remained with her eyes fixed in amazement upon his face. There was something in his manner of pronouncing this, yet more extraordinary than in the words themselves. Alarmed by his manner, and awed by the encreasing gloom, and swelling

surge, that broke in thunder on the beach, she at length turned away, and again walked towards the hamlet which was yet very remote.

Significantly, Ellena is outside the domestic refuge of the hamlet, the small rural idyll which stands in these texts as the enclave of local and familial safety. Away from domestic refuge, the 'swelling surge' she fears is not so much the oncoming change in the weather as the confusion of sexual arousal and awe in the power of the sublime.

The encounter with the sublime, however, turns into a picturesque scene. Ellena is overcome by fear and excitement, faints and turns into a picturesque object.[24] Radcliffe, however, gives agency to this enthralled feminine object. Her picturesque form moves her captor, and she thus passively facilitates her own release from the arrest of the sublime. Schedoni yields to her vulnerability, her helpless beauty – '[a]s he gazed upon her helpless and faded form, he became agitated' (p. 223) [emphasis added]:

> While he was yet unable to baffle the new emotion by evil passions, he despised that which conquered him. 'And shall the weakness of a girl,' said he, 'subdue the resolution of a man! Shall the view of her transient sufferings unnerve my firm heart, and compel me to renounce the lofty plans I have so ardently, so laboriously imagined, at the very instant when they are changing into realities!'

On the verge of success, the schematic designs of the sublime tyrant (troped as absolutist or rational regime) succumb to the sensible, the transient, the organic, feminine form. The picturesque object effects affective transportation.

The passive agency of the feminine picturesque scene in Radcliffe's texts, its capacity to transform the mechanisms of the sublime, alters the gender dynamic of Uvedale Price's characterisation of the corrective effects of the picturesque on the sublime. Whilst in Radcliffe's scene, the feminine picturesque defuses the sexual frisson, Price's description of the corrective picturesque feminizes the aesthetic to eroticize it (pp. 105–6):

> It is the coquetry of nature; it makes beauty more amusing, more varied, more playful, but also,
> 'Less winning soft, less amiably mild.'
> Again, by its variety, its intricacy, its partial concealments, it excites that active curiosity which gives play to the mind, loosening those iron bonds with which astonishment chains up its faculties.

In this configuration, the picturesque functions as release, as a corrective to the more overpowering seductions of the sublime, in ambivalently libidinous terms. The picturesque embodies a dimension of irritable movement. The picturesque eye roves across the landscape and the release is for the viewer rather than its object. A similar dynamic is suggested in Gilpin's description of the picturesque traveller who thrills to the chase of previously undiscovered objects (pp. 47–8):

> The first source of amusement to the picturesque traveller, is the pursuit of his object – the expectation of new scenes continually opening and arising to his view. We suppose the country to have been unexplored. Under this circumstance the mind is kept constantly in agreeable suspence [sic]. The love of novelty is the foundation of this pleasure. Every distant horizon promises something new; and with this pleasing expectation we follow nature through all her walks. We pursue her from hill to dale; and hunt after those various beauties with which she everywhere abounds.
>
> The pleasures of the chace [sic] are universal ... Care is left behind; and every human faculty is dilated with joy – And shall we suppose it a greater pleasure to the sportsman to pursue a trivial animal, than it is to the man of taste to pursue the beauties of nature? to follow her through all her recesses? to obtain a sudden glance, as she flits past him in some airy shape? to trace her through the mazes of the cover? to wind after her along the vale? or along the reaches of the river. After the pursuit we are gratified with the attainment of the object.

The release of picturesque travel is here described in terms of masculine sexual arousal; the picturesque scene is objectified, feminine, teasing and coy. In Radcliffe's fictions, the feminine picturesque scene is endowed with virtuous, affective agency, the power to move, to resist the arrest of the sublime.

Narrative in Contrast

Feminine agency is also figured at the level of narrative movement in Radcliffe's texts. Protagonists and readers are transported through the text by 'contrast'. In the picturesque portrait, contrast is a feature within the scene; in narrative, it is a mode of transference from one scene to another. Such contrast is temporal and spatial. Frequently visions of the future compare unfavourably with the past or the present. Valancourt's projection of his separation from Emily in *The Mysteries of Udolpho* is typical (p. 160):

> O Emily! this countenance, on which I now gaze – will, in a moment, be gone from my eyes, and not all the efforts of fancy will be able to

recall it with exactness. O! What an infinite difference between this moment and the next! Now, I am in your presence, can behold you! then, all will be a dreary blank – and I shall be a wanderer, exiled from my only home!

Scenic contrast in this instance transforms the happy present into an unhappy future, or worse, no future at all, a blank. At other moments, however, imaginative projection releases protagonists from the unbearable circumstances of their historical present, a present which is figured as a bad dream. Conversely, usually towards the close of the narrative, memories of the troubled past are figured as insubstantial, dispelled by the triumph of progress. These temporal oscillations, like the following from *The Italian*, are curious glimpses of historical narrative, linking past and future in a process of interpretation which is figured as 'romantic' (pp. 319–20):

His mind resembled the glass of a magician, on which the apparitions of long-buried events arise, and as they fleet away, point portentously to shapes half-hid in the duskiness of futurity.

As Ian Duncan suggests, at such moments 'the sensibilities of protagonist and reader' of Radcliffe's fictions 'are rushed across thresholds of experience' in a principle of '"visionary" transportation ... dynamic "contrast", or scenic change which is soon to be defined as the narrative principle of history and of modernity in versions of romance by Scott' (p. 39). Prospect and retrospect perform historical revision, and project a benign providence, the possibility of improvement, in the face of a culture which has come to believe in the malign force of history.

As I have suggested, in Radcliffe's fictions such progressive agency is gendered as feminine. Along these lines, Duncan has argued that these are romances of 'female wish-fulfillment', in which (p. 38):

the heroine's grace lies in a passive sensibility, rather than an active will to agency. We read, instead, a romance rhetoric in which desire is sublimated to drive the plot without a visible agent, by a tropological saturation of the narrative.

Duncan's reading here depends on that distinction highlighted between 'male' and 'female' emplotment of Gothic narrative. He distinguishes between the 'fatal dialectic of repression and riot' (p. 35) in the fiction of Walpole, Lewis and Maturin, where agency is figured in destructive sexual archetypes, and where individual progress is 'blocked or transgressive', and Radcliffe's depiction of a 'dialectic of privacy and persecution' (p. 37) where female desire passively enacts the transformation of the masculine will-to-power, and secures the heroine's entry into the world.

From Romance to Romance

Whilst the picturesque scene which is pursued by the male traveller is an erotic zone, an eroticism that is dependent on denied consummation, on physical 'arrest', Radcliffe's scenes sublimate desire. This sublimation is performed via the mechanisms of picturesque movement, more particularly, affective 'movement'. The attraction to tyranny (the Burkean attachment to the Gothic institution) is deflected in the establishment of a feminized domestic order.

In the eyes of a Wollstonecraftian critique, of course, the sentimental inflection in the picturesque, and the domestication of Gothic order, is tyranny under a another name; it is libido disguised as sympathy. It is prescriptive reverence to the sublime in the name of common sense and instinct. From this perspective, the picturesque enclosure is less troubling for its panoptic potential than for its complicity with the Gothic imagination. As Wollstonecraft saw it, the Burkean configuration of the familial nation betrays an attachment to the sublime aesthetic of aristocratic culture, to the chivalric romance which, in her eyes, is merely the veneer of feudal tyranny (pp. 9–10):

> I know that you have a mortal antipathy to reason; but if there is anything like argument or first principles, in your wild declamation, behold the result:– that we are to reverence the rust of antiquity, and term the unnatural customs, which ignorance and mistaken self-interest have consolidated, the sage fruit of experience: that, if we do discover some errors, our feelings should lead us to excuse, with blind love, or unprincipled filial affection, the venerable vestiges of ancient days. These are gothic notions of beauty – the ivy is beautiful though it insidiously destroys the trunk from which it receives support.

Wollstonecraft accuses Burke of being transfixed by the sublime. Radcliffe's fictions enact such 'fixation' to perform the release from arrest under the corrective agency of the picturesque; but, like Burke's romance of the Revolution, Radcliffe's fictions invest ambiguously in the arresting encounters with sublimity. Under the agency of the picturesque aesthetic, the reader and protagonists are released from fixation to move on to another scene. The narratives do not keep on moving however. Whilst they enact progress, this is not figured as the movement from the dark night of romance to the daylight of history, where things go on moving. Underwritten by the dynamic of the *Bildungsroman*, these narratives assert a good over a bad archetype. Readers and protagonists are moved from one sort of romance to another. For instance, the closing scenes of *The Mysteries of Udolpho* depict the nuptial celebration of Emily and Valancourt, and foreground the return to scenes of chivalric romance (pp. 670–71):

The feasts were held in the great hall of the castle, which, on this occasion, was hung with superb new tapestry, representing the exploits of Charlemagne and his twelve peers; here were seen the Saracens, with their horrible visors, advancing to battle; and there were displayed the wild solemnities of incantation and the necromantic feats.

Just as in the earlier texts the protagonists are wrenched from the spell of superstition and are spiralled into 'a scene of fairy-land', in *The Italian*, the restored estate is recognizably picturesque (p. 412):

The style of the gardens, where lawns and groves, and woods varied the undulating surface, was that of England, and of the present day, rather than of Italy; except 'Where a long valley peeping on the main,' exhibited such gigantic loftiness of shade, and grandeur of perspective, as characterize the Italian taste.

The house resembles 'a fabric called up by enchantment, rather than a structure of human art' (p. 413). Ellena is relieved from the material pressures of her past (she has had to turn her hand to the productive industry of needlework instead of the picturesque pursuit of sketching) to become queen of this exotic, yet quasi-English scene, and the heart of its domestic space. Vivaldi is liberated from the purgatory of the Inquisition, with its unstable, irrational (Catholic) system of value, into classical order. In *The Italian*, however, the uncomfortable contingencies of malign historical forces are not completely jettisoned.

The enchanting spell is, somewhat paradoxically, broken by Paolo's ecstatically patriotic exclamations about his return to his native landscape (p. 413):

here I am, sure enough! dancing by moonlight, in my own dear bay of Naples, with my own dear master and mistress, in safety, and as happy as almost myself; and with that old mountain yonder, Vesuvius, which I, forsooth! thought I was never to see again, spouting up fire, just as it used to do before we got ourselves put into this Inquisition!

The landscape surrounding a live volcano is less picturesque than explosively sublime; it is the scene which shifts rather than the viewer. In the aftermath of Revolution, Radcliffe offers a problematic version of new-found liberty. The private estate is vulnerable to collapse under another wave of tyranny. In the earlier texts, the sublime exists as the threat of the power-driven aristocrat, who forces the true practitioners of the picturesque into exile; the erotic appeal of the tyrant is sublimated in the new order of romance, a feminised domesticity, secured by individual agency, by picturesque movement. In *The Italian* the threat is more pervasive, surviving the death of the tyrant and postponing the final closure. In this text, the picturesque is exposed as a fragile corrective of the sublime. The sublime is the aesthetic of a contemporary history which is unyielding to the pleas of sentiment.

In the 1790s the institutions which define the Whig conception of nation need careful legitimation. Those who cling to the post-1689 liberties which define the modern British nation have to contend with the post-1789 imagining of a modern French nation, newly constituted on rationality and a text of rights. It is the work of counter-revolutionary Whigs to place a distance between 1689 and 1789, and to defend the text-free constitution, the sociability of British politics. Radcliffe's texts participate in this defence. Whilst the politics of the picturesque aesthetic in her fictions can be aligned with the modern bureaucratic gaze of the Whig establishment and with the broad church of post-Reformation culture, the privileged dynamic is not that of the panopticon or arrest. The conservative Whig imagination, which is nervous of rationalist blueprints of progress, defends British liberty with narratives of affective agency and consensus. To this end, Radcliffe's picturesque scenes foreground an improving femininity, to correct and resist the arrest of a tyrannous sublime. Such scenes distance her Gothic from the wanton fancies of modern romancers; they assert a generic line of descent from the Ancients, whose fictions could still speak to a public sphere in the language of the imagination.

Picturesque correction proves weak, however, and the national significance of Ancient romance struggles for recognition in a modern epistemology. Moreover, Radcliffe's fictions exist in a generic domain which, in the eyes of her contemporary commentators, has been hijacked by sensation seekers; the romance has been too long expelled from the public domain to make a convincing come-back. In the 1790s, its subjects progress falteringly. In subsequent readings, Radcliffe's anachronistic, genteel fancies, are consigned to remain outside the canons of national romance or novel. Radcliffe's constitutional prose romances, however, at once too polite and too vulgar to address a nation, speak of that nation's institutional uncertainty and its search for a constitutional form.

Notes

1   Benedict Anderson, *Imagined Communities: Reflections on the Origin and Spread of Nationalism* (London: Verso, 1983).

2   Ian Watt's *The Rise of the Novel: Studies in Defoe, Richardson and Fielding* (Berkeley and Los Angeles: University of California Press, 1957) has influenced a range of impressive criticism of eighteenth-century novelistic

fiction, most of which revises Watt's thesis. See particularly: Lennard J. Davis, *Factual Fictions: The Origins of the English Novel* (New York: Columbia University Press, 1983); Michael McKeon, *The Origins of the English Novel 1600–1740* (Baltimore: John Hopkins University Press, 1987); John Richetti, *Popular Fiction Before Richardson: Narrative Patterns 1700–39* (Oxford: Oxford University Press, 1969).

3   Simon During, 'Literature: Nationalism's Other?', in *Nation and Narration*, ed. Homi K. Bhabha (London: Routledge, 1990). During uses the term 'civil Imaginary', a concept inherited from Foucauldian readings of the eighteenth-century novel, to describe the realm occupied by the journalism of Addison and Steele, and the novels of Defoe, Richardson and Fielding. These writings, he suggests, share in the 'production of narratives, moral cruxes, a linguistic decorum, and character types which cover the social field of the post-1688 world' (p. 142). These texts circulate 'representations of the workings of the legal, medical and military institutions ... to provide grounds for certain reforms ... for the transfer to modern power' (p. 143).

4   Jürgen Habermas, *The Structural Transformation of the Public Sphere: An Inquiry into a Category of Bourgeois Society*, trans. Thomas Burger (1962; Cambridge: Polity Press, 1992). Davis, During and others have drawn on Habermas's important text, emphasising the ethical, rather than the political nature of the eighteenth-century public sphere and its textual constructions.

5   I have found Nancy Armstrong's *Desire and Domestic Fiction: A Political History of the Novel* (Oxford: Oxford University Press, 1978) and Ros Ballaster's *Seductive Forms: Women's Amatory Fiction from 1684 to 1740* (Oxford: Clarendon Press, 1992) particularly illuminating in this respect; the former for its suggestive Foucauldian analysis of the gendering of the novelistic domain; the latter for its intelligent critique of the predominant focus on male writers in the work of Davis, McKeon and Richetti.

6   Ann Radcliffe, *The Romance of the Forest*, ed. Chloe Chard (Oxford: Oxford University Press, 1986); *The Mysteries of Udolpho*, ed. Bonamy Dobree (Oxford: Oxford University Press, 1980; repr. 1989); *The Italian*, ed. Frederick Garber (Oxford: Oxford University Press, 1968; repr. 1990). Hereafter, page references will be included in the text. My reading of these texts is less an attempt to provide a comprehensive account of Radcliffe's fiction than to offer a way to read the significance of pic-turesque description within narrative fiction of the 1790s, as part of the broader trajectory of the reading the narration of nationhood.

7   For readings of representations of eighteenth-century British rural landscape see particularly the following: John Barrell, *The Idea of Landscape and the Sense of Place 1730–1840* (Cambridge: Cambridge University Press, 1972) and *The Dark Side of the Landscape: The Rural Poor in English Painting 1730–1840* (Cambridge: Cambridge University Press, 1980); Ann Bermingham, *Landscape and Ideology: The English Rustic Tradition, 1740–1860* (London: Thames and Hudson, 1987); Carole Fabricant, 'Binding and Dressing Nature's Loose Tresses: The Ideology of Augustan Landscape Design', *Studies in Eighteenth-Century Culture*, 8

(1979), pp. 109–35; Ronald Paulson, *Literary Landscape: Turner and Constable* (New Haven; London: Yale University Press, 1982).

8   Ann Bermingham, *Landscape and Ideology*, pp. 9–54.

9   My own understanding of the distinguishing features of the picturesque as they were defined in the 1790s are drawn primarily from William Gilpin, *Three Essays: on Picturesque Beauty; on Picturesque Travel; and on Sketching Landscape*, 2nd edn. (London, 1794) and Uvedale Price, *An Essay on the Picturesque as Compared with the Sublime and the Beautiful; And, on the Use of Studying Pictures, for the Purpose of Improving Real Landscape* (London, 1796–98). Hereafter page references will be included in the text.

10   Some of the most suggestive recent readings of the picturesque are: Malcolm Andrews, *The Search for the Picturesque: Landscape Aesthetics and Tourism in Britain, 1760–1800* (Aldershot: Scolar Press, 1989); Bermingham, *Landscape and Ideology*, especially chapters 2 and 3; *The Politics of the Picturesque: Literature, Landscape and Aesthetics Since 1770*, Stephen Copley and Peter Garside (eds) (Cambridge: Cambridge University Press, 1994); Alan Liu, *Wordsworth: The Sense of History* (Stanford: Stanford University Press, 1989); Kim Ian Michasiw, 'Nine Revisionist Theses on the Picturesque', *Representations*, 38 (1992), pp. 76–100; Sidney K. Robinson, *Inquiry into the Picturesque* (Chicago: University of Chicago Press, 1991).

11   See for example essays by Vivien Jones, Raimondo Modiano and John Whale in *The Politics of the Picturesque*, which variously recognize picturesque discourse as a restless structure of desire – appetitive, eroticised, in motion. See also Frances Ferguson, *Solitude and the Sublime: Romanticism and the Aesthetics of Individuation* (New York; London: Routledge, 1992), especially Chapter 6, 'In Search of the Natural Sublime: The Face on the Forest Floor', which captures the dynamic of picturesque description as process and catches the picturesque guide in the act of 'becoming' whilst he seeks to make himself invisible.

12   Jones '"The Coquetry of Nature": Politics and the Picturesque in Women's Fiction', in *Politics of the Picturesque*.

13   Liu suggests that picturesque landscape is the imaginary ground 'on which the rights of old property could be adjusted to the demands of new money' (p. 91); 'on which an originally feudal, agrarian machinery of rural administration could be policed by a developing urban bureaucracy' (p. 95); and 'on which Tory and Pittite could be mastered by Whig and Foxite, and thus a 'free' Britain established corresponding to the France of the very early Revolution' (p. 103).

14   *The Politics of the Picturesque*, pp. 1–12.

15   My reading of the romance revival is drawn primarily from Richard Hurd, *Letters on Chivalry and Romance: Serving to Illustrate Some Passages in the Third Dialogue* (London, 1788) and Thomas Warton, *The History of English Poetry, from the Close of the Eleventh to the Commencement of the Eighteenth Century* (London, 1779–81). See also James Beattie, 'On Fable and Romance,' *Dissertations Moral and Critical* (London, 1783) and Clara Reeve, *The Progress of Romance through Times, Countries and Manners* (Colchester, 1785). For readings of the political, cultural and literary

significance of the late eighteenth century interest in romance see particularly Ian Duncan, *Modern Romance and Transformations of the Novel: The Gothic, Scott, Dickens* (Cambridge: Cambridge University Press, 1992); Harriet Guest, 'The Wanton Muse: Politics and Gender in Gothic Theory After 1760' in *Beyond Romanticism: New Approaches to Texts and Contexts 1780–1832*, eds. Stephen Copley and John Whale (London: Routledge, 1992); Robert Miles, 'The Gothic Aesthetic: The Gothic as Discourse', *The Eighteenth Century*, 32, no. 1 (1991), pp. 39–57; Gerald Newman, *The Rise of English Nationalism: A Cultural History 1740–1830* (London: Weidenfeld and Nicolson, 1987), especially Chapter 5, 'The Literary Revolution, 1740–89'.

16   Guest, 'Wanton Muse'.

17   Miles, 'Gothic Aesthetic'.

18   This is, of course, how Mary Wollstonecraft characterised Edmund Burke in her pamphlet *A Vindication of The Rights of Men in a Letter to the Right Honourable Edmund Burke; Occasioned by his Reflections on the Revolution in France* (London: Johnson, 1790).

19   For explorations of this ambivalent generic distinction and its broader implications see, for example, Ian Duncan, *Modern Romance*; Laurie Langbauer, *Women and Romance: The Consolations of Gender in the English Novel* (Ithaca; London: Cornell University Press, 1990); Michael McKeon, *The Origins of the English Novel*.

20   George Canning, *The Microcosm*, 26 (Monday 14 May 1787) cited in *Novel and Romance 1700–1800: A Documentary Record*, ed. Ioan Williams (London: Routledge, 1970).

21   Nancy Armstrong, *Desire and Domestic Fiction*.

22   Patricia Meyer Spacks, *Desire and Truth: Functions of Plot in the Eighteenth-Century English Novel* (Chicago and London: Chicago University Press, 1990).

23   See, for instance the descriptions in *The Romance of the Forest*, p. 363 and *The Italian*, p. 412.

24   The heroines are frequently figured in terms drawn from picturesque description. They are described as half-veiled, part-concealing and part-revealing their delicate, dishevelled or agitated forms. As I have suggested physiognomic descriptions of guilty tyrants, bearing the austere expression of the patriarch, are the masculine counterparts of these wantonly innocent women. They echo Gilpin's delineation of properly picturesque representation of the human figure in his *Three Essays*, in which he privileges Milton's unadorned, dishevelled Eve, and the furrowed face of the patriarch marked by the 'rough touches of age' (p. 9).

Wordsworth's
'Tintern Abbey' in Context:
Gender, Art and Romanticism

John Williams
University of Greenwich

Wordsworth's poem, 'Tintern Abbey' (1798), contains three protagonists. There is Wordsworth at the time of writing; there is the Wordsworth who had passed the same way five years before, 'more like a man / Flying from something that he dreads, than one / Who sought the thing he loved' (ll. 71–3); and in the final section of the poem there is Wordsworth's sister, Dorothy, who accompanied him in 1798. In his essay of 1988, 'The Uses of Dorothy: "The Language of Sense" in "Tintern Abbey"', John Barrell argues that to a significant degree Wordsworth differentiates between his current self and his former self in accordance with contemporary assumptions relating to gender difference.[1] Dorothy is thus 'used' in the latter part of the poem as a receptacle where the essentially feminine sensibility of the young poet of 1793 may be preserved:

> For nature then
> (The coarser pleasures of my boyish days,
> And their glad animal movements all gone by,)
> To me was all in all. – I cannot paint
> What then I was. The sounding cataract
> Haunted me like a passion: the tall rock,
> The mountain, and the deep and gloomy wood,
> Their colours and their forms, were then to me
> An appetite: a feeling and a love,
> That had no need of a remoter charm,
> By thought supplied, or any interest
> Unborrowed from the eye.
>
> (ll. 73–84)

Barrell argues that what Dorothy is described as retaining – something Wordsworth himself has now lost in his maturity – is an ability associated in the eighteenth century mind with the limited extent of a woman's intellectual capacity: to 'think in terms only of the particular and the concrete' (Barrell, 161). In a recent essay, Ann Bermingham has argued that essentially the same assumptions may be found to hold true in the sphere of visual arts in the eighteenth century. With specific reference to Joseph Wright of Derby and Sir Joshua Reynolds, she shows how it was believed that the 'conceptual ability to abstract form from nature' was a male gift not available to women. The best a 'pseudo-creative' woman artist could hope for was to do no more than imitate the 'particular and concrete' forms of nature she encountered.[2]

Bermingham's essay points up the eighteenth-century context which Barrell claims for his reading of 'Tintern Abbey', and it is that context – with its linked items of literary and visual production – that I shall be considering. Bermingham makes specific reference to Wright's painting of 1783–4, *The Corinthian Maid*. Pliny attributed the invention of painting to the act of drawing round a man's shadow. Wright was inspired by a poem by William Hayley which described 'the soft Corinthian maid' outlining her 'lover's sleeping form'. Wright's painting is understood as an endorsement of the contemporary view of the limits of female creativity. To the woman belongs a 'primitive form of marking', the extent of her 'generative powers'.[3]

In 'Tintern Abbey' Wordsworth is reflecting on his conviction that he no longer responds to the Wye valley as a woman or a child might, registering the encounter with a spontaneous concentration on the immediate experience; his thinking now constitutes a process of reflective meditation and abstraction, 'an eye made quiet by the power / Of harmony, and the deep power of joy' (ll. 48–9). This is assumed to be the prerogative of the adult male intellect. But 'Tintern Abbey' is also registering Wordsworth's awareness of the value to the poet of both masculine and feminine attributes, and 'Tintern Abbey' may be considered as one poet's attempt to negotiate a settlement between the two in order to find 'life and food / For future years':

> And now, with gleams of half-extinguished thought,
> And many recognitions dim and faint,
> And somewhat of a sad perplexity,
> The picture of the mind revives again:
> While here I stand, not only with the sense
> Of present pleasure, but with pleasing thoughts
> That in this moment there is life and food
> For future years.
>
> (ll. 59–66)

The linking of 'half-extinguished thought' from the past with 'present pleasure' is an act of 'sad perplexity' because – in part at least – 'the picture of the mind' that suggests itself to Wordsworth does not accord with the received wisdom on the subject.

There can be no doubt that the comparison between the two perceptions of the Wye valley around which 'Tintern Abbey' revolves is gendered; Dorothy's appearance in the poem as the guardian of the young poet's manner of perception is sufficient evidence of that. John Barrell's location of the feminine principle with the ability to think 'in terms of the concrete and the particular', however, seems limited when set against the way Wordsworth specifically describes his younger self. The source of Barrell's stereotype is the anonymous *Grammar of English Language* of 1711, which draws heavily on Locke's theories of language and epistemology. The *Grammar* states that while the female mind may be expected to grasp facts, it will be incapable of understanding the principles behind those facts (Barrell, 161). What it does not indicate is the way that it was further assumed that women, bereft of the necessary intellectual rigour needed to control the process of a move into abstract thought, inevitably become a prey to emotional excess; their feelings, uncontrolled by the masculine gift of 'intellect', might be expected to run riot, making them unpredictable and irrational creatures when removed from a world of 'concrete and particular' activities. Their lives, in other words, were best fitted to the domestic round; in almost any other sphere they could justifiably be considered as children.

This latter, negative image of women as emotionally unstable and thus in need of the male guiding hand of reason, is far more prominently displayed in eighteenth-century cultural production than the more neutral (though equally patronizing) delineation of the female intellect used by Barrell for his model. In 'Tintern Abbey' the young Wordsworth of 1793 is described as emotionally overwhelmed. He is passionate, impulsive, and prone to fear; his is a feminine sensibility:

> The sounding cataract
> Haunted me like a passion: the tall rock,
> The mountain, and the deep and gloomy wood,
> Their colours and their forms, were then to me
> An appetite: a feeling and a love,
> That had no need of a remoter charm,
> By thought supplied, or any interest
> Unborrowed from the eye. – That time is past,
> And all its aching joys are now no more,
> And all its dizzy raptures.
>
> (ll. 77–86)

'Haunted … like a passion … An appetite … a feeling … a love'; these 'aching joys' are then summarized as 'dizzy raptures'. We have here someone who sounds very like the heroine of Gothic Romance, standing in need of the older, mature male intellect of Wordsworth to act as guide and mentor. We have the Dorothy of the final section of the poem in whose 'wild eyes' and 'wild ecstasies' Wordsworth can still find 'the language of my former heart' (l. 118, 120, 139), now that he has learnt 'To look on nature, not as in the hour / Of thoughtless youth, but hearing oftentimes / The still, sad music of humanity' (ll. 91–3).

Together, the older and the younger Wordsworths will make a perfect couple; together they create the poet of 'Tintern Abbey', attentive both to immediate detail and to what neither the young Wordsworth nor Dorothy could be expected to appreciate, the nature of what lies beyond the immediate and the specific, an intimation of 'The still, sad music of humanity'.

It is worthwhile, therefore, seeking to explore further the ways in which Wordsworth is gendering the image of the poet in 'Tintern Abbey', and this can be done by setting the poem in the context of recurring eighteenth-century gender stereotypes to be found in both literature and in visual art.

In Augustan portraiture of the kind made fashionable by Sir Godfrey Kneller, patriarchal emminence is conveyed by the use of an upright pose, the body angled to create the effect of the subject turning his head to honour us with his glance. While the great and the good were on occasion portrayed in their robes of high office, informal dress was frequently used, serving only to confirm the confidence with which superiority and power were assumed. What we see is in the first instance the portrait of a recognizable type; distinction between individuals is possible, but it is nowhere near as important as the process by which a common appearance confirms membership of a patriarchal elite.

Later in the century, Sir Joshua Reynolds's portrait of Admiral Keppel (1780) offers a somewhat looser, more romantic treatment of essentially the same statement. Keppel had come to epitomize the heroic, independent warrior male. He had been court marshalled twice in his career, and both times acquitted. The second trial of 1779 had been largely engineered by his political enemies at Westminster. His acquittal was accompanied by widespread demonstrations of popular support, which included this celebratory portrait where he is seen as an indomitable force, rising unaided above the tempestuous setting of his surroundings.

If, by way of contrast, we look now at Reynolds's history painting, *The Death of Dido* (1781), we see a deserted female with her despairing maidservant and a hovering angelic figure. For Dido, desertion means death. Aeneaus (the sail of his ship just visible on the distant horizon) departs to continue his great adventure, the serious, empire-building business of his life. Dido, left behind, cannot call upon the resources available to a male such as Keppel; we see her with an arm trailing behind her like a broken wing in a pose designed to state excess of emotion leading to death. Reynolds had borrowed this pose from a painting he much admired by Giulio Romano, the *Sleeping Psyche*

Admiral Keppel (1780), Sir Joshua Reynolds

of 1528. The arm thrown out and back dramatically emphasizes the weakness and vulnerability of the female subject. Romano heightened the effect by including an advancing satyr, plainly up to no good. Henry Fuseli further intensified this same image in his painting *The Nightmare* of 1782.

The distinction habitually made between male and female types was by no means always as clear-cut as these examples may suggest. In *Widdow of an Indian Chief watching the Arms of her Deceased Husband* (1785), Joseph Wright combined the fashionable Rousseauistic image

Death of Dido (1781), Sir Joshua Reynolds

of the 'noble savage' (generally depicted or described as male) with a female subject. The bereaved woman is in essentially the same situation as Reynolds's Dido; as with the *Dido*, the sea as a symbol of the man's departure is a prominent feature of the painting. But despite the contrastingly statuesque pose of Wright's subject, and her apparent stoicism, the image in no way challenges an orthodox Augustan reading of gender difference. The woman is a lone figure of tragic grief. Bereft of her warrior husband she is reduced to passive melancholy, staring sightlessly out to sea, while the smoking volcano in the middle distance may seem to presage an onset of emotional excess once the initial shock has passed.

Women do on occasion appear in eighteenth-century British art as able to stand independently of male support, but where this happens they tend to be seen as stepping deliberately outside their natural selves. Joshua Reynolds's powerful portrait of Sarah Siddons as 'the Tragic Muse' (1789) is an obvious case in point. The implication, however, is that to be more than she really is, a woman must put on an act. A somewhat less dramatic example of the same idea is Reynolds's group portrait of the Montgomery sisters as 'the Three Graces' (1773); in assuming these roles they become, we must suppose, more interesting than if they were just being themselves.

Women were not infrequently painted singly, as themselves, and in the male patriarchal pose. Pierre Mignard's portrait of the Duchess of Portsmouth (1682) is a good example of how it was frequently done without any subversion of gender roles as traditionally conceived. Mignard ensures that the role of the sitter is not in danger of being

Duchess of Portsmouth (1682), Pierre Mignard

confused with that of her male counterpart. The richness of her clothing marks out her function as essentially decorative; she is the Duke's most treasured possession, supplied with a black slave child to administer to her needs. Her passive role is thus emphasised, while the intimacy of her relationship to the child may also give the impression that she has been indulged with an expensive toy, a living doll, for a companion.

The mature male was envisaged as naturally independent, a warrior if need be, possessing the intellectual powers necessary for a statesman.

The woman, if she was to exist as an independent entity at all, could do so only through make-believe, involving at worst a morally disreputable career on the stage. Her real self became apparent when set alongside a male partner; here she could function as both a decorative appendage, and as at best a worthy manager of domestic affairs. Even here, as Samuel Johnson suggested in his 'Life of Pope', there could be no guarantee against the destructive capabilities of a woman's undisciplined mind:

> The freaks, and humours, and spleen, and vanity of women, as they embroil families in discord, and fill houses with disquiet, do more to obstruct the happiness of life in a year than the ambition of the clergy in many centuries.[4]

A further striking illustration of the close relationship between literary and visual art in the realm of gender type-casting may be supplied by comparing a passage from James Thomson's *The Seasons* with Gainsborough's double portrait of William and Elizabeth Hallet, *The Morning Walk* (1785). There is no doubt here that Elizabeth Hallet, in her fashionable clothing, is fulfilling a decorative, supporting role to her soberly clad husband. The adoring gaze of the dog in the foreground (as so often in the genre) confirms the woman's ornamental status. William Hallet may be seen, in modern parlance, to have 'done well for himself'.

In 'Spring' from *The Seasons* (1728–30) Thomson offers a literary counterpart for Gainsborough's visual image in his description of Lord Lyttelton and his wife at Hagley Park. We first find Lyttelton alone; as he walks he composes poetry, he reflects on nature, he philosophizes:

> And oft, conducted by historic truth,
> You tread the long extent of backward time,
> Planning with warm benevolence of mind
> And honest zeal, unwarped by party-rage,
> Britannia's weal, – how from the venal gulf
> To raise her virtue and her arts revive.[5]

It seems that there is nothing this man cannot do, and he does it alone.

When he is joined by his wife we see an enhancement of his state because her soul is 'attuned' to his. She introduces a more animated quality of life, perhaps; but there is equally the suggestion of something lost. When in his own company, Nature provides Lyttelton with a wide range of intellectual stimuli, much of which will be translated into practical good for the nation: 'Thy passions thus / And meditations vary, as at large / Courting the muse, through Hagley Park you stray' (ll. 906–8). In the company of his wife 'Nature all / Wears to the lover's eye a look of love' (ll. 937–8):

The Morning Walk (1785), Thomas Gainsborough

Perhaps thy loved Lucinda shares thy walk,
With soul to thine attuned. Then Nature all
Wears to the lover's eye a look of love;
And all the tumult of a guilty world,
Tost by ungenerous passions, sinks away.
The tender heart is animated peace;
And, as it pours its copious treasures forth
In varied converse, softening every theme,

You, frequent pausing, turn, and from her eyes,
Where meekened sense and amiable grace
And lively sweetness dwell, enraptured drink
That nameless spirit of ethereal joy,
Inimitable happiness! which love
Alone bestows, and on a favoured few.

(ll. 936–49)

The feminine qualities praised by Thomson are strongly reminiscent of the young Wordsworth's Dorothean self in 'Tintern Abbey'. An emotional stirring takes place marked by the words 'animated', 'lively' and 'enraptured'; but desirable as this may be, it does appear to be for Thomson an 'inimitable happiness' which is no prerequisite for the successful philosopher statesman. It is, after all, only bestowed upon 'a favoured few'; and Lyttelton, we should note, was to be found in the company of the muses and planning 'Britannia's weal' before his wife arrived to 'soften every theme'. When she does appear, her role is clearly to give (her soul 'attuned' to his), and his to take, 'You ... from her eyes ... enraptured drink / That nameless spirit of ethereal joy'.

In the latter part of the century, it becomes clear that the image of the male, or more specifically the male artist, is being extended. Popular notions of sensibility encouraged the male appropriation of what were previously characteristics understood to be symptomatic of feminine inferiority. In 1781 Sir Brooke Boothby, translator of Rousseau, poet and patron of the arts, breaks dramatically with the tradition adhered to by Kneller to have Joseph Wright paint him in the pose of the reclining female nude made familiar through works such as Titian's *Venus of Urbino* (1538). The male is now readily admitting to a degree of vulnerability formally recognized as a threat to the isolated, emotionally unstable female. The suicide of the young poet Thomas Chatterton in 1770 had swiftly established itself as an iconic model for this new man of sensibility. Henry Wallis's Pre-Raphaelite treatment of the subject in 1856 perpetuated a sympathetic, romanticized rendering of Chatterton as a young male in a state of feminized vulnerability and despair, striking the pose familiar to us from Reynolds's *Dido* and Fuseli's *Nightmare*. Like Boothby, however, Chatterton is sufficiently in control of the situation to remain fully clad to the end.

James Beattie supplied an equally influential model for the Romantic poet with Edwin, the youthful subject of his poem *The Minstrel* (1771–4). Beattie clearly intended to avoid the patriarchal male stereotype when it came to describing the young male poet:

And yet poor Edwin was no vulgar boy;
Deep thought oft seem'd to fix his infant eye.

Sir Brooke Boothby (1781), Joseph Wright of Derby

> Dainties he heeded not, nor gaud, nor toy,
> Save one short pipe of rudest minstrelsy:
> Silent when glad; affectionate, though shy;
> And now his look was most demurely sad;
> And now he laugh'd aloud, yet none knew why.
> The neighbours star'd and sigh'd, yet bless'd the lad:
> Some deem'd him wondrous wise, and some believed him mad.[6]

Wright's depiction of Edwin (1777–8) manifestly exploits the feminine side of his dreamy 'demure' nature. Beattie's poem is written in Spenserian 'Gothic' stanza form, an added challenge to Augustan classicism. For other artists, the feminization of the creative spirit continued to be a cause for concern, and in his drawing of the death of Chatterton (1775–80), John Flaxman appears to feminize Chatterton's features by way of commenting upon what for him was an immature rejection of classicism. Chatterton turns his back on the light, reaching eagerly for the bowl of poison offered by Gothic taste in the form of a hag. Flaxman was a committed classicist who became Professor of Sculpture at the Royal Academy in 1810, after ten years as an Academician.

Ann Bermingham's essay draws attention to the close relationship between visual and literary representations of gender. John Barrell has written elsewhere at length on the strong links between an evolving picturesque aesthetic in eighteenth-century visual art and its impact upon poetry, and nowhere is the influence of the picturesque more readily

Edwin (1777–8), Joseph Wright of Derby

apparent than in the opening lines of 'Tintern Abbey'.[7] The 'perplexity'
that surfaces later in the poem is indicative of the onset of a new sense of
unease on the part of the Romantic artist, now made increasingly critical
of the formula for contemporary taste by recent social and political
matters of fact. In 'Tintern Abbey' Wordsworth was recalling the aftermath of his traumatic year's sojourn in France. Nothing was ever going
to look quite the same after that. To what extent, then, is Wordsworth,
the modern poet of the 1790s with 'Simon Lee', 'The Thorn', 'The

Death of Chatterton
(1775–80),
John Flaxman

Idiot Boy', 'The Female Vagrant' and 'Goody Blake and Harry Gill' already in the printer's hands, genuinely signalling a departure from Augustan values and assumptions towards something Romantic, something substantially new?

The political ramifications of challenging Augustan values were very much a part of the aesthetic debate. Boothby holds a copy of Rousseau in his hand as he reclines in the sylvan glade, while Chatterton's ambition to write in the cause of the radical Whig interest was as well known as the contempt in which he held the cultural establishment of his day; and of course in 1798 Wordsworth was attempting to lay to rest the ghost of his younger self as a political radical in the mould of Thomas Paine. Error in political judgement was not infrequently represented in the conservative press as a manifestation of effeminacy, an unchecked emotional response to circumstances which demanded a lesson in discipline from masculine common sense.

The gendering of political radicalism in the 1790s becomes a complex process, with images of unnaturally masculine women set alongside men reduced to brute form, who may equally be characterized as having been seduced away from their masculine common sense towards the feminine tendency to act with impulsive irresponsibility. The *Anti-Jacobin* of 1797–8 illustrates how these various readings were frequently superimposed on each other. In the Introduction to the first number (November 1797), the patriot poet is described as 'a warrior'. The Jacobin of the species is by contrast one who 'rejects all restrictions in his feelings', and in consequence worships the Goddess of Anarchy 'Where'er fell Rapine stalks, or Barb'rous Discord reigns!' (No. IX, 8 Jan., p. 38). We are told that 'the coy Muse of Jacobinism' appears in many characters. We have a somewhat less than accomplished actress here, 'For in whatever disguise she appears, whether of mirth or of melancholy, of piety or of tenderness, under all disguises, like *Sir John Brute* in woman's clothes, she is betrayed by her drunken swagger and ruffian tone' (No. I, 20 Nov., pp. 3–5). In Vanbrugh's revised version of *The Provok'd Wife* (1725–6), Sir John Brute is a debauched man of quality who ensures our lack of sympathy by disguising himself as 'Bonduca, Queen of the Welchmen'. The feminine principle is being variously employed here, both for its unpredictable 'coyness' and its wildness, in order to confirm an adverse political verdict on Jacobinism.

Still no friend to political conservatism in the late 1790s, Wordsworth in 'Tintern Abbey' confirms the inferiority of femininity to a mature male sensibility, but resists any notion of it as by implication politically subversive or destructive. This is consistent with his wish to effect a reconciliation between youthful political principles, and the commitment to political justice he retained in modified form following the collapse of the French Revolution, and his disillusionment with Godwinism.

Wordsworth effectively confirms traditional eighteenth-century gender stereotypes by identifying what he needs to add to his mature male poetic sensibility as peculiarly feminine in character. There is nothing here of Mary Wollstonecraft's radical feminist demand to 'strengthen the female mind by enlarging it'.[8] Wordsworth does indeed make a gesture towards the hope that Dorothy will in due course follow him into a more mature state of mind. But if his sister's 'ecstasies' were in the end to be 'matured / Into a sober pleasure', we must realise that – if we are to believe the poem – he was prepared to will his own death as a poet (ll. 139–40). At the very least he is looking towards Dorothy's translation to masculinity, and that is not what Mary Wollstonecraft was envisaging as the goal of women deprived of proper educational opportunities.

In 1798, Wordsworth had to hand a long established cultural framework of gender reference which provided him with the dramatis personae he needed to make the composition of 'Tintern Abbey' possible. It marks a significant change in the loco-descriptive poetic genre within which Thomson was working; but despite its challenge to the Augustan model of masculinity, it contains no significant change of attitude towards the concept of femininity. If anything, it links Romanticism to a form of domestic imperialism, in which the male seeks to colonize and appropriate so-called feminine attributes in order to retain a position of dominance in creative activity within society.

Notes

The text for 'Tintern Abbey' is taken from *Lyrical Ballads and Other Poems*, ed. James Butler and Karen Green (London: Cornell University Press, 1992), pp. 116–20.

1   John Barrell, *Poetry, Language and Politics* (Manchester: Manchester University Press, 1988), pp. 137–67.

2   Ann Bermingham, 'The Origins of Painting and the Ends of Art: Wright of Derby's *Corinthian Maid*', in *Painting and the Politics of Culture*, ed. John Barrell (Oxford: Oxford University Press, 1992), pp. 154–5.

3   Ibid. pp. 137–8, 140–1.

4   Samuel Johnson, 'The Life of Pope' in *Lives of the English Poets*, ed. George Birkbeck Hill, 3 vols. (Oxford: Oxford University Press, 1905), 3, p. 234.

5   *The Poetical Works of James Thomson*, ed. J. L. Robertson (London: Oxford University Press, 1961), p. 38, ll. 926–37.

6   James Beattie, *The Minstrel; or, The Progress of Genius*, Book I (1977), Stanza XVI, ll. 136–44. From the text edited by Everard H. King, in James Beattie's *The Minstrel and the Origins of Romantic Autobiography* (Lampeter: The Edwin Mellen Press, 1992), Appendix A pp. 241–75.

7   John Barrell, *The Idea of Landscape and the Sense of Place* (Cambridge: Cambridge University Press, 1972).

8   Mary Wollstonecraft, *A Vindication of the Rights of Women* (Penguin Books, 1992), p. 107.

Wordsworth and the Aesthetics of the Walk

Robin Jarvis
University of the West of England

> Wordsworth at his best, no less than at his worst,
> is a pedestrian poet.
>
> (Seamus Heaney)

Wordsworth, as is well known, was a prodigious walker: De Quincey, who reports that the poet's legs 'were pointedly condemned by all the female connoisseurs' that he had come across, feels obliged to point out that they were nonetheless very serviceable legs, having traversed, by his somewhat mysterious calculations, 'a distance of 175 to 180,000 English miles'.[1] What is the relationship between this phenomenal mileage and Wordsworth's equally extensive output as a poet – between his walking and his writing? Wordsworth made a substantial contribution to the literature of travel: the modern preference for the early Wordsworth has made less visible such collections as *Memorials of a Tour in Scotland, 1803, The River Duddon* and *Yarrow Revisited, and Other Poems*, while chronologically-arranged anthologies have weakened the generic affiliations of any individual poems within them that have survived. There is a resumption of serious academic interest in his prose *Guide to the Lakes,* however,[2] which further illuminates his already well-documented poetic debts to the pastoral and loco-descriptive traditions. It can also hardly have gone unnoticed – to move to the area I wish to examine – how a significant number of Wordsworth's poems, including early works, were written during or about journeys undertaken on foot: *An Evening Walk, Descriptive Sketches, Salisbury Plain,* 'Tintern Abbey', *Home at Grasmere* and large parts of *The Prelude* come readily to mind. But do the pedestrian origins of these texts have more than a contingent relation to their themes and underlying preoccupations? Does a poem rooted in the activity of walking have any distinctive features regarding the kinds of observations or reflections it contains, or the ways in which they are incorporated within it? Is there any way in which pedestrianism can help determine the form and style of a literary text? In this essay I want to explore certain ways of making sense of Seamus Heaney's intriguing suggestion – the specific rationale of which I shall deal with in due course – that Wordsworth is crucially a pedestrian poet. The one text

I shall have space to focus on is his earliest walking poem, *An Evening Walk* (written in 1788–89), published along with *Descriptive Sketches*, which was written in 1791–92 but based on his walking tour of the Continent in the summer of 1790.[3]

Although some of Wordsworth's biographers and critics have, perhaps unwittingly, tended to inflate the uniqueness of his 1790 tour – Mary Moorman, for instance, claimed that 'Wordsworth and [his companion] Jones may be regarded as the pioneers of the great company who, from their day to the hikers and ramblers of our own, have claimed the right to walk for pleasure over hill and dale'[4] – it seems certain that the scope and physical severity of his expedition were exceptional.[5] It was presumably for this reason that his Cambridge friends, and his sister Dorothy (who was, of course, no mean walker herself), denounced it as 'mad and impracticable'.[6] Nevertheless, it has to be placed in the context of a vogue for pedestrianism that was undoubtedly well-established by the late 1790s. In the form of domestic tourism, this owed a lot to the formidable obstacles posed to the traditional Grand Tour (typically undertaken in a four-horsed carriage) by the Revolutionary wars.[7] However, it was taking shape well before the outbreak of war, and seems to have had, for some at least, an independent impetus, possibly politically grounded. Coleridge and his companion, Joseph Hucks, when they undertook a walking tour of North Wales in 1794, at a time when Coleridge's Pantisocratic ambitions were at their height, certainly conceived of their mode of travel as having a social-levelling dimension: Coleridge, in his first letter (to Southey) written on the tour, includes a draft of 'Perspiration, a Travelling Eclogue', in which he draws a clear distinction between the physical exposure of the walker ('scorching to th'unwary Traveller's touch / The stone fence flings it's narrow slip of shade') and the 'clatt'ring Wheels' of 'Loath'd Aristocracy', and it seems more than coincidental that he later reports that he has 'done nothing but dream of the System of no Property every step of the Way' since leaving Southey in Oxford.[8] Hucks, meanwhile, in his subsequent written account of the tour, boasts that 'all ideas of appearance and gentility' were 'entirely out of the question', and that 'if I thought I had one acquaintance who would be ashamed of me and my knapsack, seated by the fire of an honest Welsh peasant, in a country village, I should not only make myself perfectly easy on my own account, but should be induced to pity and despise him for his weakness'.[9] Radical lecturer and writer John Thelwall was another with clear political motives for his pedestrianism: his tour of southern England, serialised irregularly and anonymously in *The Monthly Magazine* in 1799–1800, was undertaken by one who found that 'every fact connected with the history and actual condition of the laborious classes' was 'important to a heart throbbing with anxiety for the welfare of the human race';[10] while his earlier publication, *The*

Peripatetic, a curious compendium of 'Politico-Sentimental Journals' recounting the wanderings of Thelwall's alter-ego, 'Sylvanus Theophrastus', persistently mobilises an activist's outrage at political abuses and social distress in a way that sharpens the elements of social criticism conventionally present in the literature of sensibility. Jeffrey C. Robinson has nicely observed that in this text 'walking signifies the restlessness, negatively the uprootedness and political drivenness, more positively the *mobility*, of the radical mind'.[11] Rather earlier, in pre-Revolutionary times, the young William Frend, later to become one of the most prominent and influential radical dissenters, undertook a walking tour of France, Germany and Switzerland. At the very least, the freedom of the walking tour seems to have fuelled Frend's spiritual conversion and politicisation, which began soon after his return.[12]

For some, then, in this turbulent decade, taking to the open road was a self-conscious political act: the flexibility, the openness to experience, and the experimental atmosphere of this mode of travel could become a natural extension of one's political prospectivism, one's readiness for change. Learning (about the real conditions of life among the lower classes, for example) was a preparation for doing. There was also the possibility of a more negative political dimension to walking: middle-class gentlemen disaffected from society for whatever reason could express their alienation by travelling in a manner clearly out of character for their class – ostentatiously distancing themselves from the Grand Tour mentality.[13] Such gestures are always somewhat showy and insecure, however, which serves to notify us that the link between pedestrianism and politics in this period is a more indeterminate one than we might assume. A now obscure pedestrian traveller like Richard Warner, for example, worried about being mistaken for a pedlar, experiences 'false shame' on encountering some 'fashionable ladies' despite having worked himself into 'a fancied heroism in this respect'.[14] Wordsworth himself, though he self-approvingly informs one correspondent of his intention to explore the west of England 'in an humble evangelical way; to wit *à pied*', is capable at another time (earlier in the decade, when his radicalism is taken by some to be firmer) of reproving a friend for proposing some open-ended shoestring travelling: 'I should not be able to reconcile to my idea of right, the thought of wandering about a country, without a certainty of being able to maintain myself, without being indebted for my existence to those charities of which the acceptance might rob people not half so able to support themselves as myself'.[15] There is a concern here for maintaining the position of an independent gentleman whilst 'acting out' (albeit very earnestly) a more lowly form of life, that is shared with other travellers of the period. There are many other pedestrian travellers in the period whose writings are politically perfectly neutral. The poet William Bowles undertook an extensive

walking tour of Scotland and the Continent in the late 1780s, and
Bowles is arguably one of the most conservative figures in English
literature. Perhaps the most reliable conclusion to draw is that the 1790s
were a transitional period in terms of attitudes to walking, and that
although a walking tour could, precisely by virtue of the endurance of
old attitudes, be a political statement, not every walking tour necessarily
was. Political signification was a kind of 'value added' vis-à-vis a form of
travel which men in the middling orders of society could now take up
innocently, if still somewhat self-consciously.

To assess the popularity of the walking tour in the Romantic period
in the light of a historically determinate politics of walking, as I have
just been doing (with due qualification), is not to account fully for such
a development, or to explain how such cultural significations became
possible. The search for such a rationale is still incomplete, I believe, but
Anne Wallace's *Walking, Literature, and English Culture* has recently
put forward a socioeconomic explanation. Wallace's central argument is
that walking could not be reconfigured and manipulated aesthetically
until it was possible to think about walking as something that was done
by choice and at leisure; and that in turn could not come about until
people had begun to be freed from the economic necessity of walking
which characterised the lives of the lower orders, and until the social
connotations of poverty, unrespectability and criminality which walking
had traditionally carried had started to be erased. The so-called transport
revolution, the first material effects of which Wallace, or the historians
whose work she cites, dates to the first decade of the nineteenth century,
cleared the ground for walking to be redefined as voluntary travel, with
the physical, mental and spiritual benefits thought to accrue to travel,
and for it to become the model for new aesthetic strategies and preferences. Prime among these is a shift from destination-oriented travel,
which correlated with the preference for stationary perspectives in art,
travel literature and topographical poetry, to process- or passage-oriented
travel, which promoted a literature committed to restoring the legibility
of a world that was being defamiliarised by alterations in perceptual
frameworks encouraged by faster and easier travel, as well as by changes
in local physical environments brought about by such factors as the
enclosure movement. Wallace's thesis deserves attention and respect,
and may well have a large contribution to make to our understanding
of the cultural history of walking in the later nineteenth-century, but my
own survey of the evidence suggests that she has backdated the deter-
mining role of the transport revolution in a a less than convincing manner.
As I have indicated, walking tours emerge as a phenomenon in the last
quarter of the eighteenth century, and have certainly established themselves by the 1790s, well before the first significant effects of the transport
revolution she discusses. The very fact that not all these early walkers

were political radicals, deliberately slumming it on principle, suggests that, in a curious reversal of Wallace's cause and effect, the ideological re-marking of pedestrianism *preceded* the material and technological changes which she claims as its preconditions. At best, these changes will have consolidated or accelerated trends that were already under way. Whether the redefinition of walking might have other material bases, or whether it should be approached as a quasi-autonomous cultural development, is something that awaits further exploration.

The general nature of the aesthetic, rather than political, questions raised by Romantic pedestrianism, can perhaps best be grasped by a counter-example from Wordsworth's *Guide through the District of the Lakes*. At the beginning of this work Wordsworth presents a topographical image that is the very negation of a pedestrian perspective on the landscape:

> I know not how to give the reader a distinct image of these more readily, than by requesting him to place himself with me, in imagination, upon some given point; let it be the top of either of the mountains, Great Gavel, or Scawfell; or, rather, let us suppose our station to be a cloud hanging midway between those two mountains, at not more than half a mile's distance from the summit of each, and not many yards above their highest elevation; we shall then see stretched at our feet a number of vallies, not fewer than eight, diverging from the point, on which we are supposed to stand, like spokes from the nave of a wheel.[16]

The imaginative hypothesis of a cloud's-eye view from which the entire region can be 'comprehended and understood at once' is one that short-circuits the temporal discovery of landscape. Wordsworth's image is inspired by a relief model of the Alps that he had seen at Lucerne, which he describes first as seducing the imagination in quite another way – 'tempting it to wander at will from valley to valley, from mountain to mountain, through the deepest recesses of the Alps' (p. 170). This is mental wandering of a kind which makes of the imagination an armchair walker; but such irresolute and tantalising footplay is overwhelmed by the 'more substantial pleasure' (ibid.) of comprehension-at-a-glance, the implied mastery of a synthesis of perceptions. However, this victory for stationary perspective (in which phrase one should recall the sense of 'station' as 'viewpoint' in the literature of picturesque tourism) is not as assured as it may seem at first. For a start, the use of a cloud as a metonymy for a fixed viewpoint goes against the grain of Wordsworth's established figural tastes: the ecstatically liberated walker who opens *The Prelude*, for example, finds in the cloud above him a metaphor for his own unpremeditated journey: 'should the guide I chuse / Be nothing

better than a wandering cloud, / I cannot miss my way' (I, ll. 17–19); while
in the beautiful fragment, 'A Night-Piece', the seemingly impenetrable
vault of wind-driven low cloud is 'split / Asunder', disclosing the illuso-
rily rapid motion of the moon and stars beyond.[17] Secondly, the very
supposition of a fixed aerial station is undercut by the deferrals attendant on capturing its perspective in writing: as Wordsworth conducts
the reader's eye up and down successive valleys, more in sympathy
with the long-distance walker than with his ideal floating observer, the
discriminations he makes are not of a kind that could be comprehended
'at a glance', but seem the product of a more scrupulous, lingering
attention. Finally, the fact that Wordsworth is compelled to move his
cloud 'four or five miles eastward to the ridge of Helvellyn' (p. 173) in
order to complete his topographical wheel, and finds, moreover, that
the vale of Coniston has to be represented as 'a broken spoke sticking
in the rim' (p. 172), is a somewhat comic deconstruction of the totalising
view afforded by his original station. What we have in the wheel image,
then, is an atemporal topographical idealism threatened at all points
with its textual dissolution – a pedestrian spirit, or something of the
phenomenal experience of actual travel, overtaking and disrupting
the aesthetic wholeness and symmetry of the synoptic view.

Mention of the literature of picturesque tourism raises the interesting
question of the relation of pedestrianism to the picturesque, which in
turn provides the obvious theoretical bridge to my discussion of *An
Evening Walk*. With regard to the political dimension of walking tours,
I have argued that there was no *necessary* connection between radicalism
and pedestrianism; but what of the *aesthetic* character of walking, within
its contemporary cultural frame of reference? Although, quite obviously, not all picturesque tourists were foot-travellers, it is arguable that
there is more than a casual convergence between picturesque theory and
the pedestrian's mode of travel and experiencing landscape.

An examination of this question must dwell firstly on the spontaneous, irregular, freely deviating itinerary of the true walker. Among
little-known Romantic walkers, The Rev. William Bingley points out at
the beginning of his *Tour Round North Wales* that the pedestrian can
'strike out of the road, amongst the mountains or morasses, in a manner
completely independent of all those obstacles that inevitably attend
the bringing of carriages or horses'; while Adam Walker declares at the
start of his *Tour from London to the Lakes* that 'there is but one way of
travelling more pleasant than riding on horseback, and that is on foot;
for then I can turn to the right and the left …'.[18] The freedom to 'strike
out' or 'turn to the right and the left' generates a route that resists
delineation, at least in straight lines. Now, it is precisely a scenery
'free from the formality of lines' – the 'lofty banks' and 'mazy course'
of the river Wye – that William Gilpin finds especially conducive to

picturesque composition.[19] It is a predilection confirmed by the doyen of Lake District guidebook-writers, Thomas West, among others:

> What charms the eye in wandering over the vale, is, that not one streight line offends. The roads all serpentize round the mountains, and the hedges wave with the inclosures. Every thing is thrown into some path of beauty, or agreeable line of nature. But to describe every picturesque view ... would be an endless labour.[20]

There thus seems to be a mutual reflection of the picturesque irregularity of lines in nature and the irregularity of the pedestrian's way: the eye discovers picturesque beauty by 'wandering' over the landscape, while the human wanderer who serpentizes round the mountains is essentially at one with his quest, has minimised his intervention in the landscape by impersonating the agreeable lines of nature.

Gilpin claims roughness as the essential quality of the picturesque, and the main point of difference between the picturesque and the beautiful. To this, Uvedale Price adds the quality of 'sudden variation', producing an anatomy of the picturesque founded on the recognition of variety and intricacy as the twin sources of pleasure in natural objects. Both Gilpin and Price, of course, write in the shadow of Burke. The latter's *Philosophical Enquiry into the Origin of our Ideas of the Sublime and Beautiful* had discussed variation as among the properties of beauty, on condition that the variation was gradual and insensible. He brought this within his physiological account of the sublime and beautiful, which distinguished between those objects or experiences that effected a violent tension or contraction of the nerves and those which caused a relaxation of the body, by noting that sharp angles bring about a 'twitching or convulsion of the optic nerve' that is inimical to beauty.[21] Eroticising this distinction in his inimitable manner, Burke writes of the gentle undulations of a woman's body (p. 105):

> Observe that part of a beautiful woman where she is perhaps the most beautiful, about the neck and breasts; the smoothness; the softness; the easy and insensible swell; the variety of the surface, which is never for the smallest space the same; the deceitful maze, through which the unsteady eye slides giddily, without knowing where to fix, or whither it is carried. Is not this a demonstration of that change of surface continual and yet hardly perceptible at any point which forms one of the great constituents of beauty?

This is consistent with the overall gender-bias of Burke's account, which, though it does not deny the existence of male beauty, regards beauty, and the 'softer virtues' of kindness and compassion, as the more

natural property of women, in contrast to the more masculine rigours of
the sublime and predominantly male virtues such as justice and wisdom.
Burke's willingness to find topographical illustrations of the feelings
excited by beauty – he compares, for example, being 'drawn in an easy
coach, on a smooth turf, with gradual ascents and declivities' to being
'hurried over a rough, rocky road' (p. 141) – further demonstrates
the close complicity between a gendered aesthetics of landscape and a
phenomenology of male desire.

When reading Gilpin and Price on the picturesque against the
background of their mutual precursor, Burke, one notices that they have
found in the picturesque a middle term that articulates the insecurity of
definition which occasionally beset the *Enquiry*, and nowhere is this
blurring of boundaries more evident than in the erotological dimension
of their treatment of landscape. Gilpin states bluntly that the division of
objects into sublime and beautiful is no more than a convenience, and
that the two are invariably mixed in picturesque art, and his description
of the picturesque traveller's pleasure in the mere *pursuit* of his object
evinces the appropriate complication of Burke's mapping of beautiful
landscape onto the female body:

> We suppose the country to have been unexplored. And shall we
> suppose it a greater pleasure to the sportsman to pursue a trivial
> animal, than it is to the man of taste to pursue the beauties of nature?
> to follow her through all her recesses? to obtain a sudden glance, as
> she flits past him in some airy shape? to trace her through the mazes
> of the cover? to wind after her along the vale? or along the reaches of
> the river?[22]

The 'airy shape', the 'mazes of the cover' and the winding vale are
perhaps consistent with Burke's inventory of beautiful qualities, but the
'sudden glance' and the 'flitting' passage of the shape are less concor-
dant with the mood of languor and relaxation appropriate to beauty.
The confusion is effected by the transformation of Burke's feminised
landscape, a woman offered up for languid contemplation, into a neo-
classical nymph who teases the male observer's roving eye. Price
provides a further interesting variation on this theme. He states that the
distinction between the beautiful and the picturesque is most obvious to
touch: following Burke, beauty inspires feelings of tenderness and
affection and a desire to touch and caress; beautiful landscape invites a
correlative sort of caressing by the eye, whereas picturesque landscape,
Price asserts, lacks this erotic appeal to the observer. However, he finds
it difficult to maintain this position as he picks up Burke's theory of the
contrasting physiology of the beautiful and sublime; the leading effect of
the picturesque is, in his account, a prurient curiosity:

it neither relaxes nor violently stretches the fibres, but by its active agency keeps them to their full tone, and thus, when mixed with either of the other characters, corrects the languor of beauty, or the horror of sublimity. But as the nature of every corrective must be to take off from the peculiar effect of what it is to correct, so does the picturesque when united to either of the others. It is the coquetry of nature; it makes beauty more amusing, more varied, more playful, but also,

'Less winning soft, less amiably mild.'

Again by its variety, its intricacy, its partial concealments, it excites that active curiosity which gives play to the mind, loosening those iron bonds with which astonishment chains up its faculties.[23]

There seems an undeniably erotic dimension to the mental play celebrated here: picturesque nature as coquette offers the lascivious aesthete a pleasurable freedom from the tedium of fixed categories or roles; she provides a 'rougher' encounter than the sensuously supine figure of beauty, without ever threatening the domination of the spectator, whilst also, by virtue of those topographically teasing 'partial concealments', warding off the fear of sublime impotence by prolonging the enjoyments of ocular 'foreplay'. The clear distinction between the beautiful and the sublime dissolves into a generalised erotic attentiveness.

To gather these threads together: I have suggested that in the literature of walking the openness and indeterminacy of the pedestrian's way may be mirrored in the variety and irregularity of line of picturesque landscape. I have also argued that it is in the nature of the picturesque, an intermediate and supplementary category, to point up the non-self-integrity of the opposed values that it bridges: for Price, picturesque roughness – as illustrated, for example, by the thorns of the rose – is the 'fringe of beauty' that demonstrates the interinvolvement of its intrinsic qualities with what is supposedly extrinsic, and which prevents its becoming what it would otherwise be: bald, monotonous and insipid. In the discourse of deconstruction, this would be viewed as the logic of the *parergon* – a term fastened upon by Derrida in his reading of Kant to denote the ambiguous function of that which is neither inside nor outside. But we do not need Derrida to see how picturesqueness throws into question the theoretical assurance of Burkean aesthetics, with its interpellation of a male connoisseur who moves between a leisurely appreciation of 'female' beauty and morally bracing Oedipal encounters with the terrors of the sublime. If, therefore, there is a confusion of gender apparent in the aesthetic characterisations of landscape predominant at the time, what lessons does this hold for the pedestrian traveller who looks to that landscape for ratification of his identity within a reciprocal relationship with nature? If the aesthetic ideal, whether in landscape or the human body, is invariably and necessarily *composite*, does this create problems of sexual identity for the walker, who refuses the masculine purposiveness of direct progress to his destination, and who relishes instead the teasing meanders and partial concealments of his route? It may well be the case that Wordsworth, for one, despite his self-promotion as a traveller who is 'free, enfranchis'd and at large', is nevertheless burdened with feelings of unworthiness and unmanliness in such a free-floating existence – leading him, for instance, in the opening of *The Prelude* to which I have alluded, to commit himself almost immediately to 'active days' and 'prowess in an honorable field'.

Alan Liu, reflecting on Wordsworth's 1790 walking tour, comments that such tours, when turned into travel literature, habitually suffer from a sense of *undermotivation*: 'a tour reduces to two points between which a break poses the problem of continuity',[24] and the logic of connection, he argues, tends to take the form of prefabricated formulae, such as an inventory of experiences of sublimity and beauty. This suggests one possible reason why travel literature of the period is prone to direct imitation and plagiarism as well as to a more random intertextuality. Charles Batten, in his survey of eighteenth-century travel literature, emphasises the degree to which convention dictated its narrative structures and descriptive resources, and underlines the irony that the 'truth' of such works was frequently determined circularly by their similarity to their predecessors, while stories that were authentic were occasionally ridiculed because they did not seem *probable* (that is, because nobody else had written about them).[25] So an undermotivation of the tour issues paradoxically in an overdetermination of the writing which the tour generates; but such insistent deference to precedent, if carried too far, diminishes the credibility of the traveller and risks denuding him/her of even the factitious sense of purpose that has been created.

However, if lack of sufficient motive of one's own risks unmanning the pedestrian traveller, some walkers nevertheless revel in this very evacuation of selfhood. Hazlitt, in his essay 'On Going a Journey', one of the masterpieces of walking literature, writes that 'it is great to shake off the trammels of the world and of public opinion – to lose our importunate, tormenting, everlasting personal identity in the elements of nature, and become the creature of the moment, clear of all ties'.[26] For him, walking unhinges the socially constructed and maintained self, places it in suspension, allowing the mind to become a screen on which the passing image is momentarily projected, overdubbed with ideas and memories generated according to strict associationist principles (pp. 144–45):

We cannot enlarge our conceptions; we can only shift our point of view. The landscape bares its bosom to the enraptured eye; we take our fill of it; and seem as if we could form no other image of beauty or grandeur. We pass on, and think no more of it: the horizon that shuts it from our sight also blots it from our memory like a dream ... So in coming to a place where we have formerly lived and with which we have intimate associations, every one must have found that the feeling grows more vivid the nearer we approach the spot, from the mere anticipation of the actual impression: we remember circumstances, feelings, persons, faces, names, that we had not thought of for years; but for the time all the rest of the world is forgotten!

Here and throughout the essay Hazlitt gives a vivid inward description of pedestrianism that is sharply opposed to the kind of lacklustre, routinised, simultaneously under- and overdetermined travel referred to above. His walking is a modest sort of emancipation, that is means-oriented rather than end-oriented, and always confined to the self. 'In setting out on a party of pleasure,' he states, 'the first consideration always is where we shall go: in taking a solitary ramble, the question is what we shall meet with by the way. The mind then is "its own place" ...' (p. 145). This allusion to Milton's Satan, however perfunctory it may be, nonetheless should make us pause for thought, since it does alert us to some possible ambivalences in the essay. If Satan's speech taking possession of hell stands, for Romantic readers of Milton, as a triumphant assertion of the self's victory over circumstance, Hazlitt's essay, vigorously upbeat though it may be, partakes of a siege mentality that never fully convinces one that solitude is as life-affirming as it is said to be. In the final part of his essay he enumerates the situations in which companionship is welcome on a walk: these include excursions with a definite end in view ('ruins, aqueducts, pictures'), and all foreign travel. Surprisingly, Hazlitt's silent luxuriating in the unchallenged sway of his own sensations and observations, on a solitary ramble, yields when abroad to an appetite for company and communication: 'In such situations, so opposite to all one's ordinary train of ideas, one seems a species by one's-self, a limb torn off from society, unless one can meet with instant fellowship and support' (p. 146). Having 'to unravel this mystery of our being at every turn' (p. 139), which Hazlitt disdains when walking in home surroundings, becomes contrarily urgent when such 'mystery' is a matter of organic national identity. This over-anxious sense of linguistic and cultural belonging, or wholeness, is seen as the precipitate of a post-Revolutionary and post-Napoleonic insularity: Hazlitt compares the joyous internationalism of the early years of the Revolution, when he first set foot 'on the laughing shores of France' and was unconscious of any 'alien sound' because he 'breathed the air of general humanity' (p. 146), to the post-war rediscovery of the prison-house of nationality.

Yet, as Hazlitt concludes his essay, another dimension to his new-found uneasiness with unaccompanied foreign travel comes into view. It is not so much the lack of an interlocutor who shares a language and a frame of reference that is troubling, but the estrangement from one's *internal* interlocutor (p. 147):

> Our romantic and itinerant character is not to be domesticated. Dr Johnson remarked how little foreign travel added to the facilities of conversation in those who had been abroad. In fact, the time we have spent there is both delightful and in one sense instructive; but it appears to be cut out of our substantial, downright existence, and never to join kindly on to it. We are not the same, but another, and perhaps more enviable individual, all the time we are out of our own country. We are lost to ourselves, as well as to our friends.

We see here, rather poignantly, the separating-out of a Romantic self, an 'ideal identity', from an ordinary, actual, 'domesticated' self. The former, self-expansively, takes pleasure in the strange, the exotic, the unas-similable, but is itself unassimilable to the homely contours of one's everyday, waking personality. There seems to be more at stake here than foreign travel, more of a general disabused reflection on the fate of the Romantic Ego. When Hazlitt says that 'we can be said only to fulfil our destiny in the place that gave us birth' (p. 147), the last phrase has the sense of Wordsworth's 'world which is the world / Of all of us', where 'We find our happiness, or not at all' (*Prelude*, X, ll. 725–27), and carries the same counter-idealising message as that passage does in context.

So Hazlitt's late-Romantic walker is one who walks to evacuate and free the self from its regular social co-ordinates, but not to stray so far, literally or metaphorically, that that society is not at hand to perform a necessary infilling if the psychological anchors wear loose.

I have been trying to identify a number of problems for the Romantic walker – a number of instabilities that inhabit representations of walking in Romantic literature. They include the voluntarily political complexion of Romantic walking; the indeterminacy of identity of the walker and walking literature, linked to their close implication in the ambiguously-gendered representations of picturesque landscape; the undermotivation of the walk coupled with an overdetermination of writing it; and the attractions and perils of enfranchising the self through walking. Need-less to say, these are but some elements of a full anatomy of a fascinating body of literature. Let me now return to the idea of Wordsworth as a pedestrian poet – or to Seamus Heaney's use of that label, which is in many ways antithetical to mine. What Heaney has in mind are Wordsworth's compositional habits – as attested, for instance, by Hazlitt in 'My First Acquaintance with Poets': that is, composing poetry whilst 'walking up and down a straight gravel-walk, or in some spot where the continuity of his verse met with no collateral interruption'.[27] For Heaney, the length of the gravel path must be roughly coterminous with a line of blank verse, and as Wordsworth crunches up and down the path the regular physical motion accommodates the prolonged equilibriums of his verse. Up-and-down walking, with no 'collateral interruptions', as he says, does not forward the journey but habituates the body to a languorous, dreamy rhythm – a rhythm that is sublimated in the slow, cumulative movement of Wordsworth's meditative blank verse.[28]

Interesting though this is, and quite possibly locally true of Wordsworth's poetry at a certain infrastructural level, what I am interested in positing is a kind of contrary accommodation of poetry to pedestrianism – a kind of textual pedestrianism that is underdetermined, freely-deviating, open to collateral interruption at every step. In looking at the erotic configurations of picturesque travel, and the risks implicit in the male traveller's identification with his quest, I have already hinted at one way in which pedestrian poetry may be inimical to stable identity. My contention is that there is a more general opposition between aesthetic forms which pedestrianism, as textual motif or metaphor if not as actual practice or literal referent, serves to articulate. This is an opposition between, on the one hand, an aesthetic practice that privileges centered structure, detail reduced to meaningful pattern, and the organic unity of a complex interdependent whole; and, on the other, a practice that is marked by seriality and contingency, fluid temporal structures of thought and perception, and a reluctance to bring individual elements under the rule of some organising Idea or intention. Theoretically at any rate, the figure of the literary walker encapsulates the possibility of the latter practice – a walker, that is, who has no ideological preconditions or intellectual agenda for his/her itinerary, but who walks in a spirit of open engagement with the world s/he passes through. Given the considerable and long-standing pre-eminence accorded to notions of organic unity in post-Romantic aesthetics, at least until the very different counter-critiques of deconstructionism and Romantic gender studies made it respectable to suspect the mystificatory potential of such ideas,[29] such a practice is unlikely to be held in the highest critical regard, but its products ask for recognition under any more inclusive account of the complexity of Romanticism.

There is a significant strand in Wordsworth's poetic output which presents an interesting study in the aesthetics of walking, and only a comprehensive study would allow me to explore the limit(ation)s of the hypothesis I have just advanced in relation to his particular case – as, indeed, only a still wider study of Romantic walking literature would allow for the hypothesis to be properly defended at all. Here there is only room to begin to plot the relevance of Wordsworth's earliest pedestrian poem, *An Evening Walk*, to this enquiry. This is a poem which used to be dismissed as an elaboration of a repertoire of stylised elements from the topographical poetry tradition, or as a close poetic cousin of the prose literature of picturesque tourism. The poem has attracted a good deal of more searching criticism in recent years – James Averill, Alan Liu, John Williams, Gerald Izenberg[30] – much of it preoccupied with the disruptive figuration of the Female Beggar two-thirds of the way through, a lingering portrait which explodes the contemplative repose of the picturesque spectator. I shall also address this passage, but before I do so I wish to tackle the question of whether or in what way *An Evening Walk* is a walking poem.

The opening lines of the poem give minimal physical presence to the solitary walker:

> Far from my dearest friend, 'tis mine to rove
> Thro' bare grey dell, high wood, and pastoral cove;
> His wizard course where hoary Derwent takes
> Thro' craggs, and forest glooms, and opening lakes,
> Staying his silent waves, to hear the roar
> That stuns the tremulous cliffs of high Lodore:
> Where silver rocks the savage prospect chear
> Of giant yews that frown on Rydale's mere ...
>
> (ll. 1–8)

The first two lines gesture at recurrent activity rather than a single walk that might become the narrative focus of the poem, and the concatenation of images from Borrowdale, Derwentwater and Rydal which follows confirms the trend to delocalised description which characterises the poem's overall trajectory. Wordsworth's Fenwick note, written in late life, which states that the plan of *An Evening Walk* was not 'confined to a particular walk or an individual place', out of an 'unwillingness to submit the poetic spirit to the chains of fact and real circumstance'[31] is in this respect perfectly accurate. Equally, the details we have here, the descriptive details that are assembled with such a cavalier approach to local geography, are of a piece with the picturesque valorisation of roughness, and so are, in a sense – and one could extend this analysis to much else in the poem – *overcoded* (to use a term of Umberto Eco's). If Wordsworth was concerned to register 'the infinite variety of natural appearances', as his Fenwick note also states, there is no point in denying that he does so with respect to, and in the terms of, long-established aesthetic conventions and preferences. This seems *not* to be a pedestrian poem in the sense of recruiting the reader's participation in the contingent, and innocently-observed, sights and sounds of an actual walk.

Indeed, as the poem continues one is granted little impression of the walk as ongoing activity. This would install a temporal dimension which, as Alan Liu has argued, Wordsworth is in fact at pains to short-circuit: as Liu points out, the verse paragraphs in *An Evening Walk* tend to organise diverse details into a 'simultaneous tapestry view', a simple descriptive present, and when there is a shift in temporal perspective, as in the transition from noon to evening in lines 85–88, it appears curiously as more of a spatial than a temporal turn, as though one could swivel one's eyes from mid-day to twilight.

To read *An Evening Walk* as a pedestrian poem, therefore, one has to posit a particular kind of what I have termed textual pedestrianism, a sort of rhetorical walking/wandering. In doing so, what swiftly becomes apparent is the extent to which walking *has* been internalised in this poem, and made the very expression of an instinct for hope and life in the process. To begin with, though, one might recapitulate the formal analogies between the picturesque foot-traveller and picturesque landscape I commented on earlier: the freedom and irregularity of line, that is, the intricacy of the pedestrian's itinerary as a mirror-image of the variety and intricacy of picturesque nature, whose eroticised appeal is predicated on perpetual partial concealment. One definition of textual pedestrianism is therefore that which stresses the insistence of half-glimpse, the fleeting penetration and withdrawal of light into and out of shade, as in the description of sunset in lines 151–74:

> And now it touches on the purple steep
> That flings his shadow on the pictur'd deep.
> Cross the calm lake's blue shades the cliffs aspire,
> With tow'rs and woods a 'prospect all on fire;'
> The coves and secret hollows thro' a ray
> Of fainter gold a purple gleam betray;
> The gilded turf arrays in richer green
> Each speck of lawn the broken rocks between;
> Deep yellow beams the scatter'd boles illume,
> Far in the level forest's central gloom ...
>
> (ll. 155–64)

Here the pedestrian is immobilised, frozen in contemplation, but the eye (of the text) is made to wander instead, seduced by the swiftly-altering view of mountain shadows, 'blue shades', 'coves', 'secret hollows' and gloomy forest that await momentary illumination. One recalls here Gilpin's strictures on landscape painting, in his Tour of the Lakes, to the effect that painting at its best does not aim 'to form an exact resemblance of nature in a *nice representation of all her minute parts*, which we consider as almost impracticable, ending generally in flatness, and insipidity; as by aiming to give those bold, those strong characteristic touches, which excite the imagination, and lead it to form half the picture itself'. For Gilpin, there is a clear analogy between the picturesque tourist's pursuit of the tantalising charms of nature and the (male) viewer's auto-erotic response to the partial concealments of the artist's representation of landscape – a masculine prerogative, it should be noted, amusingly symbolised in the phallic 'internal pencil' with which Gilpin speaks of 'administering' a suitably half-realised picture to oneself.[32]

So the eye wanders among the intricacies of the poem's descriptions. There is also a sense in which the arrested motion of the pedestrian is projected onto the outside world: the group of potters 'Winding from side to side up the steep road' (l. 110), the peasant launching himself on his sledge down the 'headlong pathway' (l. 112), the cockerel 'Sweetly ferocious round his native walks' (l. 129), the quarry-workers in the distance who 'O'erwalk the viewless plank from side to side' (l. 148), the 'violent speed' (l. 180) of the horsemen shadows on the twilight hills, all partake of the physical animation which the walker, rooted in a succession of 'stations', is not permitted to enjoy.

Stationary though he is, the world he observes is full of life and movement, and when I speak of a textual pedestrianism I refer to the way the text proceeds vigorously, turning and troping from side to side, even as the walker is at rest. Until, that is, something rather different happens in the section on the Female Beggar. It has been noticed by many commentators that this passage, together with the description of the swans that precedes and motivates it, is quite anomalous in dwelling at considerable length on a single object in the landscape, in contrast to the poem's accustomed mode of quickfire accumulation of balanced, opposing images. But it has very seldom been noticed that in turning to the Female Beggar the pedestrian observer is expressly turning *away from* observation: in spite of the fact that Wordsworth uses a language of perception ('I see her now'), it is clear beyond doubt that the Beggar is an imaginary figure, the pure product of the narrator's tormented fantasy rather than the nominal object of an encounter on either a particular or an idealised walk.[33] This is where we enter upon fully-internalised walking. Jeffrey Robinson writes that 'A paradox of the walker's fantasy and experience is that as one enters the variety and movement of the outside world, the space for interior wandering also grows', and the entry of the Female Beggar is precisely the moment in this poem at which physical wandering becomes mental travelling:

> Fair swan! by all a mother's joys caress'd,
> Haply some wretch has ey'd, and call'd thee bless'd;
> Who faint, and beat by summer's breathless ray,
> Hath dragg'd her babes along this weary way;

While arrowy fire extorting feverish groans
Shot stinging through her stark o'er-labour'd bones.
– With backward gaze, lock'd joints, and step of pain,
Her seat scarce left, she strives, alas! in vain,
To teach their limbs along the burning road
A few short steps to totter with their load …

(ll. 241–50)

Here, for once in this poem, is a sense of walking not as a perfunctory rhetorical device in the manner of 'A little onward', but as real, painful, prolonged physical progress. And yet it is an imagined journey, which Wordsworth tracks through the forest depth, where the eldest child asks questions that betray his ignorance of his father's death, along the painful road, where the mother amuses them with glow-worms, and over the lightless heath, where Death finally intervenes. One is made vividly aware of the desperate directionlessness of this walk, and of its fatal conclusion – it is more immediate than anything the poet has actually 'seen' on his evening walk. Paradoxically, *An Evening Walk* becomes most vividly a pedestrian poem when the narrator forgets he is a pedestrian at all. But there is more to it than that: a new rhetorical complication occurs when the Beggar's imagined foot-journey itself becomes allegorised as the pursuit of Hope:

And bids her soldier come her woes to share,
Asleep on Bunker's charnel hill afar;
For hope's deserted well why wistful look?
Chok'd is the pathway, and the pitcher broke.

(ll. 253–56)

Walking is synonymous with an instinct for life, while the choked pathway with which the narrator attempts to scare the woman into abandoning hope suggests the latent paralysis of his own melancholy – which, as I have suggested, his imaginative vigour and rhetorical ingenuity constantly upbraid and qualify. And what of the generic discontinuity which the swan passage, firstly, and then the Beggar episode, introduce into the poem? This is an aesthetic 'roughness' which Wordsworth makes no attempt to palliate in the completed poem, or in his subsequent revisions – a 'sudden variation' of narrative mode and style that shows the inscription at a textual level of that element of contingent surprise one might associate with a pedestrian poem proper.

Leaving the Female Beggar, Wordsworth resumes the descriptive mode in which he began the poem: there is a return, that is, to a bunching of observations (first sounds, then sights) from a stationary perspective.

But the psychologised significance of walking which the Female Beggar passage has established lingers on. The fall of night brings a crisis for the picturesque walker whose thoughts have been diverted for so long by imaginary horrors:

> Unheeded Night has overcome the vales,
> On the dark earth the baffl'd vision fails …
>
> Nought else of man or life remains behind
> To call from other worlds the wilder'd mind …
> (ll. 363–64, 375–76)

The 'other worlds' are the inner terrors which a continuation of the walk, and the world of distracting phenomena it represents, might help to dissipate. But the poet is still mentally wandering and suffering with the woman whose plight he has imagined, as the echo in the last two words makes plain: the 'wildered mind' is at one with the beggar who 'wilders o'er the lightless heath'. At this point the moon rises and crisis is averted – not, however, by literally re-opening a field of perceptions to the nocturnal walker, but by inspiring a new vision equating the onward journey with hope for the future. This is the vision of the cottage to be shared with Dorothy:

> Thus Hope, first pouring from her blessed horn
> Her dawn, far lovelier than the Moon's own morn;
> 'Till higher mounted, strives in vain to chear
> The weary hills, impervious, black'ning near;
> – Yet does she still, undaunted, throw the while
> On darling spots remote her tempting smile.
> Ev'n now she decks for me a distant scene,
> (For dark and broad the gulph of time between)
> Gilding that cottage with her fondest ray,
> (Sole bourn, sole wish, sole object of my way …
> (ll. 407–16)

Only with the thought of this future idyllic retirement is Wordsworth able to restore, in the final two verse paragraphs, a picture of a harmonious natural scene, though it is an unquiet night with which he concludes his walk and his poem. It is thus also only a metaphorised walk that is able to smooth out the poem's discontinuities and calm the poet's anxieties. Both the crisis and its resolution are phrased in the language of walking, but neither has much to do with the walk, particular or idealized, which forms the ostensible subject-matter of the poem.

An Evening Walk, therefore, is certainly a pedestrian poem, within a broad definition of pedestrian poetry. But it is a poem that makes us think of walking as an aesthetic activity above all – that invites us to look on Wordsworth as a pedestrian poet chiefly insofar as he internalised, psychologised, metaphorised or performatively allegorised the notion of walking. Walking may carry a manifestly rhetorical significance, or it may contribute to the poem a rhythm and texture – a poetics of roughness and sudden variation – that are experienced as something separate from the real-time process of the 'literal' walk. Without pre-empting the results of a fuller enquiry, I would suggest that a wider survey of Wordsworth's walking poems would reveal that he is consistently a walker in this specialised sense: *pace* Roger Gilbert's fine analysis, which sees the 'walk poem' as trying to 'erase the difference between text and experience, to assert and maintain an absolute coincidence of language and bodily sensation',[34] Wordsworth's experiments in this mode compel the reader to attend to, and interpret, walking as a conspicuously textual activity. This aesthetic conception of walking may well be capacious enough to include, as Seamus Heaney indicates, the best and the worst of Wordsworth.

Notes

1   Thomas de Quincey, *Recollections of the Lakes and the Lake Poets*, ed. David Wright (Harmondsworth: Penguin, 1970), p. 135.

2   See, for example, Jonathan Bate, *Romantic Ecology: Wordsworth and the Environmental Tradition* (London & New York: Routledge, 1991), pp. 41–51; Theresa M. Kelley, *Wordsworth's Revisionary Aesthetics* (Cambridge: Cambridge University Press, 1988), pp. 14–23; and James Buzard, *The Beaten Track: European Tourism, Literature, and the Ways to Culture, 1800–1918* (Oxford: Clarendon Press, 1993), pp. 18–31, where it is considered alongside 'The Brothers' as the opening to a much larger discussion of early expressions of the tourism/travel opposition.

3   All quotations from *An Evening Walk* are from the 1793 edition, the text used being that supplied in the Cornell Wordsworth volume edited by James Averill (Ithaca & London: Cornell University Press, 1983). All line references are included in the body of the text.

4   Mary Moorman, *William Wordsworth: A Biography. The Early Years 1770–1803* (Oxford: Clarendon Press, 1957), p. 131.

5   Donald E. Hayden, who has meticulously retraced the itinerary (albeit with the aid of a car) calculates that Wordsworth and Jones walked at least 2,000 miles, averaging nearly 30 miles a day (*Wordsworth's Walking Tour of 1790* [Tulsa, OK: University of Tulsa Press, 1983], p. 119.

6   *The Letters of William and Dorothy Wordsworth: The Early Years, 1787–1805*, ed. E. de Selincourt, 2nd ed., rev. Chester L. Shaver (Oxford: Clarendon, 1967), p. 39.

7   For the demise of the Grand Tour, see the relevant chapters in Christopher Hibbert, *The Grand Tour* (London: Weidenfeld, 1969); Richard Lambert, *Grand Tour: A Journey in the Tracks of the Age of Aristocracy* (London: Faber, 1935); and Jeremy Black, *The British Abroad: The Grand Tour in the Eighteenth Century* (Stroud: Alan Sutton, 1992).

8   *The Collected Letters of S. T. Coleridge*, ed. E. L. Griggs, 6 vols. (Oxford: Clarendon Press, 1956–71), 1: 51. 'Perspiration' is quoted from the *Poetical Works*, ed. E. H. Coleridge (London: Oxford University Press, 1912).

9   J. Hucks, B. A., *A Pedestrian Tour through North Wales, in a Series of Letters* (London: J. Debrett & J. Edwards, 1795; rpt. Cardiff: University of Wales Press, 1979), p. 5.

10 *The Monthly Magazine* 8 (1799), p. 532.

11 Jeffrey C. Robinson, *The Walk: Notes on a Romantic Image* (Norman, OK and London: University of Oklahoma Press, 1989), p. 52. This elegant monograph is one of the very few precursor-studies I have come across for my exploration of pedestrian literature. Since completing this essay I have made acquaintance with two recent books that deserve more sustained consideration than I am able, belatedly, to give them: Roger Gilbert's *Walks in the World: Representation and Experience in Modern American Poetry* (Princeton, N J: Princeton University Press, 1991), though devoted to a different body of literature, has a stimulating opening chapter treating the genealogy and aesthetic credentials of the 'walk poem' as a genre; Anne D. Wallace's *Walking, Literature, and English Culture: The Origins and Uses of Peripatetic in the Nineteenth Century* (Oxford: Clarendon Press, 1993) covers a broad sweep of the British literary tradition, and carries a strong argument as to how socioeconomic changes in the late-eighteenth/early-nineteenth centuries generated an ideology of walking which has taken lasting root in popular, as well as literary, consciousness. Her thesis is addressed briefly below. Mention should also be made of John Elder's *Imagining the Earth: Poetry and the Vision of Nature* (Urbana and Chicago: University of Illinois Press, 1985), ch. 4, which offers a fruitful interpretation of *The Prelude* as a walking poem by virtue of the ongoing, irresolvable dialectic it embodies; and David Simpson's *Wordsworth's Historical Imagination: The Poetry of Displacement* (New York and London: Methuen, 1987), especially ch. 1, which unfolds from a discussion of the short poem 'Gipsies' some fascinating speculations on Wordsworth as a writer with a 'gypsy in his soul'.

12 See the account in Frida Knight's biography, *University Rebel: The Life of William Frend (1757–1841)* (London: Victor Gollancz, 1971).

13 John Cornwell, for example, makes a comment to this effect in *Coleridge: Poet and Revolutionary, 1772–1804* (London, 1973), p. 34.

14 Rev. Richard Warner, *A Walk through Wales, in August 1797* (Bath: R. Cruttwell, 1798), p. 7.

15 Wordsworth, *Letters* (op. cit.), 168, 59. Within two months of writing the second letter, Wordsworth was on his way to France, on the strength of money advanced by his relatives!

16 *The Prose Works of William Wordsworth*, ed. W. J. B. Owen and

J. W. Smyser, 3 vols. (Oxford: Clarendon Press, 1974), 2: 171. Subsequent page references are included in parentheses in the text.

17   Quotations from both poems are from the Oxford Authors edition of Wordsworth, ed. Stephen Gill (Oxford: Oxford University Press, 1984), which prints a text of the 1805 *Prelude*.

18   Rev. W. Bingley, *A Tour Round North Wales, Performed during the Summer of 1798*, 2 vols. (London: E. Williams, 1800), I, iv; Adam Walker, *Remarks Made in a Tour from London to the Lakes of Westmoreland and Cumberland in the Summer of 1791* (London: G. Nicol and C. Dilly, 1792), preface.

19   See William Gilpin, *Observations on the River Wye, and Several Parts of South Wales, etc. Relative Chiefly to Picturesque Beauty; Made in the Summer of the Year 1770* (London: R. Blamire, 1782), p. 7.

20   Thomas West, *A Guide to the Lakes in Cumberland, Westmorland and Lancashire*, 3rd ed. (London: B. Law *et al.*, 1784), p. 105.

21   Edmund Burke, *A Philosophical Enquiry into the Origin of our Ideas of the Sublime and Beautiful* (1757; Oxford and New York: Oxford University Press, 1990), p. 140. Subsequent page references are included in the text.

22   William Gilpin, *Three Essays: On Picturesque Beauty; on Picturesque Travel; and on Sketching Landscape* (London: R. Blamire, 1792), p. 48.

23   Uvedale Price, *An Essay on the Picturesque, as compared with the Sublime and Beautiful; and, on the Use of Studying Pictures, for the Purpose of Improving Real Landscape* (London: J. Robson, 1794), pp. 86–87.

24   Alan Liu, *Wordsworth: The Sense of History* (Stanford, CA: Stanford University Press, 1989), p. 6.

25   See Charles J. Patten, Jr., *Pleasurable Instruction: Form and Convention in Eighteenth-Century Travel Literature* (Berkeley and Los Angeles: University of California Press, 1978), *passim*.

26   William Hazlitt, *Selected Writings*, ed. Ronald Blythe (Harmondsworth: Penguin, 1970), pp. 141–42. Subsequent page references are included in the text.

27   Hazlitt, *Selected Writings*, p. 60.

28   See Seamus Heaney, 'The Makings of a Music: Reflections on Wordsworth and Yeats' in *Preoccupations: Selected Prose, 1968–1978* (London: Faber, 1980), pp. 61–78.

29   A bibliography of the interface between deconstruction and Romanticism is surely unnecessary, and would be impossibly long; as regards Romantic gender studies, I have in mind especially the critiques advanced, on diverse grounds, in Meena Alexander's *Women in Romanticism* (Basingstoke: Macmillan, 1989), Anne K. Mellor's *Romanticism and Gender* (London: Routledge, 1993), and Naomi Schor's *Reading in Detail: Aesthetics and the Feminine* (New York and London: Methuen, 1987).

30   See James H. Averill, *Wordsworth and the Poetry of Human Suffering* (Ithaca: Cornell University Press, 1980), pp. 61–68; Alan Liu, *Wordsworth*, pp. 61–137; John Williams, *Wordsworth: Romantic Poetry and Revolution* (Manchester: Manchester University Press, 1989), pp. 19–35; and Gerald Izenberg, *Impossible Individuality: Romanticism, Revolution, and the Origins of Modern Selfhood, 1787–1802* (Princeton, NJ: Princeton University Press, 1992), pp. 156–61.

31   *The Poetical Works of William Wordsworth*, ed. E. de Selincourt and Helen Darbishire, 5 vols. (Oxford: Clarendon Press, 1940–49), I, 319.

32   William Gilpin, *Observations, Relative Chiefly to Picturesque Beauty, Made in the Year 1772, on several Parts of England; Particularly the Mountains, and Lakes of Cumberland, and Westmoreland*, 2 vols. (London: R. Blamire, 1786), II, 11, 13.

33   Gerald Izenberg makes this point in *Impossible Individuality*, p. 158.

34   Gilbert, *Walks in the World*, p. 4.

Frankenstein, Werther and the Monster of Love

Fred Botting
Lancaster University

> Isolate being is a deception ... and the couple becoming stable at last, is a negation of love. But what goes from one lover to the other is a movement that puts an end to isolation or at least makes it waver. Isolate being is risked, opens to what's beyond itself, to what's beyond the couple even – monstrous excess.[1]

A strange love quivers between Victor Frankenstein and the unnamed monster, producing a movement that absorbs subject and object in a terrifyingly reversible relation where ideal unity cedes to nothingness. For them, love leaps beyond limits but also encounters absolute difference: the excesses of sublime passion loose monstrous figures. Opening up questions of the self, its being, life, objects and language, love is inextricably entangled in the formation and dissolution of the western subject as it was shaped in the late eighteenth and early nineteenth centuries. In the spark of love that flickers between *Frankenstein* and *The Sorrows of Young Werther* the Romantic subject is taken to the limits of fullness and loss, transgressing all other bounds: love is both vital and fatal, presenting 'the zenith of subjectivity' and 'an extreme of solitude'.[2] In the experience of these impossible limits, however, love discloses a division at the heart of subjectivity, a division wherein negativity rends unity with the movements of desire, leaving plenitude at the level of a narcissistic fantasy that is constituted and displaced by structures of language.

The split that love tries to cover discloses, not the ideal image glimpsed by flights of amorous fantasy, but the monstrosity of subjectivity itself. Love, then, is a textual affair, bound up with structures of signification. In and between *Frankenstein* and *Werther* it is the effects of romance that both shape and displace the subject of love who is associated with the imagination, creativity and unity of Romanticism. Many readings of Mary Shelley's novel have interpreted it as a critique of male Romanticism that displays the egoism underlying Romantic ideals.[3] The homosocial identifications between male figures, the drive for unity manifested in their projects and the embedded 'chinese box' structure of the text suggest the mirror as the governing metaphor.[4]

157

Reflecting only male desires and their obliteration of all differences, especially sexual difference, the novel stresses the lethal effects of egoism and narcissism as they are defined by a patriarchal symbolic economy. While this essay shares assumptions about *Frankenstein*'s critical examination of Romantic subjectivity, it analyses the way the novel not only critiques the effects of masculine desire but examines the structural, cultural and textual issues at stake in both their production and their disclosure of monstrous excess.

Love and the One

Narcissism, however, cannot provide the grounds for an easy critique of masculinity, though it remains crucial to the formation of subjectivity. In *Tales of Love*, Julia Kristeva discusses the homological power of Eros, the ideal of Self which unifies universal and particular (p. 62). For Kristeva, the unity of the One found in Plotinus' comments on love and God establishes the condition for interiority: 'that *autou eros* that I see as the sublime hypostasis of narcissistic love was to constitute the decisive step in the assumption of inner space, the introspective space of the western psyche' (p. 111). In a secular world, the human subject falls in love with its Self, the external form constituting the ideal and perfect being, internalised as One's Self. While, for Kristeva, the subject can be captivated by metaphors as much as its own ideal image, thus leaving the binary specular frame of narcissism open to movement, the account of narcissism displays a theological structure in its ideals of unity and oneness. Such an idealised version of love implicates the Romantic philosophical tradition in the literary one.

Hegel's phenomenological system places love in a central position. In 'The Spirit of Christianity', Hegel states: 'To love God is to feel one's self in the "all" of life, with no restrictions, in the infinite. In this feeling of harmony there is no universality, since in harmony the particular is not in discord but in concord, or otherwise there would be no harmony.' Love breaks the 'might of objectivity' since it has no limits.[5]

Love unites subject and object.[6] It overcomes separation, opposition and division, partaking of the 'whole of life': 'In love the separate does still remain, but as something united and no longer as something separate; life [in the subject] senses life [in the object].'[7] Love reconciles, implicitly at least, the dialectical divisions of consciousness, articulating the 'individual divine Man' with the 'universal divine Man', the community.[8]

Feeling, the heart, provides the possibility of reconciling the subject to principles of rationality as well as community. The distinction, moreover, is framed in familial terms: the father is the figure to whom consciousness of knowing and doing belong, while the mother is linked to feeling and love. In the *Philosophy of Right*, the family again provides the image of the relationship between consciousness and love:

> The family, as the immediate substantiality of mind, is specifically characterised by love, which is mind's feeling of its own unity. Hence in a family, one's frame of mind is to have self-consciousness of one's individuality within this unity as the absolute essence of oneself, with the result that one is not in it as an independent person but as a member.[9]

Individuality has its autonomy sacrificed to the greater and essential unity of being while still sustaining its self-consciousness. Love, as 'mind's feeling of its own unity', extends, transcendentally, to encompass the totality of being; it is at once the condition and the beyond of human unity.

The image of unity proposed by Hegel's concept of love, however, depends on an experience of separation, as does the subject in the attainment of self-consciousness. Aware of this separation, the subject 'posits this [presently unachievable] unification in a future state'. Love's unity is deferred; the subject, separated from the object, encounters the distance from the ideal object of unity: 'Religion is one with love. The beloved is not opposed to us, he is one with our essential being; we see only ourselves in him – and yet also he is still not we – miracle that we cannot grasp.' ('Two fragments', pp. 262–3) Love's ideal, its divine self-image, remains distanced, ungraspable. The separation from ideal unity, however, becomes a condition for human development. Hegel uses the family to illustrate the relationship between the intuition of love, one's separation from it and the recovery of unity. Lovers, united in the manifold whole of life and love, lose consciousness of their difference from each other in the abolition of their separate selves. A child is born, testament to the union of selves and bodies, 'a seed of immortality, of the eternally self-developing and self-generating [race], has come into existence. What has been united [in the child] is not divided again; [in love and through] God has acted and created.' ('Love', p. 307)

However, while the child signifies the lovers' union with each other in the wider sphere of manifold being, the child's own unity is rather limited:

> This unity [the child], however, is only a point, [an undifferentiated unity,] a seed; the lovers cannot contribute to it as to give it a manifold in itself at the start. Their union is free from all inner division; in it there is no working on an opposite. Everything which gives the newly begotten child a manifold life and a specific existence, it must draw into itself, set over against itself, and unify with itself. The seed breaks free from its original unity, turns ever more and more to

opposition, and begins to develop. Each stage of its development is a separation, and its aim in each is to regain for itself the full riches of life [enjoyed by the parents]. Thus the process is: unity, separated opposites, reunion. After their union the lovers separate again, but in the child their union has become unseparated.

('Love', pp. 307–8)

The child functions in two different registers at once: for the parents it is a symbol of lasting union, the realisation of their greater existence in love; for itself it exists in separation, aiming to regain a lost unity that, the last sentence implies, may only be illusory. Love provides the subject with an ideal of its own unity as nostalgia and wish, a unity lost in the present and consigned to both an irrecuperable past and a distant future.

The fundamental contradiction of love appears in the renewed distancing of subject and object. Love, the ultimate and ideal unity of human consciousness, is wanting. Indeed, it exists as want:

Love's intuition seems to fulfil the demand for completeness; but there is a contradiction. Intuition, representative thinking, is something restrictive, something receptive only of something restricted; but here the object intuited [God] would be something infinite. The infinite cannot be carried in this vessel.

('Christianity', p. 253)

Love exceeds consciousness and mind is left incomplete, an incompleteness which determines the subject's want of unity, its want of an ideal and the totality of being.

Both Frankenstein and Werther are determined by the incomplete dialectic of love, subjected to the want of unity it prescribes. They both speak the exorbitant language of the Romantic imagination and indulge in passions whose ultimate object is the idealised form of self. Victor's creative enterprise, the solitude with which it is pursued and the object to which it is addressed, links him to Romantic models. Werther, similarly, speaks of the imagination and the possibility of artistic expression 'if I had some clay or wax to model'.[10] Love constitutes Werther as the consummate artist, for though unable to work he feels he has 'never been more of a painter than I am now'. As a Romantic artist, Werther identifies nature as the locus of total unity. Alone in the folds of nature, Werther feels the unifying presence of being; it elevates him, enabling his participation in the 'breath of the All-loving One who sustains us as we float in illimitable bliss' (p. 3). This unity, as with Hegelian conceptions, assumes the fusion of internal and external worlds through the animating breath of life: it is the *spiritus* that unites human and divine being in the poetry of Wordsworth and Coleridge.[11]

Such unity is found, also, in love as it presents the subject with the possibility of transcendence. Love elevates the subject himself: 'it is, after all, certain that nothing in the world renders a man indispensable save love' (p. 48). In love, Werther recovers the fullness of being which his first letter describes as having been lost. The letter states that he has left the love of his friend behind in order to escape the apparently scandalous results of his rejection of another woman who has 'entertained' him. Early in his epistolary account he recalls the loss of a woman friend whose presence elevated his own sense of being, allowing him to become 'everything I could be' (p. 6). Nature and women are the locus of love, linking the totality of being to the presence of maternal affection. Not only are women in Werther's past substitutes for lost maternal affection: Lotte is herself identified with the wonderful mother whose story has both Albert and Werther on the brink of losing consciousness.

Maternal figures predominate in Frankenstein's account of his idealised upbringing. Frankenstein is born into a family of love, the offspring of loving parents. Describing the sequence of events, that for him, culminated in his creation, Victor presents an environment that corresponds to the union of love Hegel associates with the family. His parents are united in 'bonds of devoted affection' while their child is 'their plaything and idol', a heaven-sent symbol of their unity.[12] The centre of their dutiful attentions, the 'being to which they had given life', Victor is their 'only care'. Later, with the addition of an orphan girl to the family, the harmonious tones of Victor continue. She is another version of him: 'the passionate and reverential attachment with which all regarded her became, while I shared it, my pride and delight' (p. 35). Elizabeth is an extension of Victor, a mark of his wish for completion, sign of his mother's love, a gift, a 'pretty present' (p. 34). She is, however, also a dangerous supplement, a sign of his lack in that she fulfils his mother's wish to have a daughter (p. 34). Not the object of absolute love, Victor is incomplete because he is not a girl.

Victor, the 'seed' and symbol of his parents' love, is left wanting the unity that it leaves in the past and promises in the future. His creative project, furthermore, stays within the bounds prescribed by the familial metaphor. Frankenstein pursues feminine nature in order expropriate the knowledge, both carnal and metaphysical, that will enable him to understand its hidden laws and possess the secret of life. He describes his victory over nature as the achievement of the 'summit of his desires'. In this 'most gratifying consummation' he reaches the pinnacle of subjectivity and the end of his 'painful labour' (p. 52). His penetration, consummation and labour signal the attainment of totality, success in reproduction, conception and creation. His identity is ideal, his union complete: beyond gender distinction, having absorbed the roles of lover, father, mother and child, no differences block the overwhelming fusion of the transcendent moment, no opposition or separation impedes the rush to continuous being. Like the Hegelian love-child or the Wordsworthian child, he has superseded his parents and fathered himself.

The plenitude that swells within Frankenstein as he enjoys this moment of idealised erotic self-union lead to boundless speculations of a metaphysical nature, speculations whose object is the divine form of the self (p. 54):

> No one can conceive the variety of feelings which bore me onwards, like a hurricane, in the first enthusiasm of success. Life and death appeared to me ideal bounds, which I should first break through, and pour a torrent of light into our dark world. A new species would bless me as both its creator and source; many happy and excellent natures would owe their being to me. No father should claim the gratitude of his child so completely as I should deserve theirs.

The aspirations to absolute paternal power are uttered with a passion that is both erotic and catastrophic. Wanting no less than the summit of being, the human realisation of divinity wherein the control of self and others is absolute, he transcends all limits. Being divine and human, creator and source, origin and end, cause and object of total love, he imagines the eroticised ideal of self. The images of natural energy, the hurricane and the flood, signal the catastrophe of amorous passion, the 'enthusiasm' that shatters all bounds in the first flush of love.

Want

Love, however, is predicated upon loss: the separation from parental figures of unity for Hegel, the risk of isolate being for Bataille, and, for Frankenstein and Werther, the loss of self-presence associated with maternal and natural being. The fullness Frankenstein projects produces not the lasting union of self-copulation: the realisation of his creative power instead reopens the divisions that he imagined he had transcended, producing a reaffirmation of oppositions and differences and a repetition of his separation from his ideal. The creation of life does not deliver the fantasy of homogeneous and total existence, but presents an uncontrollable flood of heterogeneity. As the monster stirs with life the creator is horrified by its physical incongruity, his failure perceived in distinctly aesthetic terms: the creature's ugliness negates the visions that inspired its creation. This embodiment of life in full repulses the creator. The monster presents the inverted image of Frankenstein's narcissistic project; its animation overturning the creative ideals in a process of complete and monstrous reversal: beauty cedes to ugliness, hope to disappointment, success to failure, attraction to repulsion. As the passage continues further reversals dismantle the visionary world: fleeing the creation, Frankenstein sleeps to dream a nightmare in which his fiance turns into the worm-ridden corpse of his mother: death, decay, and sexual difference turn eroticism into continual catastrophe, fragmenting being, separating subject from object rather than enabling their unification. Frankenstein notes how his world has turned upside down. The inversion of poles from life to death, union to separation reopens the gap and arouses the subject's sense of absolute loss. Mimicking the convulsions that brought the creature to life, Frankenstein's throes of despair constitute an unavowed recognition of his own monstrosity.

Werther, too, is possessed by a monstrous figure, undergoing the dramatic reversals characteristic of the Romantic subject of love. Bereft of the tiny acknowledgements a lover depends upon, Werther's bright vision of the world is replaced by a bleak prospect. Bliss and fullness once produced in sympathy with nature now cause 'unbearable torment', the infinity of being remains a memory that exacerbates his sense of total separation: 'it is as though a curtain has been drawn from before my soul, and the scene of eternal life is being transformed before my eyes into the abyss of the of the ever open grave' (p. 52). Life turns to death, being to nothingness, as nature becomes a consuming destructive force rendering all beings transient and mortal entities. The figure of the monster dominates this vision: 'I see nothing but a monster, eternally devouring ...' (p. 52). Unity dissolves, self is lost: 'I cannot, I cannot regain command of myself. Wherever I go I encounter an apparition which totally deranges me' (p. 90). The appearance of the monster, for both Werther and Frankenstein, signals the decomposition of their narcissistic fantasy.

In *Frankenstein*, the appearance of the monster constitutes the turning point, the moment of complete reversal which discloses the negativity inherent in Romantic idealism. Life, presence and unity confront death, absence and difference, situating the subject in a world, not of love, benevolence and completeness, but of desire, loss and insufficiency. Werther is utterly without a place, his love of self having taken him beyond all symbolic, social relations, beyond reason and prohibition as is evident from his discussion with Albert (p. 61). Frankenstein's love has also transgressed all conventions, boundaries and laws to leave him isolated and apart. The monster magnifies this condition: more solitary, more separate, with no social bounds or familial bonds, the creature has no recognised place except as outcast. Significantly, it is the monster who severs all Frankenstein's ties with the human community: killing his bride and causing the death of his relations, the creature magnifies the egotism rather than the grandeur of the creator's project. The separation, moreover, emphasises the desire and violence at the heart of the idealist project.

Alexandre Kojève's rereading of Hegel underlines the movements of negativity and desire by examining the function of the master-slave dialectic in the formation of the subject. For Kojeve, self-consciousness cannot exist without a desire that is orientated towards a non-natural object, 'toward something that goes beyond the given reality'. Not an object in the sense of a static entity, but 'the revelation of an emptiness, the presence of the absence of reality', it is desire itself which constitutes a subject entirely different from the 'animal I', a subject constructed, consumed and created in and by desire. Since desire realises itself in the negation of a given reality, this subject will produce itself by its actions: 'it will be (in the future) what it was (in the past), this negation being accomplished with a view to what it will become.'[13] The subject is thus 'an emptiness which receives a real positive content only by the negating action that satisfies Desire in destroying, transforming, and "assimilating" the desired non-I' (p. 4). The negation of objects also involves a risk in which animal desire can be transformed into human desire: 'man's humanity "comes to light" only if he risks his (animal) life for the sake of human Desire' (p. 7). Human desire thus depends, not on a world of objects, but on other desires, the desires of others. Human or social reality exists as 'a set of Desires mutually desiring one another as Desires'. In this way, Kojève explains, desire produces 'a free and historical individual, conscious of his individuality, his freedom, his history, and finally, his historicity' (p. 6). Humans desire 'the Desire of the Other'; they wish to be desired, loved, recognised as beings possessing human value, as individuals. To attain this position, however, demands a struggle, a fight in which a being's life is risked in order to be recognised by the Other. The struggle for prestige or mastery is the key moment in this process: the victor achieves the position of master while the loser takes the role of slave and 'must give up his desire and satisfy the desire of the other: he must "recognise" the other without being "recognised" by him' (p. 8). As well as being perceived by the master as a slave, s/he also perceives her/himself as such.

This dialectic emerges as the basis of Frankenstein's project and his relationship with the monster. Taking the form of a struggle with feminised nature, whose 'citadel' he imagines he can conquer, the object of desire, the secret of life, is shaped by the Other, the goal of the world's wisest men (p. 52). His desire for mastery means that he risks his physical life, making himself seriously ill during his experiment. It also depends on the recognition of the 'new species' he creates: the recognition of these 'slaves', however, is insufficient to sustain his sense of mastery. It is only at the end, too late for Frankenstein, that he encounters an equal: Walton's recognition provides the image of his own desire. The master's position, as Kojève observes, is redundant. The sense of mastery, moreover, crumbles: Frankenstein cannot recognise his creation, and nor does the creation recognise the master. In the Alps, the strength, agility and eloquence of the monster subjects the creator to his demand, not for Victor's recognition, but for the recognition of another, a female mate. Initially Frankenstein acquiesces to the demand. With the half-finished female monster before him and the eyes of the creature upon him, he rebels, destroying the new creation. At this point, the angry monster makes explicit the reversal that has occurred in their relationship, calling the creator a slave (p. 167).

Given Frankenstein's act of resistance, this is a belated cry of mastery. It the leaves the pair within the master-slave dialectic, an incomplete dialectic which they play out in the remainder of the novel in a mutual, exclusive and reversible pursuit of the other. In the process Frankenstein is severed from all ties but those with the monster. It is, at last, an exclusive, if unresolved relationship, a dialectic without sublation. In the precipitation of one towards the other, however, they are erotically bound together in the momentum of true love. Indeed, 'the one you fight is the one you admire the most'.[14] As Frankenstein's double, the inverted form of the creator's ideal image, the monster constitutes the embodiment of his desire and, simultaneously, the resistance that activates it.

Love depends on the other. For Werther, it is Lotte's love that supports his recognition of himself as his own ideal: 'Loves me!', he declares, 'how the thought exalts me in my own eyes! How I – I may tell you, perhaps, for you can sympathise with such an emotion – How I worship myself since she loves me' (p. 36). Made possible by the other's recognition, the idealisation opens to the infinite union desired by the subject. Like Frankenstein, it is nature and the totality it represents that is the ultimate object of desire (p. 31):

> Oh! friend, when the world grows dim before my eyes and earth and sky are absorbed into my soul like the form of a beloved, I am often consumed with longing and think, ah! would that I could express it, would that I could breathe on to paper that which lives so warm and full within me, so that it might become the mirror of my soul as my soul is the mirror of the eternal God! My friend – but it is beyond my power, and I succumb to the splendour of what lies before me.

As the physical world recedes under the longing gaze of the Romantic subject a transcendental dimension unfolds as its horizon and object of voracious introjection. Beyond difference, divine in its plenitude, the oneness that is imagined also involves the loss of identity, a sacrifice to the Other and absorption in its sublime splendour. Consuming and consumed, the subject remains dislocated in the momentum of a strange and impossible fusion.

It is a fusion that offers, not life in full, but absence and death. What Werther wants is not a specific object, but like Frankenstein, the infinity of being. 'Love', as Bataille argues, 'is a desire to possess an object as great as the totality of desire' (*Guilty*, p. 152). As the summit of a subject's desire, love activates the passionate momentum that exceeds dialectical resolution. Bataille takes the negativity at the core of the Hegelian system further than Kojève. What he terms 'unemployed negativity' does not reconcile opposition at a higher level but 'breaks closed systems' (*Guilty*, pp. 123–4). Extreme states of experience display the movements and effects of negativity. The joy, the ecstasy of love is the consummation of the self in a passion that takes it outside itself towards its object which is neither being nor nothingness:

> This object, chaos of light and shadow, is catastrophe. I perceive it as object; my thought, however, shapes it according to its image, at the same time that it is its reflection. Perceiving it, my thought sinks into annihilation as into a fall wherein one emits a cry. Something immense, exorbitant, is liberated in all directions with a noise of catastrophe; this emerges from an unreal, infinite void, at the same time loses itself in it, with the shock of a blinding flash.[15]

The catastrophe, exploding consciousness, liberates the separate subject, not in a unifying fusion with a determinable object or ideal, but in its sense of absolute loss, its plunge into an overwhelming torrent of negativity. This is the condition which befalls Frankenstein after the creation of the monster, his enthusiasm of discovery inverted. Werther, too, sees 'eternal life' transformed 'into the abyss of the ever open grave' (p. 52). The abyss into which subjectivity dissolves is the 'yawning gap' that love opens between subject and object (Bataille, *Inner*, p. 59). The 'yawning gap' also opens a wound in the narcissistic ego, the 'principle of insufficiency', that mocks being with its incompleteness (Bataille, *Inner*, p. 81). Incompleteness puts all assumptions of unity into question. Unity is rendered 'unavowable' and lost; being is lacking; the subject left wanting.[16]

Death

These poles of unity and dissolution chart the limits, the extremes of possibility for the subject, as it remains separated, dislocated by the momentum of its excessive passion. The mirror, reflecting the subject from where it is not, discloses an impossible ideal. The narcissism of amorous passions leave subjectivity between an other that it cannot efface and an Other which it cannot grasp. There is a last, negative direction, however, for union, the fatal path of Narcissus, sacrificing himself to his image. At the fatal rendezvous of life and death, the love of self-mastery, control and possession is sacrificed to the Other on the condition that the subject will be free from its subjection to the forces of desire, loss and separation. The beyond that love promised, the transcendence of limited and alienated existence and an ecstatic entry into a world of being and self-presence turns, in the force of the passion it looses, into absolute abandonment to the Other. The totality of being becomes the totality of dissolution. As Bataille notes, the attempt of the ego to exceed itself, to surpass its solitary and isolated state by uniting with another in the 'pure eroticism' of love's passions or in bodily sensuality produces an intensity that leads it towards death.[17]

In *Passion and Society*, Denis de Rougemont discusses the intimate connection between of love and death:

> Romance only comes into existence where love is fatal, frowned upon and doomed by life itself. What stirs lyrical poets to their finest flights is neither the delight of the senses nor the fruitful contentment of the settled couple; not the satisfaction of love, but its passion.[18]

Articulating love and death in an explosive dynamic, passion uncouples, disconnects, the subject from all fixed relations of law, reason or society in a metaphorical flight to a higher state of being, the beyond and finality of all desire: 'Passion requires that the *self* shall become greater than all things, as solitary and as powerful as God. Without knowing it, passion also requires that beyond its apotheosis death shall indeed be the end of all things' (p. 260).

In his instant of self-destruction, Werther imagines the 'perpetual embrace' guaranteed by the divinity. But the violence of his death transgresses every limit of subjectivity and a refusal to serve any master. The '*non serviam*' is, Bataille notes, the devil's motto, the resistance that determines the lethal condition of human life, the satanic sovereignty that refuses all forms of subjection.[19] At last exceeding law and reason, Werther becomes sovereign and dies. His Satanic rebellion against all law, brings him close to the monster who, along with Werther, identifies Milton's Satan as an appropriate model. It is Frankenstein's monster, a more perfect form of Werther (more perfect because he is more hideous and rejected), who presents a more complete gesture of gloriously pathetic and heroically tragic self-sacrifice. The destructively vital passion that sustained his relationship with another being in an dialectic without resolution ends with the death of Frankenstein. The creature mourns the creator's demise, another's death moving him beyond the limits of his demand for love to disclose a desolate space of subjectivity. As Blanchot, discussing Bataille's notion of 'inner experience', observes, this space disturbs the boundaries of selfhood: 'Death, the death of the other, like friendship or love, clears the space of intimacy or interiority which is never (for Georges Bataille) the space of a subject, but a gliding beyond limits' (*Community*, p. 16).

With the death of the creator, the monster accedes to the Other's desire, destroying himself. Sacrificing himself to the Other, an act of relinquishing and giving, the monster performs the culminating moment of the creator's project, the consumption of being.[20] In this attenuation of the human subject's sacred position, the monster's act affirms the effervescence at the moment of its evanescence (Bataille, *Religion*, pp. 52–3). The monster's solitude is complete, as his last words, addressed to his dead creator, acknowledge (p. 223):

> 'Blasted as thou wert, my agony was still superior to thine; for the bitter sting of remorse will not cease to rankle in my wounds until death shall close them for ever.' 'But soon,' he cried, with sad and solemn enthusiasm, 'I shall die, and what I now feel be no longer felt. Soon these burning miseries will be extinct. I shall ascend my funeral pile triumphantly, and exult in the agony of the torturing flames. The light of that conflagration will fade away; my ashes will be swept into the sea by the winds.

This act, the monster promises, will take place at the Pole, the literal and metaphorical object of Walton's and Frankenstein's desire. There, in a cataclysmic reversal of the Romantic creator's project, the monster plans to fulfil the final joyous ecstasies of the human subject, becoming one with the Other. Death heals the wounds of subjectivity. In an overwhelming fusion and rending of opposites, fire and light amid ice and darkness, life and death entwine in a joyous embrace, a total consummation of self and Other, achieved at the moment the subject achieves ultimate mastery, self-possession and autonomy in an act of destruction. The ashes remain as the trace of an isolated being now at one with, dissolved in, the greater being of Nature. 'The path of my departure was free' as, in his reflections on *The Sorrows of Young Werther*, the monster quotes this line from P. Shelley's 'Mutability'.

Achieving absolute freedom, the monster offers a glimpse of the sovereign desire of the subject. At the end of *Frankenstein*, the reader, suspended between the impossible poles charted by the novel, follows Walton's disillusioned gaze at the monster disappearing in darkness and distance. The monster's promise remains to illuminate his departure with an intensity that testifies to the persistence of Frankensteinian desire and the negativity that underlines its sovereign wish:

> To remain a man in the light requires the courage of demented incomprehension; it means being set on fire, letting go with screams

of joy, waiting for death, acting in a realization of some presence you don't and can't know. It means becoming love and blind light yourself, and attaining the perfect incomprehension of the sun.

(Bataille, Guilty, p. 20)

But the monster only promises to immolate himself. And how many promises are kept in *Frankenstein*?[21] It is a death the novel leaves unrepresented.

For Werther, death completes love's selfish sacrifice. It both ruptures and completes the narcissistic fantasy of unity, attenuating the divine at the expense of life. However, Werther's passion, though endlessly stating the will to exceed all limits, repeatedly teeters on the brink of the sacrificial and apotheotic moment. In speaking of suicide, he continually retreats from the act. For him it has a different end (p. 116):

> For the last time then, for the last time I open these eyes. They are alas! to see the sun no more; it is hidden by a dark and misty day. Mourn then, Nature! thy son, thy friend, thy lover nears his end.

Nature is enjoined to mourn an ideal figure, Werther himself, who, though imaginarily already eclipsed, is not yet physically lost. Werther indulges in quite a number of last moments and mournful speculations of the loss of his own ideal. In the anguish of repeated last moments the subject hangs on passionately, waiting for some word of reprieve from the Other. Unable to attain the ecstatic heights of being that are intimated in his relationships with Nature and Lotte, he pleads for their understanding, their recognition. Addressing Nature as a lover and demanding suitable rites of mourning, Werther shows that he cannot conceive of his demise by projecting himself, as powerful absence, into a future in which he will have no vital part. Indeed, as he goes on to say to Lotte, he has no conception of the meaning of 'the last' or to 'pass away' (pp. 116–17).

The inability to conceive of finitude displays the recalcitrance of narcissism. Werther hangs on to the dream of his ideal and infinite self. This belies his gestures of sacrifice and statements of utter dissolution: 'Friend, I am lost! She can do with me what she will' (p. 88). Werther, however, does not submit to her will. Rejected, he keeps coming back. His returns, and especially his explanation of self-sacrifice, have little of the ring of true devotion about them. Instead, in the insinuations of responsibility (stating that it was she who provided the means of death), in describing the death of another lover (Lotte was not the first and only!) and in the visions of her suffering, Werther sets out to hurt her. The aggressive tone of his last letters construct a childish wish to punish her for her rejection of him. He taunts and threatens her with his own death, his last weapon in his fight to win her recognition. It is also the last gesture of a subject glimpsing the impossibility of mastery: to have effects on others bears some precious, pathetic testimony to his continuing powers. The vain cry of 'She is mine! You are mine!' only repeats his lack of mastery (p. 118).

The repeated and vain gestures of mastery with which Goethe's novel draws to a close, situate Werther as a resolutely narcissistic being. His gestures, the projections and mournful recuperations of his idealised image, produce a game of mastery, of rejecting and returning the lost object of love in an effort to overcome the trauma of separation. For Freud, the child's 'fort/da' game attempts to overcome the 'distressing experience' caused by the disappearance of the love object of the narcissistic ideal ego.[22] Werther, it seems, predicates his ideal on the wish to recuperate the lost figure of his own ego. As Lacan observes, the mother is central to Werther's narcissism: the object, Lotte cuddling a child, provides 'an entirely satisfying' image for the *anaclitic* narcissism as it coincides with his own fundamental image.[23] Throughout the novel, maternal figures are linked to the subject's ecstasies. Albert and Werther are brought to the brink of ecstasy by Lotte's relation of the story of a wonderful mother. In another letter Werther asks his friend not to send any books. Not wishing to add to the 'ferment' his heart is already in, Werther is content with the 'lullabies' of Homer. The maternal songs that soothe a child to sleep offer a cure to the restless changeability of his 'sick heart' where other books enliven or excite, rousing the fluctuations of extreme desire. With Werther's last words the mother is firmly placed at the centre of the beloved image: after death he will be united with Lotte and her mother (p. 128).

The mother occupies a central place in Frankenstein's world. Idealised, her loss forms the site on which Frankenstein's desires take their particular form: to conquer death is to overcome her death and recuperate her, while to 'give birth' to life is both to fulfil her desire for a daughter and to occupy the place of the mother. Frankenstein's nightmare, however, presents the irrecuperable maternal loss: his mother, after his act of creation, remains dead. As the absolute condition and limit of life, death signals the impossibility of his narcissistic fantasy, anaclitically invested in the figures of Elizabeth and his mother. Immortality, unconditional love, life and being are replaced by absolute and irreparable loss. This limit describes the shift Freud observes in the significance of the double. For the ideal ego of primary narcissism the double provides intimations of immortality, but in secondary narcissism the double takes on the function of ego ideal as a 'harbinger of death'.[24] At the turning point of Frankenstein's catastrophic creation, the double has altered its position from primary to secondary narcissism, from promise of divine immortality to monstrous finitude.

Passion of the Signifier

While love seems to define Romantic subjectivity as profoundly and
inescapably narcissistic, its effects exceed the closure of the mirror. For
Lacan, the subject of love is a narcissistic entity whose sense of unity
remains imaginary and emerges in a master-slave dialectic with its own
image. However, the narcissistic subject is doubled and introduces
effects of signification that enable and exceed the very constitution of
the subject. Love, as it highlights and displaces the possibility of being
raises, for the subject, questions of its imaginary unity by providing an
image which though reflecting like a mirror and thus profoundly
narcissistic opens on to symbolic relations: 'It's one's own ego that one
loves in love, one's own ego made real on the imaginary level' (*Seminar
I*, p. 142). In the mirror, as in love, the subject glimpses and identifies
with the total form of itself in an act of mastery that remains imaginary
because it misrecognises the other, the image, as itself. The subject has
not yet achieved mastery over the motor coordination of its body even
though psychological mastery is, in the mirror moment, anticipated.[25]

The mastery of an ideal ego is assumed before the fragmented desire
(and body) is regulated in the dimension of the symbolic. The mirror's
specular relation is, for Lacan, a mirage whose illusory status is manifested
in the look of love: 'when in love, I solicit a look, what is profoundly
unsatisfying and always missing is that – You never look at me from
the place from which I see you'. The imaginary, like love, remains a
deception:

> As a specular mirage, love is essentially a deception. It is situated in
> the field established at the level of the pleasure reference, of that sole
> signifier necessary to introduce a perspective centred on the Ideal
> point, capital I, placed somewhere in the Other, from which the
> Other sees me, in the form I like to be seen.[26]

Love discloses the subject's dependence on the Other, the 'locus of
signifying convention' (*Ecrits*, p. 173). An imaginary phenomenon, love
and its narcissistic subject is relocated as a symbolic construction, an effect
of linguistic and cultural practices, dependent on speaking subjects
amorously addressing an Other from whom they want a reply, a sign of
recognition.

The master-slave dialectic's structure operates in a symbolic framework as well: the Other for whom the slave works prescribes the rules
that determine the latter's existence and identity (*Seminar I*, pp. 146,
222–3). Love, like narcissism, is divided between symbolic and imaginary registers. The ideal ego of primary narcissism is associated with the
latter, the ego ideal with the former. In the imaginary register the loved

object is confused with the ego ideal. Functioning as the phallus, the ego ideal with which the subject identifies guides it beyond imaginary captation and binds it within symbolic relations (*Seminar I*, pp. 134, 112, 141). In the symbolic, the subject enunciates a demand, a demand that it wants to be loved for everything which composes it, a demand in which it is recognised in the fullness of its being. This demand remains bound up with the functions of signification rather than tied to the real being: 'it is at the centre of the signifiers – insofar as the final demand to be deprived of something real is essentially linked to the primary sym-bolization which is wholly contained in the signification of the gift of love.'[27] Wanting the gift of love from the Other, a presence that is at once its own self-presence, the subject goes on wanting the impossible since it is a gift that the Other, absolute in its differential condition, cannot give. Instead, in the hollow, the gap opened up by the subject's exorbitant demand, desire is activated and displaced. The ego ideal or super-ego situates the subject as 'always wanting to elevate himself to the dignity of the ideals of the father, of the master, and who imagines that that is how he will attain the object of his desire.' The mastery that is imagined, however, places the subject in an unstable and reversible position, subject to the Other and the image, the other; 'the funda-mental position of the ego confronted with its image is indeed this immediate reversibility of the position of master and servant.'[28]

Love, in the movement it enables between imaginary and symbolic, between primary and secondary narcissism, sustains a generally disrup-tive momentum:

> Love is a phenomenon which takes place on the imaginary level, and which provokes a veritable subduction of the symbolic, a sort of annihilation, of peturbation of the function of the ego-ideal. Love reopens the door – as Freud puts it, not mincing his words – to perfection.
>
> (*Seminar I*, p. 142)

Such perfection glimpsed in the peturbation of the symbolic opens on to a 'beyond' of language. Words of love produce 'a rupture in the system of language'.[29]

For Lacan, the perturbation, the rupture and the beyond it discloses, associate love with the sacred, an imaginary beyond that remains para-doxically beyond the imaginary dimension:

> The primary imaginary relation provides the fundamental framework for all possible eroticism. It is a condition to which the object of Eros as such must be submitted. The object relation must always submit

to the narcissistic framework and be inscribed in it. Certainly it transcends it, but in a manner which it is impossible to realise on the imaginary plane. That is what introduces for the subject the necessity of what I would call love. A creature needs some reference to the beyond of language, to a pact, to a commitment which constitutes him, strictly speaking, as an other, a reference included in the general or, to be more exact, universal system of interhuman symbols. No love can be functionally realisable in the human community, save by means of a specific pact, which, whatever the form it takes, always tends to become isolated off into a specific function, at one and the same time within language and outside of it. That is what we call the function of the sacred, which is beyond the imaginary relation.

(Seminar I, p. 174)

At the limits of language, which as Other cannot be transcended, the subject of love finds transcendence. Erotic love, 'the universal presence of a power binding subjects together' and passionate love, 'a sort of psychological catastrophe', meet at this seam of imaginary, symbolic and beyond (*Seminar I*, p. 112). The sacred becomes the ultimate imaginary object that remains ungraspable, impossible, something that functions in the mode of anamorphosis: 'what we seek in the illusion is something in which the illusion as such in some way transcends itself, destroys itself, by demonstrating that it is only there as a signifier' (*Ethics*, p. 136). Love, through the sacred, discloses the field of the Thing 'onto which is projected something beyond, something at the point of origin of the signifying chain, the place in which doubt is cast on all that is the place of being' (*Ethics*, p. 214). This locus displays love as a textual thing, enmeshing the subject in a network that it imagines it can transcend. It also, however, severs love from its associations with being and human presence, signifying the emptiness of the subject of language.

Romance Metaphor

Discussing the structures of the courtly romance, Lacan elaborates on the 'inhuman character of the object of love', on how it supplants living beings with the movement of desire and signifiers: 'this love that led some people to acts close to madness was addressed at living beings, people with names, but who were not present in their fleshly and histor-ical reality … they were there in any case in their being as reason, as signifier' (*Ethics*, pp. 215–16). The romance, like the literature that suc-ceeded it, situates love in relation to a thing that cannot be symbolised, a thing which lies as the ungraspable remainder of the subject of language,

with which it desires reunification but which stays forever out of reach
for the I who is subject to 'the passion of the signifier' (*Ethics*, p. 143).
It is the thing as lost self, as the ambivalent double constantly posited
by poetic creation which deploys a 'form of sublimation specific to art'
that 'consists in positing an object I can only describe as terrifying, an
inhuman partner' (*Ethics*, p. 150).

It is this thing, this double, that emerges in the writings on love by
the poet Percy Shelley. Love presents an imaginary ideal. Describing the
'miniature' of 'our entire self' that inhabits our intellectual nature,
the 'ideal prototype', the 'portrait our external being' and an 'assemblage
of the minutest particles of which our nature is composed', Shelley's
torrent of images is interrupted by an asterisk before further elaboration's describe the internalised and homomunculic image of love's
dream as 'a mirror whose surface reflects only the forms of purity and
brightness; a soul within our soul ...'[30] The imaginary totality of love
unites internal ideal with external form: love seeks the subject's own
ideal object – its self. Interrupting this description of the union of inside
and out, of self and ideal in a state of complete being, however, the asterisk
directs the reader to a footnoted expostulation: 'these words are ineffectual and metaphorical. Most words are so – No help!' The imaginary
encounters that ambivalent thing, metaphor, and thence the insufficiency
of being at the limits of language, the words of love that rupture the system of words. Metaphorical substitutions become ineffectual, the Other
is called for to deliver, recognise and stabilise love. This goes against the
metaphorical momentum of the signifier, leaving Shelley stranded
before the Other who will not rescue him with an answer to his cry.

The metaphors that were ineffectual in the representation of love
for Shelley become, as the cry for help – a cry, words, addressed to the
Other – suggested, its very essence. Love's language is, in the words of
Kristeva, 'impossible, inadequate, immediately allusive when one would
like it to be most straightforward; it is a flight of metaphors – it is literature' (*Tales*, p. 1). In the wanderings of metaphor the subject's identity is
risked, its limits disappear to put the very identity of the speaking
subject in question:

> Finally, to speak of love may be, perhaps, a simple condensation of
> speech that merely arouses, in the one spoken to, metaphorical
> capabilities – a whole imaginary, uncontrollable, undecidable flood,
> of which the loved one alone unknowingly possesses the key ... what
> does he understand me to be saying? What do I understand him to be
> saying? Everything? – as one tends to believe in those moments of
> merging apotheoses, as total as they are unspeakable? Or nothing? –
> as I think, as he may say when the first wound comes and unsettles
> our vulnerable hall of mirrors ...

Vertigo of identity, vertigo of words: love, for the individual, is that sudden revelation, that irremediable cataclysm, of which one speaks only after the fact.

(Tales, p. 3)

With words love takes on its true force, opening the subject up to the effects of the Other. With words, also, the imaginary, narcissistic structure of love and subjectivity enters a different dimension of impossible being, raising the subject to a zenith which is its apotheosis in the Other.

The Other, as 'the very space of metaphorical shifting', forms the locus in which the subject has, and loses, its being. At stake, for the subject is its very unity, a unity which Kristeva associates with metaphor. For the amorous subject the object is a metaphor that crystallises its fantasy of unity in contrast to the phantasmatic narrative in which desire is articulated *(Tales, p. 31)*. Metaphors, however, remain distinctly uncanny in their effects. For Lacan, it is metaphor that serves to connect the subject to the signifying chain: causing a 'creative spark' that 'flashes' between signifiers, occulting but preserving one, metaphor constitutes the imaginary point of suture between subject and symbolic. The occulted signifier, however, remains only metonymically connected to the chain *(Ecrits, p. 157)*. The position of the subject depends on the articulations of signifiers: 'Now what is a signifier? ... A signifier is that which represents a subject. For whom? – not for another subject, but for another signifier' *(Four, p. 198)*. What is uncanny, then, about metaphor is that it allows the subject to identify a place in the chain of signifiers, a place in which it finds itself other to itself, in which it substitutes another image for itself, but where, also, it is subjected to movements, passions that are not its own. For Derrida, the uncanniness of the uncanny is inextricably bound up with metaphor as it discloses 'a process of interminable substitution' and castration anxiety (which for Lacan is the point of the subject's inscription in the symbolic), that 'non secret of seminal division that breaks into substitution.'[31] For Helene Cixous, the anxiety of the uncanny engenders 'an infinite game of substitutions' which leads to displacements, an 'insidious movement, through which opposites communicate. It is the *between* that is tainted by strangeness.'[32] The double, ambivalently moving between life and death, fantasy and reality, marks the strange space in which subject sees itself in horror as an effect of language. Signalling the subject's subservience to the ego ideal and to a final, fatal difference it cannot transcend, the double forms the figure of the subject's occultation in signification.

Romance Reading

In *The Sorrows of Werther*, the protagonist comes to the fore as a subject of letters. The epistolary structure of the narrative serves to highlight

the displacements of amorous utterance even as they shape the intimations of inner space and enable the Romantic postures assumed by
Werther. Love's text, integral to amorous experience as it is, nonetheless
frustrates Werther's amorous insistence on the absolute, constituting
and displacing his exorbitant longing for the beyond. Words exert their
ambivalent, monstrous power to excite the subject to ecstasy and plunge
him into despair. At the moment Werther believes he has won the love
of Lotte he exclaims: 'Oh! may I, can I express the Paradise that lies in
these words? – that she loves me' (p. 36). The paradise of the Other's
recognition does not, however, always fill hollow words.

The demand for love, presence and unity uttered in words, but to
their beyond, signals a demand that remains too great for the Other
to respond. In the face of the silence of the Other, Werther attempts to
efface the hollow distance in a return to the plenitude of the imaginary.
Words fail him when he tries to describe the perfection of Lotte. The
failure of words to adequately match up to an idealised reality is already
a conventional romantic trope for expressing the inexpressible, for
broaching the sacred. Werther, however, takes this convention to its
limit. As he confesses to his addressee, constructing the intimacy of the
moment's poignancy, 'between ourselves, since I began this letter I have
been three times on the verge of laying down my pen, saddling my horse
and riding off ...' (p. 13). Ellipsis in the letter suggests he has just done
so. When the narrative resumes he says he has. Werther, retreating from
the symbolic, frustrated with the inadequacy of writing, succumbs to the
irresistible lure of the imaginary.

Rejecting the letter in favour of the spirit, Werther locates love solely
in the imaginary register. The distinction, however, is made after he has
been deeply moved by Lotte's description of the death of her perfect
mother: 'That is what she said. Oh! Wilhelm! who can repeat her words,
how can the dead cold letter depict the divine efflorescence of her
spirit?' (p. 58). It is ironic that Lotte has just affected Werther by using
dead cold letters, the mirage of her spirit being one of their effects. But
even as he repeats the patterns of romantic convention, he encounters
the uncertainty that binds him to them. Describing his beloved as an
angel, he goes on to utter doubtfully, 'By heaven, everybody says that of
his mistress! Doesn't he?' (p. 13). Throughout the novel his imaginary
ideal encounters the barriers of convention. Indeed, it is in romantic
convention that the exorbitance of love is sustained. For the conventions of love demand the subject's sacrifice to all but the idealised object.
The breaking of all symbolic prohibitions on attachments with engaged
women or on suicide remains central to love's imperative. Werther's true
love, indeed, lies in the structure of his letters, in his addresses to the
Other that is the locus of all romantic conventions. As Werther shows,
love must speak, for in speaking the subject realises himself and his love,

empties himself of all but his love. In the epistolary address the Other remains near despite the unbridgeable difference that it never ceases to expose. The Other is Werther's true love: 'What a night that was! Now, Wilhelm, I can surmount anything. I shall not see her again. Oh! that I cannot fly to your breast, tell you amid a thousand tears and transports all the emotions which are assailing my heart' (p. 56). The addressee, his frequently expostulated friend Wilhelm, occupies the place of the Other who understands, recognises, knows and loves. While the world might misunderstand Werther, the Other will recognise the soul that is laid bare before it. In the appeal to the Other one finds one's love by identifying one's ideal communicant. For Frankenstein, in a loving expostulation to his dead friend Clerval, the absent addressee provides the site for a moment of pure presence and ideal communication. In the opening to *The Prelude* Wordsworth apostrophises the ideal friendship of Coleridge and later, in 1850, associates that friendship with the breeze, the gentle messenger that binds poetic enunciation with the pervasive breath of eternal nature.

The lover's speech seems to deliver amorous presence in full. It seems to exceed the specular ideal. In the remarks that precede one of Werther's amatory expostulations the words both question and fill specular uncertainty: 'No, I am not deceiving myself! I can read in her black eyes a real interest in me and my destiny' (p. 36). Love's presence, love's specular communication, is not immediate, it appears, but depends on the subject's interpretation, on a wishful reading of the significance of love's look. It is a reading that both suspends and sustains erotic uncertainty with a frisson crucial to passion and desire, directing energies towards the place of the look, the Other. The novel, in contrast to Werther's insistence on speech and presence, attends to the writing and reading that enable love to appear. The ultimate moment of passion in *Werther* occurs as a direct effect of reading. On Werther's last visit to Lotte, after he has determined to die, the latter finds herself unable to carry out her injunction not to admit him. Compromised and confused by his presence, Lotte suggests that he reads. The reading from *Ossian* with its stormy scenes, passionate addresses and images of solitude, love and death has profound effects on the pair. The tales bring forth their own misery in a flood of recognition and tears. With a passion that sweeps away all bounds of decency and dissolves all self-possession, Werther clings to Lotte in a desperate embrace. Hands, cheeks, lips touch before Lotte regains her self-possession and pulls away, fleeing to the next room and locking the door. Departing without a single word of farewell from Lotte, Werther never sees her again.

In the context of the late eighteenth-century it is neither unimportant nor surprising that *Ossian* is the text that inspires the overflow of romantic passions. *Ossian*, a forged collection of Gaelic fragments, 'translated' by James Macpherson and published in 1759, participated in the changing aesthetic sensibilities of the eighteenth century, part of a broad literary and scholarly endeavour recovering or reconstructing old English, Scottish, Welsh and Irish poems and tales.[33] The Romantic or Gothic revival grew and changed shape in the course of the eighteenth century. The terms 'romance' and 'gothic' associated the revival with styles of writing that countered the prevailing neo-classical taste for aesthetic productions in the Greek and Roman mode by a recourse to older national traditions. Linked to feudal culture and customs, and freedoms, passions and energies deemed barbarous by Augustans, the literature evoked lost worlds, magical beings and mysteries, and, using wild natural landscapes and images, produced the excitement, wonder and awe associated with the developing taste for sublime objects and emotions. In the process romance began to assume meanings of love and adventure.

It was not only old poetry and tales that were collected, fictionalised and popularised. Prose fiction, developed from imported French romances began to blend 'antient and modern romance', as Horace Walpole put it in the preface to *The Castle of Otranto* (1764), to produce narratives set in a chivalric past but attuned to the developing middle-class tastes in the present. For the neo-classical critical establishment these kinds of fiction caused serious moral and aesthetic concern. Not only did they lack the formal regularity, symmetry, uniformity and proportion demanded by neo-classicism, but, by presenting a succession of wonderful events and characters, distorted the distinctions between virtue and vice that fiction was supposed to inculcate in its subservient didactic role in the upholding of eighteenth-century moral values. In the aesthetic artifices of romances and Gothic novels, moreover, the naturalness of manners, behaviour, and moral sentiments that were drawn from social life as proper models for imitation were rendered artificial themselves. For critics, romances and, often indiscriminately, the realistic novels of Fielding and Richardson, were monsters, an alarming 'new species' of writing.[34] Unnatural, aesthetically and morally deformed, romance fictions abused rather than perpetuated the useful functions of monstrosity: to display vice in all its repulsiveness in order to affirm the boundary between and necessity of virtue. Many fictions, for critics of the eighteenth century, undermined these boundaries, a sign of the dangers fiction posed not only for aesthetic production, but for social reproduction.

In the concerns expressed by critics about the corrupting effects of romances on the morals of susceptible young, and particularly female, readers there emerged the threat of the complete deterioration of home, culture and society.[35] Presenting 'a very unfit model for imitation' and producing 'a desire of resembling the fictitious heroine of a novel', fictions led to readers becoming 'entirely corrupted by the giddy and

fantastical notions of love and gallantry' or habituated to 'loose principles and immodest practices'.[36] They disrupted domestic orders,
constructing ideals that cannot be realised and leading to the, mostly
female, rejection of paternal authority and domestic duty, 'perverted
with chimerical ideas of romantic love' or '*crying for the imaginary distress
of an heroine*, while their children were crying for bread.'[37] The
metaphorical language of the romance exceeds the prescriptions of
neo-classical aesthetics and morality in producing powerful identifications. Metaphor becomes the real monster to 'transport the reader
unprofitably into into the clouds, where he is sure to find no sold
footing, or into the wilds of fancy, which go for ever out of the way of
human paths.' There is no return, morally, socially or aesthetically, on
the investments of reading. Romance metaphors produced the dangerous spectre of a 'monster of the imagination' spreading uncontrollably
across all symbolic boundaries.[38] The reception and success of *The
Sorrows of Young Werther* inspired a flood of imitations and numerous
outpourings of critical concern as well as fears of suicide epidemics and
bans in various European towns.[39]

Reading Monsters

The reverberations of passionate excess evident in the spark between
Ossian and *Werther* continue beyond any single text of love or romance:
the repetition of passionate signifiers opens onto a field in which fiction,
in the eighteenth century, became a site of anxiety. In *Frankenstein*,
written when the popularity of the Gothic romance was on the wane,
and thus eschewing most of its extravagant features and formulas, the
effects of reading and writing are not only repeated, but staged and re-
examined. Full of accounts of reading and its effects, the writing of
Frankenstein foregrounds the structures that form subjectivity and
monstrosity. The epistolary narratives that make up the text disclose the
dependence of subjects on others, speakers on listeners and writers on
readers. The text discloses, moreover, the reversibility of these relations
as writers become readers, speakers become listeners, in the manner of the
monstrously reversible relation between Frankenstein and the creation.
Such a structure bars the subject from a singular and autonomous
position. Moreover, it does not remain within the bounds apparently
prescribed by its narrative frames: its 'chinese box' structure is over-
turned by the monster who does not stay encased in others' narratives.
Breaking the frames imposed by Walton's and Frankenstein's accounts,
the monster appears, at the end of the novel, and directly addresses
Walton and his departed creator, then to disappear beyond the stories'
incomplete frames. The text, then, does not present the narcissistically

contained image of closure and unity. Its disunity deforms it, presenting a monster in the terms of neo-classical aesthetics, a monster that reanimates the monstrous reversibility and unrepresentability of the figure it makes manifest. The monster remains both text and thing, an embodiment of ambivalent romance metaphors that exceed the finality of narcissistic closure in the symbolic passions of love.

The monster's position as Frankenstein's double discloses the uncanny ambivalence of metaphor. It is a creation made possible by Frankenstein's romance identifications. The mysteries and miracles promised by the alchemists and by Waldman's romanticisation of science lead to the torrential overcoming of boundaries and the vision of a new species. Both terms were used repeatedly in the eighteenth century to describe the flood of novels threatening to overwhelm proper aesthetic and social boundaries. Moreover, in Frankenstein's speculations on the dangerous propagation a female monster might spawn, he echoes fears about the spread of feminised fiction in the period. As text, the monster causes the duplication of romance anxieties, as ambivalent thing, as double, it confirms them. For Frankenstein, the monster is more than an alter-ego: the double inverts, completes and exceeds the human creator's project.

In the moment of its animation the monster presents the creative subject with a reflection of its narcissistic fantasy in a state of decomposition, an inverted image of the mirrored ideal. Reversing the antinomies governing Frankenstein's project, turning life into death, dissolving fullness and unity, replacing love with loathing and benevolence with violence, the monster fulfils the dream that is also a nightmare. More solitary, stronger and more passionate, however, it is the monster who proposes a glorious and sovereign end that completes, exceeds and undermines his creator's. In the demands he places on Frankenstein, the monster also undermines the position of mastery that is assumed. He demands of the Other what cannot be given, asks questions to which the creator has no answers and thus exposes his limitations, affirming the difference and alterity that Frankenstein can neither negate nor transcend.

With these demands the monster constitutes itself as more than the passively resistant and distant alter-ego, or narcissistic antitype. To make them, it has to speak. In speaking the monster becomes more monstrous still. Assuming, eloquently, a defining capacity of the human subject, the monster disrupts the naturalness of human identity as much as the human creator subverts the naturalness of nature: in creating a living thing from dead parts, Frankenstein Romantically transgresses the supposedly natural distinction of life and death; in taking the position of a human subject, the monster, conventionally out of nature and inhuman, dislocates humanism. Moreover, the monster's speech, enabled by his reading, Volney's *Ruins* in particular, continues to interrogate radically the very nature, legitimacy and stability of human identity, authority and institutions. Humans, and the institutions they inhabit, emerge as divided entities, 'so virtuous, and magnificent, yet so vicious and base' (p. 119).

By speaking independently, the monster exceeds the creator's narcissism by taking critical positions made available by a variety of textual identifications. He lives and, in living, elaborates, a different condition of incomplete subjectivity. A living thing, rather than an imaginary projection, recognised, albeit negatively by others, the monster exists beyond Frankenstein. While he wants a recognised place in a community of others, his desires are not, like Frankenstein, predicated on the assumption of absolute self-unity. Disrupting the supposed interiority of subjectivity, the monster breaks the mirror, in more ways than one, that Frankenstein holds before himself, shattering the imaginary unity of inside and outside that guides his passionate and narcissistic project: the monster, like the language his textuality foregrounds, figures the extremity of subjectivity. Unlike Frankenstein, the monster has no sense of imaginary integrity and is prevented from misrecognising the mirror image as an ideal projecting beyond symbolic frameworks. He cannot (mis)assume a unified, prelinguistic self: his only ideals are shaped in symbolic relations. When the monster sees his reflection in a pool of water he is horrified, making no jubilant assumption of specular identity. For the monster, the specular relation is inadequate, hence his appeals for recognition to the blind father of the de Lacey family and his symbolic blinding of Frankenstein, covering his eyes before he tells him his story in the Alps.

But the monster has already 'seen' his reflection in the responses of Frankenstein and other humans, their repulsion constituting the moment of nonrecognition that he repeats when he looks at his image in the pool. The monster's origin, as an assemblage of different narratives as well as bodily pieces, comes from textual identification rather than a body image. He discovers the secrets of his birth in laboratory notes he finds in the pocket of a coat he stole from the scene of his creation. However, before he can understand them, he must learn to read, uncover the secrets of that 'godlike science of letters' used by humans. This is done from the position of a voyeur. Through a crack in the wall, the monster watches a fallen bourgeois family. Moved by, though not understanding, the scenes he sees, it is only when a foreigner, Safie, the son's beloved, arrives, that the monster has the opportunity to learn and identify with human symbolisation. Safie is taught to speak the de Lacey's language. The monster is an avid student too, learning, at last, the meanings of the arbitrary sounds he had heard uncomprehendingly for so long. Acquiring language second-hand, subjectivity remains a purloined state, for ever outside, emanating from the external world of signifiers: his identity is always someone else's. It is also purloined in the sense that it is never legitimated by an other person, never recognised by a community of distinct speaking beings. Though he has adopted a place in the symbolic by learning language, it is not a social place.

His understanding and critique of the human social world from which he has been excluded and his own position comes from books. These texts offer him a variety of identities, thus leaving him dependent on the metonymic relations of others' narratives. Finding a package of books which Peter Brooks describes as 'a kind of minimal Romantic *cyclopedia universalis*',[40] the monster reads them, identifying with characters whose position appears similar to his: Milton's Adam and Satan, Goethe's Werther. The other text he enjoys, Plutarch's *Lives*, elevates him 'above the wretched sphere of my own reflections, to admire and love the heroes of past ages' (pp. 128–9). These figures, like the heroes of romance, provide a temporary sense of imaginary, metaphorical unity. In contrast, Adam, and the complaint that forms the epigraph of the novel that was dedicated to William Godwin, reflects the position of the creation in regard of the creator. Like Adam, the monster wants some reason, some meaning for being. While Adam's separate existence is akin to the monster's, everything else about him is, the monster laments, different. Satan seems a more appropriate figure: as outcast barred from the world of the phallic signifier, he rebels against it, venting his anger in acts of destruction: he burns down the De Lacey's cottage and kills members of Frankenstein's family. Echoing Satan's cry of 'evil be thou my good' in the phrase 'evil thenceforth became my good', the monster locates the rejection as the moment in which he turned into the other he was supposed to be, doing the violent, irrational, destructive and inhuman things a monster should do. The monster thus moves from the abjection of a being utterly excluded from, yet subordinated to, the symbolic order, to the sovereignty of a being who agonisingly relishes his exclusion and turns its violence back on the system that enforced it.

In the figure of Werther, however, the monster discovers a model that is less mythological. The story enlightens many 'obscure subjects', offering the monster 'a never-ending source of speculation and astonishment'; it provides the monster with 'lofty sentiments and feelings, which had for their object something out of self', a better image than the bourgeois domesticity of the De Lacey's. Werther, moreover, provides the ideal: 'I thought Werter himself a more divine being than I had ever beheld or imagined; his character contained no pretension, but it sunk deep'. In the spark of identification between monster and Werther, the former displays the patterns of Romantic reading. The books 'produced in me an infinity of new images and feelings, that sometimes raised me to ecstacy, but more frequently sunk me into the lowest dejection.' Duplicating the passionate extremes of the narcissistic

Romantic subject, the monster performs a strange repetition in which Werther, the very image of his creator, becomes his own ideal. His love obeys the prescriptions of *The Sorrows of Werther*'s preface: 'You will not be able to withhold your admiration or love for his mind and character or your tears for his fate' (p. 1). Indeed, all his textual models repeat prescribed patterns from romance and Romanticism: ancient heroes, Miltonic rebels, and sensitive souls and Promethean artists, present objects of love that direct the monster's desire and destiny. While the path of the monster's departure is free, there is, he observes, no one to 'lament his annihilation'. In the mourning of an ideal loss in Werther, an act he repeats on Frankenstein's death, he is already bound to their fate, his identity established by way of their metaphors, his destiny prescribed by the flight of the signifier.

His duplication and his repetitions, however, disclose a difference in his patterns of Romantic reading. While his mourning performs the blessing that Frankenstein wished of his 'new species', and the promised death the apotheosis of the creator's wishes, the way the monster, like the novel, stages processes and effects of reading, suggest critical differ- ences. The monster says that he read all the volumes as a 'true history' (p. 129). In reading literary texts literally, however, he signals problems in Romantic patterns of metaphorical identification. While his state- ment appears as an attempt to stabilise distinctions between literal and figurative language that his acquisition of language's arbitrary system put in question, inserting a distance and difference between fiction and reality, it only continues the problems, for the subject, of metaphorical movement. As monster, an unnameable entity with a variety of names, he serves as a metaphorical substitute and as an embodiment of the metaphors guiding others' projects. At the same time his being and his identity can only be negatively metaphorised as he opens metaphor to metaphoricity. He tries, nonetheless, to make his reading of *Werther* literal, but fails: 'as I read, however, I applied much personally to my own feelings and condition. I found myself similar, yet at the same time strangely unlike to the beings concerning whom I read, and to whose conversation I was a listener' (p. 128). Finding both similarity and difference, the monster remains doubled, unable to efface the gap that separates him from and binds him to others or to separate the literal and metaphorical dimensions of language. The strange dissimilarity of others is not effaced by his identification; he does not collapse in an ecstatically narcissistic union with his textual ideals. Reading, for him, encounters the ambivalence of language's uncanny. Providing doubles for the double, as his textual substitutes do, only accelerates the momentum of metaphorical reversibility.

Figures of identification provoke further destabilising questions for the subject, the monster: 'My person was hideous, and my stature

gigantic: what did this mean? Who was I? What was I? Whence did
I come? What was my destination?' Partial, unsatisfactory answers come
from other texts, but the monster continues questioning. Literal reading
becomes critical reading as, on the basis of his formative texts, the monster moves beyond questions of self and interrogates the insufficiency of
logocentric language and the systems it shapes. In demonstrating
the effects of doubled language, the monster moves beyond bodies,
characters and persons to critique the figures and structures of human
institutions. This is a position that the fractured frame structure of
Frankenstein establishes for the reader: by staging reading in the story,
the epistolary structure of multiple first-person narratives simultaneously invites personal identification and displaces it, to leave no secure
position at the end. Indeed, the final reader of the letters in the text,
Walton's sister, Margaret Saville, never appears in the novel: a marginal
and uncertain reading position remains the destination of the letters.
A critical distance is established, questioning the limits of the Romantic
subject of love and interrogating, also, the structures, conditions and
effects of its textual reproduction.

The double reading may also be that of Mary Shelley. Examining the
significance of *The Sorrows of Young Werther* in *Frankenstein* and Mary
Wollstonecraft's letters, Roswitha Burwick argues that Shelley's use of
Goethe's text is influenced by her mother's development of a female
Werther figure and her romantic disappointments. For Burwick, the
textual interimplication is gendered: Goethe's authoritative and one-
dimensional mode is opposed to Shelley's organic and multidimensional
story.[41] While the mother remains as a figure of loss, Burwick avoids
pursuing this line of interpretation, which would serve to restore the
author as an object and end of critical narcissism, the ideal image,
the metaphor substituting for text, arresting its movement and meaning.
But biography remains intricately textual.[42] Her mother remains a figure, known through letters, a life in writing which generates writing.[43]
In contrast to the narcissists represented in the novels, for whom the
mother signifies a lost, ideal unity that can be recovered, *Frankenstein*
leaves the mother as a figure, an inevitable loss in the structuring of
subjectivity. The maternal figure becomes a metaphor generative
of metaphoricity rather than the locus, the object, for the enactment of
mastery. At the time, however, in cultural formations of the period the
paternal metaphor was undergoing something of a crisis, suffering a loss
of singularity, credibility and legitimacy as a result of revolutionary
shocks to and radical incursions against its authority. Burke's account of
the French Revolution is dominated by images of violated feminine
beauty and oedipal antagonism towards the father.[44] The horror and
the threat demands their vigorous repulsion in the name of good
(paternal) order, a return to values of monarchy, tradition and family.

In Romanticism, for Wordsworth and Percy Shelley particularly, the space of the paternal metaphor is incompletely filled by the ideal figure of the poet, a solitary figure shadowed by the effects of narcissism. In *Frankenstein's* scrutiny of the narcissism that haunts Romantic subjectivity all its supports and assumptions – nature, poet and the ideal human figure – are open to suspicion and the doubled effects of monstrosity. Indeed, in the critical space of double reading it sustains, in the differences it examines and questions rather than expunges or resolves, *Frankenstein* discloses, to adapt Jean-Francois Lyotard's familiar phrase, an incredulity towards paternal metaphors.

Notes

1 Georges Bataille, *Guilty*, tr. Bruce Boone (San Francisco: Lapis Press, 1988), p. 158.
2 Respectively, Julia Kristeva, *Tales of Love*, tr. Leon S. Roudiez (New York: Columbia University Press, 1987), p. 5 and Roland Barthes, *A Lover's Discourse*, tr. Richard Howard (New York: Noonday Press, 1978), p. 1.
3 See Mary Poovey, '"My Hideous Progeny": Mary Shelley and the feminization of Romanticism', *PMLA* 95 (1980), pp. 332–47; Anne K. Mellor, *Mary Shelley* (London: Routledge, 1988); Margaret Homans, *Bearing the Word* (Chicago and London: Chicago University Press, 1986).
4 Joseph Kestner, 'Narcissism as symptom and structure: the case of Mary Shelley's *Frankenstein*', in *The Nature of Identity* (Tulsa: University of Oaklahoma Press,1981), pp. 15–25.
5 G. W. F. Hegel, 'The Spirit of Christianity', in *Early Theological Writings*, tr. T. M. Knox (Philadelphia: University of Pennsylvania Press, 1948), p. 247.
6 G. W. F. Hegel, 'Two fragments on love', trans. H. S. Harris, *Clio* 7 (1978/9), 257–65, p. 261.
7 Hegel, 'Love', *Early Theological Writings*, p. 305.
8 G. W. F. Hegel, *Phenomenology of Spirit*, tr. A. V. Miller (Oxford: Oxford University Press, 1977), p. 478.
9 G. W. F. Hegel, *Philosophy of Right*, tr. T. M. Knox (Oxford: Oxford University Press, 1952), p. 110.
10 Johann Wolfgang von Goethe, *The Sorrows of Young Werther*, tr. Michael Hulse (Harmondsworth: Penguin, 1989), p. 55. All further references, cited in brackets in the text, will be to this edition.
11 M. H. Abrams, 'The correspondent breeze: a Romantic metaphor', in Abrams (ed.) *English Romantic Poets* (Oxford: Oxford University Press, 1975).
12 Mary Shelley, *Frankenstein*, ed. M. K. Joseph (Oxford: Oxford University Press, 1969), p. 33. All further references, cited in brackets in the text, will be to this edition.
13 Alexandre Kojève, *Introduction to the Reading of Hegel*, tr. James Nichols Jr. (New York: Basic Books, 1969), p. 5.

14   Jacques Lacan, 'Desire and the interpretation of desire in *Hamlet*', *Yale French Studies* 55/6 (1977), 11–52, p. 31.

15   Georges Bataille, *Inner Experience*, tr. Leslie Anne Boldt (New York: State University of New York Press, 1988), p. 73.

16   Maurice Blanchot, *The Unavowable Community*, tr. Pierre Joris (Station Hill Press: New York, 1988), pp. 2–7.

17   Georges Bataille, *Literature and Evil*, tr. Alastair Hamilton (London: Calder and Boyars, 1973), pp. 16–17.

18   Denis de Rougemont, *Passion and Society*, tr. Montgomery Belgion (London: Faber and Faber, 1956), p. 1.

19   Georges Bataille, 'Open Letter to Rene Char', *Yale French Studies*, 78 (1990), 31–43, p. 34.

20   See Georges Bataille, *Theory of Religion*, trans. Robert Hurley (New York: Zone, 1989), pp. 48–9.

21   See Beth Newman, 'Narratives of seduction and the seductions of narrative: the frame structure of *Frankenstein*', *English Literary History*, 53 (1986), pp. 141–61.

22   Sigmund Freud, 'Beyond the Pleasure Principle' (1920), *Standard Edition* XVIII, trans. James Strachey (London: Hogarth, 1955), pp. 1–64.

23   Jacques Lacan, *The Seminar of Jacques Lacan: Book I*, tr. John Forrester (Cambridge: Cambridge University Press, 1988), p. 142.

24   Sigmund Freud, 'The Uncanny' (1919), *Standard Edition* XVII, tr. James Strachey (London: Hogarth, 1955), 218–56, p. 235. Also, Mladen Dolar. '"I shall be with you on your wedding night": Lacan and the uncanny', *October*, 58 (1991), pp. 5–23.

25   See Jacques Lacan, *Ecrits*, trans. Alan Sheridan (London: Tavistock, 1977), pp. 1–7 and *Seminar I*, p. 79.

26   Jacques Lacan, *The Four Fundamental Concepts of Psychoanalysis*, trans. Alan Sheridan (Harmondsworth: Penguin, 1997), p. 103.

27   Jacques Lacan, *The Ethics of Psychoanalysis*, trans. Dennis Porter (London: Routledge, 1992), p. 150.

28   Jacques Lacan, *The Seminar of Jacques Lacan: Book II*, trans. Sylvana Tomaselli (Cambridge: Cambridge University Press, 1988), p. 265.

29   Jacques Lacan, *The Psychoses*, trans. Russell Grigg (London: Routledge, 1993), p. 55.

30   Percy Bysshe Shelley, 'Essay on Love', in David Lee Clark (ed.), *Shelley's Prose or the Trumpet of Prophecy* (London: Fourth Estate, 1988), p. 170.

31   Jacques Derrida, *Dissemination*, trans. Barbara Johnson (London: Athlone, 1981), p. 268, n. 67.

32   Hélène Cixous, 'Fiction and its phantoms: a reading of Freud's *Das Unheimliche* (the "uncanny")', *New Literary History*, 7 (1976), 525–48, pp. 536, 543.

33   See Arthur Johnston, *Enchanted Ground* (London: Athlone, 1964); Gillian Beer, *The Romance* (London: Methuen, 1970); Hugh Blair, *A Critical Dissertation on the Poems of Ossian* (1765), (New York: Garland, 1970).

34   Ioan Williams, *Novel and Romance 1700–1800* (London: Routledge, 1970).

35   Peter de Bolla, *The Discourse of the Sublime* (Oxford: Blackwell, 1989), p. 260.

36 William Cumberland, *The Observer* 27 (1785); Henry Pye, *A Commentary Illustrating the Poetic of Aristotle* (1786); T. Row, Letter, *Gentleman's Magazine* xxxvii (1767); Anon., Letter, *Gentleman's Magazine* (1788). In Williams, pp. 333, 337, 272.

37 Richard Berenger, *The World* 79 (1954), in Williams, p. 214; J. L. Chirol, *An Enquiry into the Best System of Female Education* (London, 1809), p. 234; in de Bolla, p. 260.

38 Review of *Peregrine Pickle*, *The Monthly Review* (March 1751), in Williams, p. 162.

39 See Michael Hulse, Introduction to *Werther*, pp. 11–15.

40 Peter Brooks, *Body Work* (Cambridge: Harvard University Press, 1993), p. 205.

41 Roswitha Burwick, 'Goethe's *Werther* and Mary Shelley's *Frankenstein*', *Wordsworth Circle* 24 (1993), pp. 47–52.

42 Barbara Johnson, 'My monster/my self', *diacritics* 12 (1982), pp. 2–10.

43 Marc A. Rubenstein, '"My accursed origin": the search for the mother in *Frankenstein*', *Studies in Romanticism* 15 (1976), pp. 165–94.

44 See Ronald Paulson, *Representations of Revolution (1789–1820)* (New Haven and London: Yale University Press, 1983), and Chris Baldick, *In Frankenstein's Shadow* (Oxford: Clarendon, 1987).

List of Illustrations
and Acknowledgements

p. 124   Sir Joshua Reynolds, *Admiral Keppel*, 1780. Reproduced with permission of the Tate Gallery, London.

p. 125   Sir Joshua Reynolds, *The Death of Dido*, 1781. Reproduced with permission of Penguin Books Ltd, Harmondsworth.

p. 126   Pierre Mignard, *Louise de Kéroualle, Duchess of Portsmouth*, 1682. Reproduced with permission of the National Portrait Gallery, London.

p. 128   Thomas Gainsborough, *The Morning Walk*, 1785. Reproduced with permission of the National Gallery, London.

p. 130   Joseph Wright of Derby, *Sir Brooke Boothby*, 1781. Reproduced with permission of the Tate Gallery, London.

p. 131   Joseph Wright of Derby, *Edwin*, 1777–8. Reproduced with permission of Hambros Bank Limited, London.

p. 132   John Flaxman, [*Death of Chatterton*] *Thomas Chatterton Taking the Bowl of Poison from the Spirit of Despair*, 1775–80. Reproduced with permission of the Department of Print and Drawings, the British Museum.

The Collected Essays of John Goode

Edited by Charles Swann
and with an introduction by
Terry Eagleton

1848 and the Strange Disease of Modern Love

Amours de Voyage: The Aqueous Poem

Adam Bede

'The Affections Clad with Knowledge':
Woman's Duty and the Public Life

'Character' and Henry James

The Pervasive Mystery of Style:
The Wings of the Dove

Hardy and Marxism

Sue Bridehead and the New Woman

Woman and the Literary Text

Feminism, Class and Literary Criticism

Gissing, Morris, and English Socialism

William Morris and the Dream of Revolution

Now Where Nowhere: William Morris Today

The Decadent Writer as Producer

Writing beyond the End

Margaret Harkness and the Socialist Novel

Mark Rutherford and Spinoza

D. H. Lawrence

'The Uninteresting Actual Frog:'
or Is There Life After Postmodernism?

ISBN 1 85331 068 9

*For a complete list of Keele University Press and Ryburn
books in print, please write to Keele University Press,
Keele University, Staffordshire ST5 5BG, England*

EU Authorised Representative:

Easy Access System Europe Mustamäe tee 50, 10621 Tallinn, Estonia

gpsr.requests@easproject.com

Printed and bound by CPI Group (UK) Ltd, Croydon, CR0 4YY

09/06/2025

01897303-0001